A
VISITOR'S GUIDE
TO
THE ANCIENT
OLYMPICS

A
VISITOR'S GUIDE
TO
THE ANCIENT
OLYMPICS

Neil Faulkner

YALE UNIVERSITY PRESS
NEW HAVEN AND LONDON

For information about this and other Yale University Press publications please contact:
U.S. Office: sales.press@yale.edu   yalebooks.com
Europe Office: sales@yaleup.co.uk   www.yalebooks.co.uk

Designed and typeset in Rotis by Peter Ward
Printed in Great Britain by Hobbs the Printer Ltd, Totton, Hampshire

Library of Congress Cataloging-in-Publication Data

Faulkner, Neil.
  A visitor's guide to the ancient Olympics / Neil Faulkner.
     p. cm.
  Includes bibliographical references and index.
  1. Olympia (Greece : Ancient sanctuary) 2. Olympic games (Ancient)
3. Greece—Social life and customs—
To 146 B.C. 4. Greece—Civilization—To 146 B.C. 5. Olympics. I. Title.
  DF261.O5F38 2012
  796.480938—dc23
                                          2011035476

A catalogue record for this book is available from the British Library

10 9 8 7 6 5 4 3 2 1

CONTENTS

ILLUSTRATIONS AND MAPS

MAPS

ACKNOWLEDGEMENTS

I am very grateful to the following four friends who have taken the trouble to read the text and make critical comments: Stephen Batchelor, John Taylor, and Fran and Vernon Trafford. The text has been much improved thanks to their efforts. David Bellingham, another old friend, kindly supplied some authentic Ancient Greek vocabulary.

Thanks are also due to Mark Edwards for preparing a striking set of 'black-figure' athletes based on original Greek art, and to Ian Bull for translating my sketches and instructions into five crystal-clear plans.

I am also grateful to Rachael Lonsdale, Associate Editor at Yale University Press, for her valuable suggestions, and to Yale's two anonymous academic reviewers, both of whom have been exceptionally conscientious and supportive critics.

PREFACE

What was it like going to the Olympics 2,400 years ago? Instead of London 2012, how about Olympia 388 BC? Would a modern visitor to the ancient Olympics find it all very familiar, or would he (virtually no women were allowed in) be overwhelmed with culture shock?

In the Olympic Stadium, there were no stands and no shade: you sat on a grassy bank under the searing heat of the midsummer sun. Naked athletes competed in foot-races, the pentathlon, horse- and chariot-races, and three combat sports: wrestling, boxing, and the almost no-holds-barred *pankration*, the crowd's favourite, because there were virtually no rules and it was all blood and pain.

Half the Olympic programme was given over to religious ritual: processions, hymn-singing, incense-burning, gory animal sacrifice, and strange incantations by exotically-attired priests. The Olympic site was not just a sports stadium; it was part-sanctuary, part-art gallery, part-heritage trail. In the Temple's inner sanctum, behind a dazzling colonnaded façade, sat a colossal gold-and-ivory statue of Zeus, divine master of ceremonies. Outside was a mountainous heap of ash: an altar formed of a thousand sacrifices. All around were shrines, altars and statues.

Fringe events included philosophy lectures, poetry readings, and sundry charlatans and cranks offering to predict the future. The nightlife was yet more exotic. No-one got any sleep, as parties went on through the small hours, and hundreds of prostitutes, both women and boys, were busy touting their services until dawn.

The Olympic Village was a vast, tented encampment, with inadequate water supplies, heaps of stinking refuse, and huge, open, improvised latrines. The air was alive with millions of flies, mosquitoes and wasps. By the end, no-one had washed properly for a week, and you could smell the Games a mile away.

Welcome to the ancient Greek Olympics. A stranger in a foreign land, a time-traveller visiting another age, a sports fan and a pilgrim at a once-in-a-lifetime extravaganza, you are going to need a guide-book. This is it. It tells you everything you need to know about such essentials as how to get there, where to stay, and what to eat; about the historical background and rich history of the Games; and about the celebrities, the contests, and the rituals that make up the ancient Olympic programme.

I am inviting readers to adopt a role: that of a tourist visiting the Olympics in 388 BC, much as tens of thousands of tourists will visit the London Olympics of AD 2012. My assumption is that the reader may know little or nothing about ancient Greece, but that he or she wishes to learn something now – because of the London Olympics, and because these, like all Olympics, are a conscious imitation of things presumed to have happened as long ago as 776 BC.

The book is written in the form of a travel guide. I wanted readers to imagine themselves to actually be there. So you must allow yourself to believe it is 388 BC – 2,400 years ago – when the ancient Olympic Games were at their peak. As far as I have been able – as far as the evidence allows – I have attempted to reconstruct the Games exactly as they might have been in that year.

My approach is not an altogether 'reputable' academic procedure. It involves four things that would be inadmissible in writing a scholarly paper for a learned journal. The first is to draw heavily on what we know *generally* about ancient Greece in reconstructing what might have happened *specifically* at the Olympic Games. Let me give an example. We probably know as much about ancient Athens as we do about the rest of the ancient Greek world put together. We know a lot, for example, about what the ancient Athenians ate and drank, and about their meal-times and table manners, whereas we know very little about these matters at the Olympics. To imagine that eating at the ancient Olympics was in many ways similar to eating in the ancient city of Athens is quite a leap. But in the absence of any other evidence, it seems legitimate if the aim is to give the reader a sense of what it might have been like on the basis of the little we do know. At any rate, it is either that, or leave great gaps.

The second sin is the temporal equivalent of the first. If it is questionable to assume that practices recorded for another place can simply be transferred to Olympia, it must be equally questionable to assume that practices first recorded at another time can simply be transported back to 388 BC. To retain the food theme, can the dishes described by the fourth-century BC gourmand Archestratos of Gela (in Sicily) be taken as evidence for what might have been eaten at the beginning of the century at Olympia? The same defence applies as before: I have chosen to run with the evidence available in order to make the composite picture as full as possible.

The third sin is to ignore all academic controversy and uncertainty, such that matters on which scholars are agreed and matters on which they argue are left indistinguishable in the text (though you can find good summaries of the debate and evidence if you follow up the references). Let me give one or two examples to illustrate the depths of depravity to which I have sunk. Though we are certain which events were included in the ancient Olympic programme, we are not certain on which days they took place. A guide-book that cannot even tell you whether the foot races are on day three or day five is not much use – but to introduce the haziness would break the illusion of present time. If we were actually there, we would know. In some cases of uncertainty I have been able to pass over the matter in silence, but in other cases, when it could not be avoided, I have plumped unequivocally for one of the alternatives.

The fourth sin may be the worst. It is to make use of what R.G. Collingwood called 'the historical imagination'. This does not mean making things up in the manner of a novelist. It does mean filling in some of the gaps in the historical and archaeological record with some informed guesswork. What would it have been like living for a week in the ancient Olympic Village? There are passing comments in the ancient sources – about the heat, the flies and the lack of adequate water, for example. The fuller picture that I offer incorporates those observations and builds upon them on the basis of common sense and 'historical imagination'.

Enough of sin. I have chosen it – with all its consequences – so we may as well enjoy it. As best I can, I have tried to describe the ancient Olympic Games as I think they might have been, drawing on direct evidence, near-contemporary parallels and historical imagination. Any reader can readily check the relationship between evidence and claim by reference to textual notes and the relevant sources. I hope that scholars and students will enter into the spirit of the book, and take it for what it is: a sincere attempt to reconstruct a past historical reality as a lived human experience. And I hope that general readers, especially those new to ancient Greece, will enjoy it as an introduction to another world.

Neil Faulkner
July 2011

A NOTE ON THE PRESENTATION OF ANCIENT GREEK WORDS

There is no standardised way of rendering Ancient Greek words in modern English script. Most letters are the same, and many sounds similar, but there are some awkward differences. With some very familiar names – like Aeschylus or Socrates – I have retained the conventional, Latinised form. But in most cases, I have adopted a form closer to the Ancient Greek, using, for example, 'k' in place of 'c' (for Ancient Greek has no 'c'), 'ch' for the Greek letter chi (pronounced like 'ch' in loch), and 'ai' rather than the Latin diphthong 'ae'.

In one particular matter, I have tried to avoid following the almost universal practice of rendering upsilon, the Ancient Greek 'u', as an English 'y'. This strange convention merely encourages mispronunciation. Unfortunately, it is so deeply embedded in the literature that it would merely compound confusion to alter well-known names, so Odysseus, for example, remains Odysseus. With ordinary words, however – those given in italics – I have transliterated upsilon as 'u'.

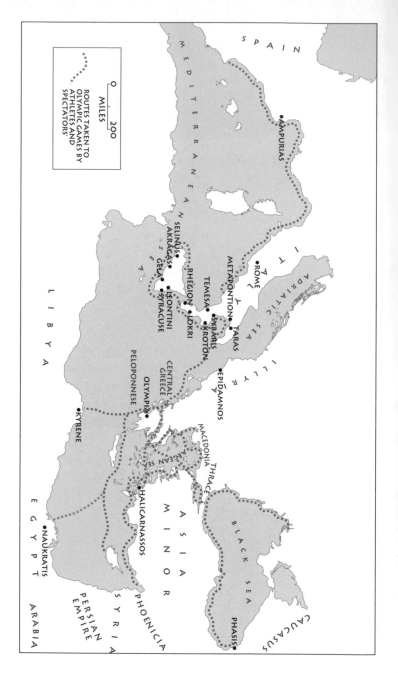

Map 1. Map of the Greek world showing city-states and other places mentioned in the guide and the routes taken by athletes and spectators attending the Olympic Games.

1 THE BASICS

GETTING THERE

OVERLAND

So you want to go to the Greek Olympic Games? You may be disconcerted to learn that getting there is far from straightforward. This may be the premier event in the Greek sporting calendar, but it takes place in a remote rural backwater located a good distance from any major thoroughfare.

The Games are hosted by the city of Elis, a minor state tucked away in the northwestern Peloponnese, and Olympia itself, the sacred site where the contests are held, lies some thirty-six miles to the southeast. This means the site is a long way from all the major Greek cities. If you are coming from Central Greece, Athens is 120 miles distant, Thebes 110; if from within the Peloponnese, Corinth is seventy-five miles away, Argos and Sparta both sixty. (These distances are approximations: there are no accurate long-distance measurements in ancient Greece.)

The actual travelling distance is much longer, as few of the roads are straight, and many wind through hill country. The 'roads', moreover, are atrocious – just rough tracks – which makes travelling in any sort of vehicle slow, uncomfortable and expensive. Carts drawn by mules, oxen or horses (in ascending order of cost) are available for hire, but usually only for short distances across local plains; you will then have to walk the hill-country and hire again on the far side. An alternative, especially if you are heavily laden with baggage, is to hire a donkey or mule, which may take you the whole way. The problem – apart from the expense – will be finding one, with tens of thousands of people on the move. Anyone on a tight budget is likely to find themselves walking. You can certainly assume that those passing you on the road on horseback or in horse-drawn chariot are rich.

The Greeks are used to walking. Life is simple, most people relatively poor, and the terrain arduous, so it is often the best way. People tend to reckon the distances between places in walking-time. The workers in the Peiraieus Harbour consider a trip to Athens and back, around nine miles in total, an easy day. An army is expected to march between fifteen and seventeen miles in a day. The thirty-six mile procession from Elis to Olympia at the start of the Games takes two days. If you are a good walker, you can probably manage fifteen to twenty miles a day, even on cross-country tracks.[1]

Is it safe? This is the question that everyone asks. Greece is divided into some 1,000 independent city-states. Many are bitter rivals, warfare is endemic, and it is quite common for there to be several local wars being waged in different parts of Greece at the same time. To give an idea, over the last century Athens has been at war three years out of every four.

Despite this, travelling across Greece to the Olympics is relatively safe. Because Greek armies are citizen-militias made up of ordinary farmers, military campaigns are usually restricted to spring and summer – that is, between sowing and harvest. Most campaigns do not result in pitched battle, and if they do, it is often by pre-arrangement between belligerents. Even when territory is being laid waste, with crops cut down and buildings demolished, civilians are rarely targeted, and religious sanctuaries hardly ever plundered.[2] Moreover, anyone en route to the Olympics is considered a pilgrim, under divine protection, such that any kind of hostility or violence amounts to violation of a strict religious taboo.

It is as well to know this, since travelling any distance overland will involve crossing numerous borders, and in some cases passing through actual war zones. The borders are unmarked and unguarded. Passports do not exist. But during the Games, the land is under a Panhellenic 'Sacred Truce', which effectively guarantees safe passage through the territory of any state to all those going to or coming from Olympia. The Sacred Truce does not – as some people naïvely imagine – mean that the fighting stops. Rather, it allows the Games to take place *despite* the fighting, as they did throughout the long and bitter Peloponnesian War between Athens and Sparta in the late fifth century BC.

Even so, you should take care. State authorities maintain order inside city precincts, but they do not police the local countryside. Brigands are not unknown in the more remote areas, and many live not only outside the laws of men, but also without regard for the precepts of the gods. There are places in Greece where the protective mantle of the Sacred Truce is somewhat ragged.[3]

BY SEA

The alternative is to go by sea. Due to the parlous state of the roads and the expense of overland travel, water transport, wherever possible, is always first choice in ancient Greece. An ox will consume the equivalent of its own load in a month of haulage work; over the same period, the crew of a ship will consume only a tiny fraction of their cargo.[4]

Olympia is only nine miles from the sea, and the River Alpheios, which runs past the site, is navigable for light craft. Even if you are coming from other parts of mainland Greece, it may be preferable to go around the coast by ship than to travel overland. But if you are coming from any of the islands or the colonies, there is, of course, no choice but to travel at least part of the way by sea.

There are no passenger ferries. All Greek sailing ships are designed to take cargo. They are small, short, broad-beamed, wind-dependent, and vulnerable in a storm. Average speed in favourable conditions is around five knots.

1. An ancient merchantman. Going to the Olympics by sea usually means perching on top of the cargo.

On the other hand, the crew is small and space ample, so the ship can carry everything it needs, and once at sea you may not need to put into port until you reach your destination.

You will see large rowing vessels, which are much faster, cruising at seven or eight knots, and capable of up to thirteen knots in short bursts. But these are triremes – warships – built for speed and power rather than ocean-going voyages. The whole of the inside of the hull is taken up with wooden benches to accommodate 170 rowers, with minimal space for carrying water and provisions, and none at all for passengers. You cannot get to Olympia on a warship. And you would not want to. A trireme is likely to take on water and sink if a storm gets up. The journey would take longer because the vessel has to beach every night. And the stench of 170 heaving, sweating, tight-packed bodies inside the hull during high summer can be overpowering.

That is not to say that conditions on the trading vessels employed as ferries during the Games are pleasant. Ship-owners are liable to charge extortionate prices for nothing more than a perch on top of the cargo. For anyone on a tight budget, it will almost certainly be a matter of creating your own improvised berth, either in the gloom of the hold or on the open deck above, taking a chance on the personal hygiene of whoever pitches up as proximate neighbours.

Once aboard and on the move, there is a premium on endurance, patience and tolerance. Assuming favourable winds all the way (unlikely), the voyage takes at least a day from Corinth, two from Athens (including being hauled across the Isthmos), and five from Syracuse in eastern Sicily. From the most distant Greek cities – Ampurias in Spain, or Phasis on the Caucasus side of the Black Sea – the journey can take a fortnight.

The only way to cut the journey time would be to go direct, across open sea, but it is virtually impossible to persuade a Greek skipper to risk this, even in the fairly storm-free summer months. Hugging the coast is dangerous enough: a sudden squall can drive any sort of Greek vessel onto the rocks. Nervous passengers will spend much of the voyage praying to Poseidon for deliverance and pouring libations over the side. Of course, if coming from Naukratis in Egypt or Kyrene in Libya, there is no choice but to cross the Mediterranean. The libations will then be more generous.

So, going by sea, you are in for the long haul. You will be lucky if the ship is more than twenty metres long. It will have hurdlework above the gunwales designed to increase capacity, and the skipper can be guaranteed to have packed the vessel to maximise profit, perhaps taking on a mix of passengers and cargo (there being a captive market at the destination). With the crush onboard and the swaying of the vessel, sleep is virtually impossible. Expect to arrive at Olympia exhausted.[5]

Poor transport links are the key reason the Olympics tend to be a Western Greek event, with disproportionate numbers of athletes and spectators coming from southern Italy, Sicily and the Adriatic. The Olympics is one of four top festivals – known as the 'crown' games – but they are the least accessible. The Isthmian and Nemean Games, both on the opposite side of the Peloponnese and easily reached by sea, tend to attract Eastern Greeks from the island and coastal cities of the Aegean, while the Pythian Games at Delphi are best supported from Central and Northern Greece. Nonetheless, despite occupying the worst location, Olympia has achieved an unchallengeable position as Greece's premier sports festival (see pp. 126ff).[6]

Map 2. City-states and other places in Old Greece mentioned in the guide.

When you finally arrive, Olympia, nestled in a hollow surrounded by gentle hills, can look idyllic. The leisurely River Alpheios runs in multiple streams through a wide flood-plain on the southern edge of the site, while its narrow tributary, the Kladeos, runs beside the western boundary. The northern side is dominated by a steep-sided conical peak, the Hill of Kronos. The whole region is rich with cornfields, vineyards, olive groves and cattle pasture. Whether you have come over the rugged mountain passes of Arkadia or have island-hopped by sea, Olympia may seem a good place to have come to.[7]

But you may not have noticed, being wholly preoccupied

with the traffic jam and the crowds, as hundreds of carts and chariots, thousands of mules and horses, and tens of thousands of people nudge their way into the Olympic Village sprawling along the north bank of the Alpheios. At least there is no ticket barrier – the Olympic Games are free. But that is not to say they are cheap and easy. You will need to have come prepared. This may be the biggest religious and sporting festival in ancient Greece. There may be

ALPHEIOS AND ARETHUSA

Western Greeks, especially Syracusans, think of a visit to Olympia as a homecoming. The link between the western Peloponnese and Sicily is mythologised in the story of Alpheios and Arethusa.

Arethusa was a nymph, huntress, and follower of Artemis, goddess of the wild woods and virgin huntress. One summer's day, hot and tired from the hunt, she came upon the River Alpheios, running clear and cool, shaded by poplars and willows along the bank. She stripped off and dived in.

Looking up from the depths was the river god. Aroused by the beauty of the naked nymph swimming above, Alpheios surged upwards in a whirl of foaming water, groping towards Arethusa.

Startled and terrified, the nymph sprang onto the bank and fled, leaving her clothes hanging on a tree. Alpheios pursued her. The chase continued over plain and mountain, until, as the nymph began to flag, the river god closed the gap, his shadow upon her, his panting loud behind.

In the final seconds, Arethusa appealed to Artemis for deliverance, and in an instant the goddess had shrouded her in dense mist. Here she hid, while Alpheios, tormented by lust, flailed for her in the vapour, calling incessantly, 'Arethusa! Arethusa!'

Artemis did not desert her charge. The nymph dissolved into water and was transformed into a stream. The stream flowed down through the earth, running under the sea from the Peloponnese to Sicily, and then resurfaced on the island of Ortygia in Syracuse. The spring of Arethusa still feeds fresh water into a pool beside the sea.[8]

100,000 spectators staying for a week. But there are *no* facilities of any kind. Everyone has to fend for themselves.

DISTANCES, WEIGHTS AND MEASURES

Distances are calculated in ancient Greece using measures of length based on parts of the body. The basic unit is the foot (*pous*). Unfortunately, neither the foot nor its various subdivisions and multiples are stable quantities, varying from place to place. Because of this, the *stadion* of 600ft (which gives its name to the running track) is 192m in length at Olympia (under the state authority of Elis), but only 178m long at Delphi (under the inter-state authority of the Amphiktyonic Council). Generally speaking, short distances are measured in feet, longer distances in *stadia*.[9] The lengths of journeys, however, tend to be described in terms of the *stathmos*, a vague measure of both distance and speed that approximates to between fifteen and seventeen miles, the ground an army is expected to cover in a day's march.

Weights and volumes are equally unstable quantities. Do not assume you have been ripped off by a stall-holder until you have got used to the local standard. Weight measures are the obol, the drachma (six obols), the mina (100 drachmas), and the talent (sixty minas). But be aware that the Attic obol weighs only two-thirds that of the Aiginetan obol (0.72g as against 1.02g).

Volume measurements are vaguer still. The basic units are the cup (*kotule*) and the corn-measure (*medimnos*). Different sizes of cup are used in different places, and the range is as wide as that for the obol, between 210ml and 330ml. A handy ready-reckoner is that Greeks consider four cups to represent one man's daily ration of grain. The cup is the standard measure used in retail – the corn-measure (equal to 192 cups) is used only in wholesale – so it is the cup with which you will need to familiarise yourself.[10]

MONEY

There are no banks, credit facilities or even paper currency in ancient Greece. All commercial transactions involve coins or barter. The monetary system is based on coins of real metallic value and standardised weight. There are no tokens – that is, coins without intrinsic value which are nonetheless accepted in exchange because they are backed by state authority. An ancient Greek coin, assuming it is not a forgery, is worth exactly what it says it is worth – but with the usual caveat that actual weights, and therefore values, vary.

The talent and the mina represent quantities too large to be coined; they are used only as expressions of value. The coins in use are drachmas (minted in silver), obols (usually minted in bronze), or multiples and fractions thereof. The following table lists the coins you are likely to encounter:

tetradrachma (or stater)	four drachmas
tridrachma	three drachmas
didrachma	two drachmas
drachma	
tetrobol	four obols, two-thirds of a drachma
triobol (or hemidrachma)	three obols, half a drachma
diobol	two obols, one-third of a drachma
trihemiobol	one and a half obols
obol	one-sixth of a drachma
hemiobol	half an obol, one-twelfth of a drachma

You need to be aware that there are two main monetary standards in use, the Aiginetan and the Attic (or Euboic). The latter is more widespread, but it is the former that is used across the Peloponnese and therefore at Olympia. Local traders will, however, accept Attic currency, but if you carry it you will need to remember that the exchange rate is four Attic obols – not six – to the Aiginetan drachma. It is also worth knowing that both Persian and Phoenician silver circulates in ancient Greece. The following table gives the approximate exchange rates:

to the Aiginetan drachma : 1.42 Attic drachmas
to the Persian siglos : 1.24 Attic drachmas
to the Phoenician shekel : 1.63 Attic drachmas

Unfortunately, there is no real alternative to carrying all the money you need with you, despite the inevitable risk. Even so, be prepared to haggle and barter. Coins of low denomination did not exist in Greece at all half a century ago, and there are still desperate shortages of small change, especially in remote backwaters like Olympia. Simple transactions can degenerate into complex negotiations involving exchange rates and/or value in kind.[11] Do not expect shopping to be straightforward.

How much money will you need? A drachma is a good day's pay for a labourer, and visitors on a tight budget should be able to get by on this, even allowing for overcharging by traders in the Olympic Village. But if you choose not to walk, and if you plan to live it up during your stay, you will need much more.

DATES AND TIMES

The only Panhellenic calendar used in ancient Greece is that supplied by the Olympic Games themselves. The first recorded Olympics were held in the year that we now know as 776 BC, and then every four years after that. Each Olympic festival is named after the victor in the *stadion* (the 600ft sprint). So if a Greek says to you 'in the Olympiad of Xenophon of Corinth', this means 'in 464 BC', because it was in that year that Xenophon won the Olympic sprint. Go to a recitation of *The Peloponnesian War*, the extraordinary new book by the Athenian historian Thucydides that is the talk of the chattering classes, and you will find it employs an Olympic chronology.[12]

At home, however, each city-state tends to use its own system of dates based on the names of senior elected officials. The chronological framework for Athenian record-keeping, for example, is provided by the sequence of annually elected archons (the word simply means 'ruler'). To say 'in the archonship of Solon' means 'in 594 BC'.

Each year is divided into twelve lunar months. This reflects the deep religious significance attached to the lunar cycle. However, as everyone knows, the lunar and solar cycles are out of sync. The lunar cycle lasts for twenty-nine and a half days, so months calculated on this basis will slip by eleven or twelve days every solar year, such that the relationship between months and seasons would soon break down. The Greek practice is to insert an intercalary month every other year (so there are, in fact, twenty-five months spread over two years). Unfortunately, there is no standardisation: the names of the months vary from city-state to city-state, as do the arrangements for the intercalary adjustment.[13]

Months are not divided into weeks, and there are no days of the week. Instead, Greeks identify the day in one of two ways. They divide the month into three lunar sections

– waxing, full and waning – and then number the days in each.[14] Alternatively, they distinguish between work days and festival days. All festivals are essentially religious events, and they range from affairs of the family to those of the village, the state, and such pan-Greek extravaganzas as the crown games. Most regular monthly festivals are sufficiently small-scale as not to impede normal working, but annual festivals, whether local or state, involve a holiday for most people. The Athenians – famous as partygoers – have some sort of festival taking place every other day, and the typical citizen takes one day as holiday in every seven. It hardly needs saying that the religious calendar varies, not just from city-state to city-state, but from village to village. There is no way of talking about a specific day of the month that will be universally understood.[15]

The Greeks are very imprecise about the time of day. They tend to work – in a fairly laid-back way – throughout the hours of daylight, and they reckon time by using dawn, midday and dusk as reference points. More precise reckoning can be achieved by consulting a sundial or a water-clock, but these are oddities rather than everyday conveniences.[16] And why bother? No-one else will be keeping strict time, so you may as well take it easy and go with the flow. Leave your time-obsession and other neuroses at home when you head for the Games.

LANGUAGE

The Greeks are defined largely by their language. They make a sharp ethnic and moral distinction between themselves, those who speak Greek (known as *Hellenes* in their own language), and everyone else, all of whom are lumped together in the convenient catch-all category of 'barbarians' (*barbaroi*). As a visiting barbarian, you can expect to be well received. Strict rules of hospitality and

SOME HANDY GREEK WORDS AND PHRASES

Hello/Goodbye	*Chaire* (sing.), *Chairete* (pl.)
Please	*Ei soi dokei*
Thank you	*Charin echo soi*
Sorry	*Sugguothi moi*
How are you?	*Pos echeis?*
Good luck to you!	*Kale tuche soi!*
Cheers!	*Propino soi* (sing.), *humin* (pl.)
Which way to the nearest vacant camping space?	*Poi hai eggutatai kenai skenai?*
Is this water okay to drink?	*Potimo touto to udor?*
Where can I buy food near here?	*Pou entautha sitia oneisthai?*
Where can I find a doctor?	*Pou hiatrou heuriskein?*
Where is the best place to take a dump around here?	*Pou entautha kallista chezein?*
How much for a quickie?	*Boulomai binein hos tuchista – poson esti?*
When does the next event start?	*Pote archetai hō husteros agon?*
Get out of my sunlight!	*Ekpodon choreite moi!*
Is that Plato?	*Ho Platon autos?*

One	*Eis*	Six	*Hex*
Two	*Duo*	Seven	*Hepta*
Three	*Treis*	Eight	*Okto*
Four	*Tessares*	Nine	*Ennea*
Five	*Pente*	Ten	*Deka*

protection apply to strangers. It is an offence to the gods to do gratuitous harm to a stranger, and 'guest-friendship' (*xenia*) is a relationship hedged with taboo and almost mystical in its intensity. However, not being Greek, you will be regarded as a cultural inferior, and must be prepared to bear the occasional put-down with good grace.

A linguistic complication is the existence of numerous local dialects. Most Greeks can make themselves understood to other Greeks readily enough, but local pronunciation and colloquialisms can cause problems for the non-native speaker. Broadly, there are two groups of closely related dialects, the (newer) Northwestern and Doric on the one hand, and the (older) Arkadian, Aiolic and Ionic on the other. The Attic speech of the Athenians, for example, is an Ionic dialect, whereas the Lakonian speech of the Spartans is Doric. Greeks are acutely aware of such differences. Athenian plays sometimes include Spartan characters speaking with thick regional accents. The conventional Athenian view of Spartans is that they are uneducated, reactionary and thuggish. The Greeks can be shockingly racist about other Greeks, let alone 'barbarians'.

The Eleans speak Northwestern Greek, and the Olympics still draw their crowds disproportionately from the local region, so expect this to be the dialect you hear the most.[17] But all the dialects of Greece will certainly be represented during the festival.

HEALTH

Minor ailments are common at Olympia. The festival takes place in mid-August, the hottest time of year, and the sanitary conditions are dire. In most places, particularly in the Stadium and the Hippodrome, there is no shade. Heat-related problems – sunburn, headache, dehydration and sunstroke – are common. The philosopher-scientist Thales of Miletos is reputed to have died of sunstroke at Olympia.[18] Also common are stomach upsets, since the place is awash with refuse and sewage which contaminate the water supply and provide sustenance for millions of flies. Expect food poisoning, and worse.

A third worry is infection by others. With around 100,000 people packed together for a week in a crowded camp-city and sports complex, disease spreads easily, and there is always the chance of something really nasty getting a grip. The Great Plague that afflicted war-time Athens in the years 430-27 BC killed around a third of the city's population. For anyone visiting Greece, especially in high summer, the recorded symptoms give food for thought.

The disease seems to have worked its way down the body. First came fever, inflammation of the eyes, bleeding from the mouth, and foul-smelling breath; then sneezing, hoarseness and coughing; next, stomach aches and violent vomiting; and finally burning skin, eruptions of pustules and ulcers, a raging thirst, uncontrollable diarrhoea, loss of feeling in the extremities, and sometimes blindness and total memory loss, such that friends went unrecognised. It could have been any one of a number of diseases, including measles, typhoid and pneumonic plague.

If you do have a serious problem and need medical help, there are various options, not all to be recommended. Medicine is a bitterly contested field in Greece, and practitioners divide into two main camps.[19]

HIPPOKRATIC DOCTORS

The followers of Hippokrates of Kos take an essentially scientific-rationalist approach. They are not strong on diagnosis because, with dissection of corpses tabooed on religious grounds, they have not had the opportunity to study how the body actually works. They are guided by

GLOIOS

You may be offered *gloios* for sale in small ceramic bottles. This is medicine, not food, but is of highly questionable value. *Gloios* is a mixture of oil, sweat and dust that has accumulated on the bodies of athletes during exercise, practice and training. It is collected when athletes scrape themselves down with a *stlengis* (strigil) after completing their routines. There seems to be some confusion over whether it is primarily an ointment or a potion. Presumably, it is relatively harmless – though unpleasant and perhaps somewhat anti-social – when used as the former; consumption, on the other hand, is not to be recommended.[21]

rather vague notions of the body being composed of various 'elements' that need to be kept in 'balance'. Methods include dieting, exercise, bloodletting, surgery and purgative drugs. On the other hand, the observation of injuries, diseases and the curative properties (or not) of various treatments has enabled them to accumulate an impressive store of trial-and-error knowledge. The most conscientious and experienced Hippokratic doctors can be very good indeed. Needless to say, this is reflected in their fees.

Public doctors are the best. To be awarded one of the few official appointments is a mark of the highest distinction for a doctor. At Olympia, however, any public doctors are likely to be busy dealing with athletic injuries, and you will probably need to see a private practitioner. Most doctors fall into this category, either with a shop in the city, or working as an itinerant travelling with portable medicine case and instruments from village to village. You should find a good number of them set up in temporary stalls in the Olympic Village for the duration of the Games.

Those on a tight budget need to be wary. According to the great Hippokrates himself, only a minority of the medical profession can be described as 'good doctors', while the lower end of the fraternity grades imperceptibly into the ranks of sundry drug-sellers, potion-makers, magicians and out-and-out crooks. A basic test is whether

ASKLEPIOS

Asklepios is the semi-divine son of the god Apollo and the mortal woman Koronis.

While pregnant with Apollo's child, Koronis slept with an old flame, and her infidelity was reported to the god. Enraged, Apollo persuaded his sister, Artemis, archer-goddess of wild nature and the hunt, to destroy Koronis with her deadly arrows. When Apollo saw the corpse, beautiful and bloody, he was filled with remorse. Though he could not resurrect his lover, he asked Hermes, god of the death-passage – amongst much else – to cut the foetus from the womb and give it life.

Apollo taught his son the arts of healing, and then arranged his further education by apprenticing him to Cheiron the Centaur, half man, half beast, but learned in medicine. Asklepios became skilled in surgery, the use of drugs, and the occult mysteries of resurrection.

With a phial of the Gorgon Medusa's life-giving blood, he set about negating death and snatching victims from Hades, lord of the Underworld. Some say that Asklepios was paid in gold by those he restored to life, others that he was a philanthropist. Either way, Hades complained to Zeus, and Zeus destroyed Asklepios for *hubris*, along with his latest patient, in the blast of a thunderbolt.

In revenge, Apollo killed three one-eyed giants known as 'Cyclops', who lived on the slopes of Mount Etna in Sicily and worked as armourers and fortress-builders for Zeus. Apollo was condemned to a year's hard labour, but his son, Asklepios, was revived, deified and elevated to Mount Olympos, residence of the gods, in conformity with an ancient prophecy which Zeus now honoured.

So young Asklepios, equipped with a snake-talisman, his symbol of healing, is revered by both Hippokratic doctors and Asklepian priests – but they bicker endlessly over his true allegiance, the former claiming it for science, the latter for superstition.[23]

or not your man has provided himself with a well-lit location for examinations and a good stock of medicines, clean bandages, fresh water and surgical instruments.[20]

ASKLEPIAN PRIESTS

The second class of practitioners is comprised of the priests of various health cults, principally that of Asklepios, but also of Hygieia (goddess of health), Eileithyia (goddess of childbirth) and Apollo (god of light, prophecy, music, the arts, male beauty, and also – two important sidelines – plague and healing). The greatest of the healing centres is that at Epidavros in the northeastern Peloponnese, where the sick are treated in one of two ways: they might 'incubate' in a special dormitory and be visited by Asklepios in the form of a dream; and/or they might be approached by one of Asklepios's sacred snakes. In either case, the result might be an immediate cure, or the interpretation offered by one of the priests might lead to a cure. It is customary for the suppliant to dedicate cakes, other offerings, and ceramic models of the malfunctioning body part in the Sanctuary.[22]

Almost any Greek deity can be called upon in a medical emergency, so expect there to be a colourful variety of priests offering their services as intermediaries, ranging from highly respectable Asklepians to the crackpots and charlatans of the mystic fringe.

ACCOMMODATION

There are no hotels or boarding houses at Olympia. The authorities provide none, and it is not profitable for entrepreneurs to fill the gap, since the site is really busy for only one week in every four years. Most of the time Olympia is staffed by a small group of religious functionaries and groundsmen, with visitors reduced to a slow trickle of pilgrims and sightseers. At the festival, everybody camps. Come prepared.

Dictators, diplomats and the rich tend to advertise their presence with large tent-pavilions decorated with colourful hangings, often erected in the more prominent locations close to the Sanctuary at the centre of the site. In these, they will host banquets for the great and good, especially when there is a victory to celebrate. Most people, on the other hand, have to claim a pitch and improvise a shelter amidst a sprawling camping-ground of awnings, tents and shacks extending along the Alpheios or down one of the tracks leading to the site.

With up to 100,000 seeking accommodation, if you arrive relatively late you may find yourself making camp several miles from the Stadium. For some, this is a matter of choice. There is less tolerance of rowdy behaviour close to the Sanctuary, and the police (*Mastigophoroi*: Whip-bearers) are more active in this area. If you want a relaxed 'alternative' atmosphere, camp further out. On the other hand, if you are travelling light and do not mind humping your stuff around, you can simply sleep rough each night wherever takes your fancy.

The discomfort is compounded by the searing heat of a landlocked valley in high summer, and the dust, garbage and flies generated by a vast shanty town. Getting enough water to drink – never mind wash – is a permanent preoccupation. The authorities sink temporary well shafts for the festival, but there are never enough of them. The rivers, shrunken by the summer heat, are soon flowing with any amount of filth and disease. To get clear of the contamination you will have to walk several miles.

Further misery is inflicted by the swarms of mosquitoes that breed in the fetid pools and channels of the valley at this time of year. As well as the irritation of bites, and the risk of infection if you scratch at them, there is a real danger of malaria.

Toilet facilities are nonexistent. There are attempts to direct people to certain areas, but the reality is that nowhere is really clean. With tens of thousands packed together, sweating all day and reluctant to wash in the polluted channels of the river, coupled with the heaps of refuse and excrement rotting in the heat, the simple truth is that the Olympic Village festers and stinks.

Of rest and sleep, expect little. As well as the impediments of hard ground, lack of space, summer heat, foul smells, itching bites and gippy tummy, there is the noise, which never really stops. At every hour of the night until dawn, someone on the campsite nearby will be raucously (and drunkenly) partying. No-one sleeps properly. Most spectactors view the Games through the leaden haze of exhaustion.[24]

Why do the authorities do nothing to improve facilities? They do. They pray to Herakles and Zeus.

ZEUS: ZAPPER OF FLIES

Herakles, semi-divine hero and mythic founder of the Games, was pestered by flies while making a sacrifice at Olympia. In his irritation, he appealed to his father, Olympian Zeus, lord of the heavens and king of the gods. It is not recorded how helpful this was, but true to the tradition, centuries later Zeus *Apomuios* ('Averter of Flies') is still worshipped at the Sanctuary.

It has not made any difference. There are still millions of flies. Even Zeus, it seems, cannot counteract the effects of Olympia's insanitary squalor.[25]

2. A symposium – a male drinking party – in full swing. Hundreds will be held in large tents during the Games.

EATING AND DRINKING

The ancient Greeks eat four meals a day. Breakfast (*akratisma*) usually consists of bread dipped in undiluted wine along with some olives or figs. Lunch (*ariston*) is also a light meal, typically bread with some cheese, olives and figs. Tea (*deilinon*) is optional and really just a snack to keep you going until the main meal of the day. This is dinner (*deipnon*), and it involves the full ritualised rigmarole of Greek eating and drinking.[26]

THE STAPLE (*SITOS*)

A full meal consists of three elements: the staple (*sitos*), the relish (*opson*), and the drink, invariably watered wine (*oinos*). *Sitos* is usually barley bread, but this is prepared and baked in a variety of ways, and often contains added ingredients such as fat, herbs, milk, oil and the seeds of flax, poppy and sesame. It can also be fried or used to make pies. Meat, fish, vegetable and cheese pies are common fast foods. *Laganon*, a sort of baked wheat-cake, is often available as an alternative to bread. When the Greeks talk about *sitos*, then, they have in mind the main fill-up food that gives a meal its bulk. The contrast they make is with the more expensive, tasty, fat- and protein-rich food that peps it up and makes it a proper meal – which they call *opson*.[27]

THE RELISH (*OPSON*)

Beef, lamb and pork are not considered everyday foods. They tend to be reserved for special occasions, and are rarely served outside the context of ritual feasting, when the meat of sacrificial animals is available. Heroes – whether Homeric or Olympian – might dine regularly on meat, but ordinary mortals usually make do with fish. The rich, as usual, are an exception, and meat is often served at elite dinner parties.

If you do insist on meat, the choices are likely to be game, goat and offal. The sausages and pies can be excellent, and the range can be wide, including chicken, duck, goose, partridge, pelican, thrush and swan, and also hare, turtle and wild boar.

But the dominant food is fish, which is available in great variety and to suit all budgets. Preserved fish (*tarikhos*) tends to be cheap, with salted mackerel and tuna among the tastier options. Fresh fish is usually more expensive, but there is a considerable variety, from anchovies, sprats and other small fry at the cheaper end, and such delicacies as blackfish, conger eel, dogfish, gilthead bream, grey mullet, lobster, red mullet, sea bass, sea perch, shark and swordfish at the other. Or, if you want to try something different, there is either *glaukos* ('grey-fish') or *karabos* ('heavy-armed crayfish').

Certain cuts are especially prized by Greek fish-lovers: the belly and some parts of the neck and shoulders of tuna;

and the heads of conger eels, sea bass and *glaukos*. But it is the eel (in all its constituent parts) that seems to drive the locals into ecstasies.

Cheese is considered very much a second-rate 'snack' food, although it can sometimes be an ingredient in the finest meat and fish recipes.[28]

SICILIAN CHEFS

The Sicilian Greeks, along with the Sybarites of southern Italy, are considered the greatest chefs and gourmands. Among the island's famous chefs is Mithaikos, author of a widely-read cookbook; even Plato talks of him. If you wish to try a simple recipe, here is one of his for the preparation of ribbon-fish: 'Cut off the head of the ribbon-fish. Wash it and cut into slices. Pour cheese and oil over it'.[29]

VEGETABLES (*LAKHANA*)

Meat and fish can be fried, roasted, braised or stewed, and typically are served with both staple and vegetables. The latter include lentils, broad beans and other pulses, various edible grasses like notchweed, along with leeks and bulbs, cabbage, mallows, mushrooms and black mustard. Among the salad vegetables are artichokes, rocket, lettuce, nettles, radishes and boiled courgettes. A wide variety of herbs is also used to season food.

Many foods, especially vegetables and herbs, are prized for supposed medicinal qualities. Lettuce and rocket function as aphrodisiacs. Cabbage helps headaches. Basil is an insect repellent. Saffron deals with stomach upsets, sage with snakebites. Whether these and other herbal remedies work is an open question, but often enough it is all there is.

Yet more dubious are various food superstitions. Lentils cause distension. Broad beans weigh down the stomach and damage the intellect. Cow's milk facilitates conception. Eating the testicles of a hare will guarantee a male child. Much of this nonsense is the lore of cranks, but some of it has deep roots in religious tradition, so if you do not want to cause offence, play safe and keep quiet when you come across it.[30]

DESSERTS AND SWEETS (*TRAGEMATA*)

Ancient Greeks consider honey the nectar of the gods. They use it for flavour and sweetness in both savoury and sweet dishes, and of special note is a wide variety of honey-soaked cakes, pastries and pancakes, often with seeds, nuts and/or dried fruit as additional ingredients. Because of its sacred character, honey is also widely used in ritual, including the special beverages consumed during religious festivals.[31]

WINE (*OINOS*)

The Greeks drink watered wine. Anyone who drinks beer or undiluted wine they consider *barbaros*.

The wine flows freely in the Olympic Village. The 'tavern' (*kapeleion*) can range from an elaborate pavilion with facilities for sitting and dining, to nothing more than a slave-girl with a cart. Keep alert for short measures, over-watering, and charging for high quality while serving low.

Undiluted wine is likely to be around fifteen per cent or more alcohol, but the Greek practice is always to add water. It usually has bits of grape and vine debris floating in it, so it will need straining before drinking. Be prepared for distinctive aromas and tastes – the result of storage and transportation in amphoras sealed with pitch or resin, and sometimes, in the case of local farm produce, in the skins of goats and sheep. Wine is either white, 'black' (equivalent to red), or 'amber' (equivalent to rosé). White and amber can be sweet or dry, while black can be made 'medium'.

Cheap local wine is likely to cost around an obol for three cups' worth, so even a budget-conscious traveller on a drachma a day could easily get plastered. At the other end of the spectrum are top imported wines from such places as Chios, Lesbos, Magnesia, Mende and Thasos. Fine wine can send Greeks into raptures. 'With Mendean wine,' croons the Athenian playwright Hermippos, 'the gods themselves wet their soft beds. And then there is Magnesian, generous, sweet, and smooth, and Thasian, upon whose surface skates the perfume of apples; this I judge by far the best of all the wines, except for blameless, painless Chian'.[32]

MUG, CUP OR DRINKING-HORN?

Wine is served in different types of cup. The Spartan *kothon*, a heavy military-type mug, is increasingly popular, especially among the rich, who admire its right-wing chic. It is as well to be aware that the defeat of Athens at the end of the Peloponnesian War in 404 BC (less than twenty years ago) was widely perceived as a setback for democrats everywhere. Sparta is certainly the dominant power in Greece at present, and because of this, in some circles, the Spartan style has become fashionable, sometimes abrasively so. The *kothon*, due to its size, is also associated with excessive drinking. If you use one, people may read into it more than you intend.

Moderate drinkers and self-conscious democrats tend to prefer the delicate *kulix*, a shallow drinking-cup. If you want something a bit more substantial, but without the connotations of the *kothon*, you might choose a *kantharos*, a deep drinking-cup especially associated with the wine god Dionysos. Or you may prefer a horn-shaped vessel, a *rhuton* or *keras*, both of which have ample capacity, plus a touch of the barbarian-exotic, not to mention the picnic-site advantage that the pointy end can be poked into the ground.[33]

It is common to eat nibbles with wine, either savoury (*hales*) or sweet (*tragemata*).[34]

FROM FAST FOOD TO FEASTS

The simplest way to eat is to buy ready-cooked fast food from one of the numerous vendors in the Olympic Village. Be aware that food vendors, especially fishmongers, have a dubious reputation for cheating. A favourite device is regularly drenching their fish in water to make them look fresher. Do bear in mind that 'fresh' fish arriving from the coast is likely to be at least a day old by the time it reaches you at Olympia.

Self-catering is difficult on your own. Fish and other meat tends to be sold whole or in large cuts (remember the lack of small change), and you will also need to rig up a cooking fire, so self-catering works best as part of a group. It will also give you more confidence when it comes to haggling over price, which is more or less universal. To give an idea, at the top of the range you might have to pay four obols for an octopus, five for a grey mullet, eight for a barracuda, and perhaps as much as eighteen (three drachmas) for a large eel.[35]

Option three for dinner is to get yourself invited to someone else's dinner party (called a *sumposion* or, as we tend to say, 'symposium'). This might be easier than you would expect since the Greeks are very hospitable, strangers are under divine protection, and creating 'guest-friends' is the main form of social networking. The symposium is an all-male drinking party where the guests recline on couches, enjoy good food and wine, sing to the accompaniment of panpipes and the lyre, and engage in learned and witty conversation. Hired entertainment can include poets, musicians and dancing girls. If there are other women present, they are likely to be *hetairai* (courtesans). Some of the male 'guests' might also turn out to be prostitutes. Unless you are prepared, the whole thing can be a bit of a culture shock.

Official feasting takes place in the evenings of the second, third and fifth days. On Day Three, when 100 oxen donated by the host city of Elis are sacrificed to Zeus (see pp. 221-2), there should be enough for everyone. Private victory parties, often on the last night, usually organised by the horsey set to celebrate a win in the chariot-race, can also be lavish enough to feed large numbers. Alkibiades, the famous (and scandal-ridden) Athenian aristocrat who won the chariot-race in 416 BC, paid for enough roast ox to feed everyone at the Games.[36]

TABLE MANNERS

Even without an obol to spare, you are unlikely to starve at the Olympics. But to keep your place at table, it is worth knowing the basic etiquette. Food comes first, then the tables are cleared and re-set for the drinking. You recline on your left arm, using the left hand for bread only, and you use the right to take food from the communal dishes before you. Remember the rule: *sitos* with the left, *opson* with the right.

Spoons are occasionally used for sloppy foods, but never knives or forks. Plates are sometimes provided, but often not, and napkins never. Bread is multifunctional – staple, scoop, saucer and sponge.

Needless to say, it is bad manners to pig yourself or get blotto. *Opsophagoi* (roughly 'fish-loving gluttons') and *philopotai* ('wine-loving drunks') are disapproved of. On the other hand, to some degree it depends who you are with and the time of night. Do not be surprised to hear drunken fops being rowdy in the small hours. But they will not be popular.[37]

SEX

WOMEN AT THE GAMES

Men cannot take their wives to the Olympic Games: there is an inviolable ban on attendance by married citizen-women. By what seems a strange quirk, on the other hand, they *can* take their unmarried daughters. This is almost certainly because, in a dim and distant past, only virgins were pure enough to participate in the local fertility rites of goddesses like Demeter or Hera (see pp. 84ff), and

ATALANTA

A famous myth concerning the relationship between women and sport is that of Atalanta. Stories like this will often be alluded to in passing comments, and will sometimes be the subject of intense, even impassioned, debate. It is as well to have some familiarity with the major myths relevant to the Olympic Games – of which there are many.

Because her father wanted a son, Atalanta was abandoned and exposed on a hillside. But she was rescued by Artemis, goddess of wild nature, and reared by a clan of huntsmen, who trained her from babyhood in running, wrestling and the chase. She grew into a formidable huntress and athlete. Uninterested in men and

marriage, she would kill to protect her virginity.

In the hunt for the Kalydonian Boar, she took her place in the line with the men. When the great beast was flushed out, it charged the hunters, killing some, scattering others. But Atalanta wounded it behind the ear with an arrow-shot and it scurried off.

'That is no way to hunt,' sneered Ankaios. 'Watch me!' As the boar charged again, he stood his ground and swung with his axe, but he misjudged, and in an instant he was impaled, castrated and disembowelled.

It was Meleager who inflicted the fatal blow, a javelin cast into the right flank, which caused the beast to flail in pain their presence is therefore sanctioned by ancient religious tradition. That said, no self-respecting Greek father would risk the chastity and reputation of his maiden daughter at the Games. Nor would he want her there cramping his style: at one level, the Games are like a gigantic stag party. So, in practice, with one or two notable exceptions, the wives and daughters of Greek citizens do not attend.

The main exception is the Priestess of Demeter of the Earth-bed (*Chamune*). She, indeed, has a special seat, the very altar of the goddess she serves, situated on the north side of the Stadium. Like the theoretical admission

and drive the blade into its heart.

But Meleager was besotted with Atalanta, so he gave her the pelt that was the champion hunter's reward, saying, 'You drew first blood, and had we left the beast alone, it would soon have succumbed to your arrow.'

She was later seduced by Meleager, and gave birth to a son. But, still in denial of her womanhood, she left him exposed to die on a hillside, to be found by shepherds and given the name Parthenopaios, 'son of a pierced maidenhood'.

Atalanta, in short, was a threat to the patriarchal order.

Her father, finally willing to welcome her home, now sought a husband for her. She resisted, insisting that any suitor for her hand should first beat her in a foot-race, and if any tried and failed, she would kill them.

Melanion, as love-struck as Meleager had been, appealed to Aphrodite, goddess of love, for help. She supplied three golden apples, advising her protégé to throw them beside the track during the race. Sure enough, Atalanta, distracted and delayed by the baubles, was pipped to the post by Melanion.

Forced to marry, she still resisted male lust. Her defiance of both Aphrodite and patriarchy now destroyed her. She finally succumbed to Melanion in a precinct of Zeus, defiling its sacredness. In punishment, Zeus turned the lovers into a pair of lions, unable ever again to consummate their love.[40]

of maidens, the actual presence of the Priestess is almost certainly a relic of ancient fertility rites.[38]

The other exception to the male-only audience is women getting in disguised as men. It is easy to imagine motives: mothers wanting to see their sons compete, women eager to admire the male talent, or simply curious about the biggest sports event in the calendar, and so on. The one recorded case concerns a woman called Kallipateira (or Pherenike) from Rhodes, the daughter of a boxer, who accompanied her son, Peisirodos, to the Olympics disguised as his trainer. When he won, she leaped over the barrier in her excitement and exposed herself. The authorities let her go unpunished, out of respect for her father, her brothers and her son, all Olympic victors – but they took the future precaution of requiring trainers to go naked like athletes.[39]

This does not mean there are no women around in the Olympic Village. Far from it. There are two sorts of women in ancient Greece: those with whom you cannot copulate in legal and physical safety (respectable citizen-women), and those with whom you can (slaves, foreigners, barbarians and professional prostitutes). And, of course, there are tens of thousands of men. So, for those who wish to make it so, the Olympic Games can be a sex-fest.

STRAIGHT SCENE

You will discover that sex is very much on sale in the Olympic Village during the festival, and that there are services to suit all budgets; as in all things, you travel first-class if you can afford it, and economy if your means are more modest.

Rich men may be accompanied at the Games by either a live-in concubine or an *hetaira* with whom they have a current relationship. Otherwise, they may buy in the services of one or more *hetairai* for an evening's entertainment.

3. A prostitute and a prospective client. Erotically-attired dancing girls are often hired for a symposium.

Hetairai are classy professional 'companions' or 'escorts', many of whom work independently, maintaining their own houses out of the 'gifts' they receive from admirers. Often intelligent and educated, always seductive and manipulative, an *hetaira* will be expensive, whatever sort of relationship you have with her.

Much cheaper and far more numerous are the *pornai* (common prostitutes). Some work for pimps (*pornoboskoi*) in proper brothels, often spinning and weaving by day, and selling sex by night. Spinning and weaving are considered 'women's work', associated especially with respectable citizen-women, since they take place in the seclusion of the women's quarters in the sexually segregated Greek home. Expect, therefore, to see scantily-clad *pornai* working spindles and looms as you amble around the Olympic

Village – a scene which carries a heavy erotic charge for Greek citizen-men. Come back at night and you will see them arranged in a semicircle, half-naked or draped in diaphanous fabric, awaiting inspection by drop-in clients. A well-appointed 'fuckery' (*kineterion*) may have partitioned cubicles available once a selection has been made.

Cheaper still are street prostitutes, some of them slave-girls owned by pimps, some desperate creatures eking out a lonely living in the shadow-land on the margins of society. This can be a dangerous world of competition, haggling, punch-ups and, not least, misogynist violence, which often lurks just beneath the surface in this deeply patriarchal society.

Needless to say, there is a big difference between *pornai*, who deal in quick sex and are paid for the deed, and *hetairai*, who are paid for the evening, and may or may not grant their favour at the end of it, depending on mood, the generosity of the 'gifts' with which they have been plied, and, to be blunt, whether they fancy it with the bloke in question.

Prices can range from one obol to 1000 drachmas. Typical prices might be two or three obols for a quickie with a street prostitute, one or two drachmas for the pretty flute-girl among a troupe of entertainers, and as much as 100 drachmas for a top-flight *hetaira*. But price also depends on position (sexual, that is).

The bottom end of the market (so to speak) usually means the *kubda* (bent-over, rear-entry), with the *lordo* (woman bent back, rear-entry) pricier, while the *keles* or racehorse (man on his back, woman on top, front-entry) is very expensive.

Three words of warning. First, disease is rampant; it is certainly true in general terms, and possibly so of venereal disease specifically. Second, be aware that any sex on offer is a commodity – that is, you will have to pay. Third, do not assume that all women you meet are potentially available.

In other words, expect to encounter *hetairai*, even *pornai*, who are already accounted for – and for all you know, the bloke might be an Olympic wrestler.[41]

NAKEDNESS

Male-on-male sexuality is a normal feature of Greek culture. Greek men are commonly bisexual. It is standard practice for citizen-men, assuming they have either the looks or the money, to sleep at different times with their wives, female prostitutes, male lovers (often teenage boys), and male prostitutes. For many, spending a week at Olympia away from home is an opportunity for a sex holiday.

The Games are certainly conducive to this. Athletics is homoerotically charged. This starts with two simple facts: all athletes are relatively young men at the peak of physical condition; and all athletic exercise, training, practice and competition are performed naked. So deep-rooted is this aspect of Greek athletics that the word for 'training-ground' (*gumnasion*) is derived from the word for 'naked' (*gumnos*). Not the least of Olympia's attractions for a good proportion of spectators is the stunning display it affords of bronzed male beauty completely exposed.

Why the nakedness? Many explanations are offered. Some say the Spartans started it when they began anointing their bodies with oil before gymnastic exercise. Some contend that it was the Athenians, who passed a law making nakedness compulsory after a runner leading in his race tripped and fell when his loincloth unravelled. Others report that the example was set in the Olympiad of 720 BC, when Orsippos of Megara also lost his loincloth, only in this case he went on to win the race. Or maybe it was Akanthos of Sparta who did this. And so on. In other words, none of the Greeks is sure when and why athletic nakedness began. The one thing that is certain is that it was not always so: Homer's heroes did not strip off for games, so the practice dates from some time after around 750 BC.[42]

Three explanations are worth pondering. The first is purely practical. The standard personal kit of every athlete is an oil flask (*aryballos*), strigil (*stlengis*) and sponge (*spongos*). That is because the Greek practice is to coat one's skin with oil before exercise, to scrape the oil, sweat and dust off afterwards, and then to wash down at a basin. The oil acts as a sunblock and keeps dirt out of the pores, but it makes a mess of any clothing. The simplest thing by far is to wear nothing at all.[43]

The second possibility is that nakedness has ritual significance. Rites of passage that involve passing from one state of being to another require the casting off of one identity in order to assume an alternative. One way of doing this is to change clothes – and to symbolise the liminal state between identities by going naked. The Olympic Games are rooted in the rituals and symbolism of the fertility cults. Perhaps athletes entering the Games shed their old skins and appear naked before the god in order to emerge purified and transformed by the festival's end.

A third guess is that nakedness is somehow linked with the spirit of democracy. All Greeks are citizens of a city-state (*polis*) where they enjoy legal protection and political rights. The extent of actual democracy varies, but brazen flaunting of wealth goes down badly everywhere. So egalitarianism – more or less – is the political fashion in Greece. And nothing levels men more completely than to be stripped of all fine clothes and accoutrements and to appear naked at the starting gates, rich and poor, side by side, in the Stadium.[44]

Oiled bodies. Ritual purity. The democratic spirit. All three, perhaps, are facilitated by athletic nakedness.

GAY SCENE

Olympia offers a surfeit of homosexual opportunities. Pederasty – the erotic love of adult males for adolescent boys – is widely practised in Greece. Indeed, the most idealised gay relationship is that between a mature male and a virginal teenager, with the former pursuing and attempting to seduce the latter. The symposium is a traditional setting for such endeavours, and it is common to see older and younger men paired on couches. There is often a flirtatious undercurrent to the symposium's mix of witty conversation, singing to the accompaniment of lyre or pipes, and playing party games like *kottabos* (tiddlywinks: flicking dregs of wine from empty cups at some sort of mark). Surprisingly strong and enduring relationships may result.[45]

A book by Ion of Chios called *Visits* records in passing some current seduction techniques. The boy serving the drinks at a party on Chios caught the eye of Sophocles,

4. Locker-room seduction. Older men hang around gymnasia and sports festivals in the hope of a pick-up.

the famous Athenian playwright (aged around fifty at the time). 'Do you want me to drink with pleasure?' he asked. The boy did. 'In that case, take your time when you approach me to fill my glass, and do not be in a hurry to withdraw.' The boy blushed. Later, Sophocles asked the boy to blow some vine-debris from his cup, seizing the opportunity thus contrived to steal a kiss.[46]

The hired entertainment may include boys as well as girls among the dancers and musicians. *Kithara* (lyre) players are considered especially desirable. Some may not be available, some may already be accounted for, but more often than not the impresario doubles as a pimp willing to sell his troupe's sexual services at a suitable price. At the top of the range, a boy might cost as much as 300 drachmas – a year's wages for many Greek workers.[47]

More casual pick-ups might be made where athletes are working out. Sport is closely bound with the Greek cult of the male body-beautiful. Moreover – notwithstanding much evidence to the contrary – physical beauty is assumed to correlate with intellect and moral virtue. Since male lovers are desired for all three attributes, it is little wonder that the gymnasium is traditionally associated with both voyeurism and courtship (see pp. 118ff).

Older men will often be seen watching the naked youth exercise in the gymnasium while homosexual couples (or would-be couples) will agree to train and wrestle together. Here, too, *kinaidoi* ('little buggers') sometimes hang out. The term is street slang and its meaning is broad and vague, but it usually implies an effeminate man, seductively dressed, parading availability, sometimes for money. The most important thing about a *kinaidos* is that he offers himself in the passive role. In the patriarchal culture of the Greeks, he who penetrates asserts dominance; to be penetrated by a social inferior is considered degrading and emasculating.[48]

The Athenian philosopher Plato applauds pederasty as the basis for bonds of friendship which inspire higher thoughts. The poet Theognis of Megara writes of the happiness of exercising naked in the morning and then spending the rest of the day with a boy lover. Many Attic painted pots depict athletes bearing young men's names with the adjective *kalos* – so-and-so 'is beautiful'. Other scenes show mature men chasing young athletes with traditional courtship gifts like cocks and hares. The Athenian playwright Aristophanes has a father upbraiding a male friend for not making advances towards his son upon returning with him from the training school.

In short, homosexuality and the gymnasium are inseparable in Greece. Statues of Eros, god of male desire and sexual education, often stand in training schools. Disapproval of pederasty, by contrast, is considered one of the more benighted aspects of barbarism.[49]

ZEUS AND GANYMEDE

The gods lead the way in Greece. Zeus seems to be Heaven's premier sexual athlete, with some 120 recorded female conquests.[50] But he also likes boys.

His most famous homosexual infatuation was with a youth called Ganymede, the son of King Tros, the founder of Troy, and said to be the most beautiful boy alive. Zeus was besotted when he first caught sight of him. Swooping down to the plain of Troy disguised as an eagle, he grabbed the boy and swept him up to Heaven, where he made him cup-bearer to the gods and bedfellow to himself.

Zeus sent Hermes to compensate King Tros for his loss with gifts of a golden vine and two horses, and assurances that Ganymede was happy in his new role, serving nectar to the gods from a golden bowl, and that he would escape old age and live forever.[51]

THE FRINGE: POLITICS

The main entertainment at the Games is provided by the official religious pageants and the athletic competitions, but numerous fringe events provide endless distractions.

Many other games festivals integrate contests in music, poetry, drama and dance into their main programmes. The Pythian Games at Delphi – sacred to Apollo, god of music – includes contests in the playing of, and singing to, both the *kithara* (lyre) and the *aulos* (flute-like pipes). The Panathenaic Games at Athens – dedicated to Athena, patron goddess of Greece's city of culture – does the same, and also has contests in something called 'fiery' dancing.[52] Olympia, though, sticks resolutely to an exclusively athletic programme, consigning all visiting musicians, dancers, poets and other arty types to the fringe. They remain undeterred, however, for even the fringe at Olympia guarantees an audience. Because of this, you will never be bored during the Games: someone, somewhere, is always putting on a performance.

The Games are especially popular with right-wing intellectuals. There are two main reasons for this. Greece is sharply divided between 'oligarchs' (essentially upper-class conservatives who support the status quo) and 'democrats' (lower-class radicals who want more power for ordinary citizens and a more equal distribution of wealth). The main antidote to democratic sentiment is to shift attention away from divisions between rich and poor by stressing what the Greeks call *homonoia* – literally 'same-mindedness' or, in political terms, the unity of the Greeks. It boils down to whether you think the main enemy is at home (the Greek aristocracy) or abroad (the Great King of Persia). Olympia is especially popular in right-wing circles because it is a Panhellenic ('all-Greek') festival that glosses over inter-Greek animosities.[53]

Secondly, Olympia is about sport, and sport in Greece

is ineradicably tainted with elitism. The reason is simple: you need leisure to train, and you need money to train well. The city gymnasium is traditionally the place where well-born young men hang out. That is why philosophers hold court in and around the place: it is where their paying clientele are to be found. So the gymnasium is a kind of finishing school, providing both physical and intellectual education, for the gilded youth.

Significantly, the Greek word *schole* actually means 'leisure'. Implication: you get a proper education only if you belong to the leisured classes. Result: most athletes are 'well-born' (as the Greeks choose to put it, somewhat tactlessly). Everyone else – presumably 'badly-born' – is too busy making a living.[54]

In a nutshell, sport is both nationalistic and elitist, so Olympia is a good place for patriotic recitations. Herodotus, for example, the famous historian of the Persian Wars, delivered lectures from the back porch of the Temple of Zeus. His big theme was the unity of Greeks from different city-states in the desperate struggle to throw back the invaders.

Gorgias, a well-known philosopher from Sicily, also turned up to bang the war drum. He lectured at Olympia in 408 BC to the effect that Greek should not fight Greek, one city-state against another, but instead should direct their aggression against the territory of 'barbarians'. Nothing like a foreign war to unite the country.[55]

Yet more exciting can be the appearance of a famous war hero. Themistokles, architect of the decisive naval victory over the Persian invasion fleet at Salamis in 480 BC, relished the applause of the crowd at Olympia when he pitched up four years later. He took the opportunity to denounce Hiero, tyrant of Syracuse, for staying out of the great patriotic war. This was very much playing to the crowd.

The Sicilian tyrants, by the way, are obscenely rich, so they can afford the best horses, vehicles and charioteers. In consequence, they often win the horse- and chariot-races. Their victory parties are lavish and often open to all. They hire the best poets, sculptors and mint-masters to advertise their successes in verse, bronze and on coins. It does them little good: no-one really likes them. Themistokles knew his audience.

THE FRINGE: CULTURE

Still, every artist has to make a living, so if the man can pay, you hold your nose and get on with it. Expect to see many leading artists touting for work at Olympia, often giving free displays of their skills to all and sundry. Pindar of Thebes, the greatest composer of victory odes, was, in his day, a regular at the Games (see pp. 188-90). Myron of Athens, sublime sculptor, the creator of the famous *Diskobolos* ('Discus-thrower'), also sought commissions at Olympia (see pp. 190-1).

Even scientists sometimes turn up to publicise their work. It is, it seems, the place to be seen if you want to make any sort of name for yourself. The astronomer Oinopides of Chios, for instance, presented the results of a lifetime spent observing the stars to the assembled crowd at Olympia, discoveries that he had recorded for posterity on an inscribed tablet that you can still see on display in the Sanctuary today.[56]

Along with the occasional top-flight cultural celebrity, you will come across a good many 'rhapsodes' (professional reciters) at Olympia, men with good memories, loud voices, clear diction, and unfaltering delivery. They are usually older men – a full beard and a few grey hairs lend authority in the Greek world – and they can often be seen positioned on a low platform, standing erect, with chest out, the right arm outstretched and resting on a long walking-stick. Most of them can give a fair rendering of at least some of the classics – Homer especially – but they can also be hired for command performances, of a new victory ode for example.[57]

A similar species are the 'rhetors' (professional orators) who are often hired by cities or tyrants to publicise important achievements or benefactions. For instance, an endowment at Olympia – a refurbishment, new facilities, a dedicatory statue – is a good way to raise one's profile. Often this will be in celebration of a glorious military victory. But there is little point if no-one knows about it. So the grand occasion will be marked with a ceremony, a religious sacrifice (all such endowments are technically offerings to Zeus or another of the gods), and perhaps a public address by a hired rhetor. Needless to say, the tedium of such self-advertisement by the great and good is usually best avoided.[58]

Olympia offers both the peak and the pit. Not every artist is a genius. The Games attract hundreds of jobbing performers and wannabes. Sanctuary and Village are full of third-raters: philosophers who are banal, shallow and dull; poets whose verse is plodding and lifeless; doctors who are quacks, scientists who are charlatans, and a motley assemblage of acrobats and jugglers, singers and dancers, magicians and fortune tellers. These merge imperceptibly into the general throng of wine traders, pastry cooks, flower vendors, souvenir sellers, and all sorts of smelly pedlars hawking every kind of tourist tat.

Take care in the bustle and throng. Apart from the obvious danger of getting skinned by some local wide-boy, the competition between petty entrepreneurs can sometimes turn nasty. There have even been punch-ups between the students of rival philosophers.[59]

Most celebrities and performers at Olympia are keen to draw attention to themselves. Modesty is not the Greek way. But there are exceptions. Top celebs have sometimes been known to mingle anonymously with the crowd. When Plato attended the Games, he was already the best-known philosopher in Athens, but the men he shared a tent with did not know who he was. He passed his time among this group of strangers, sharing food, conversation and entertainment, without ever mentioning Socrates, his famous teacher, the Academy, where he had established a school of higher education, or his own formidable scholarly reputation.[60]

SOUVENIR TOYS

What should you take back for the children? You will see all sorts of toys on sale in the Olympic Village, partly for fathers to take home as gifts, partly because adults play with them too.

A wide variety of balls is sold. They may be small or large, covered in cloth or leather, stuffed with sand, earth, flour, wool, horsehair, feathers, rags, string or sponge, and they may be dyed or painted bright colours – red, blue or gold.

Many different games are played with balls. For example, a small hard ball covered in leather and stuffed with material is used in a game of snatching and grabbing (harpaston being the name of both specialised ball and the game for which it is designed). An alternative version uses a soft ball instead. Other team games include a version of hockey, one that involves piggyback riding, and several that require opposing players to throw and catch the ball.

Small balls are often sold in sets of three for juggling. Then there are yo-yos and tops, of bronze, terracotta

Hopefully, the foregoing notes will be of some help in enabling you to keep body and soul together during your week-long stay at Olympia. But you are going to need a mental map, so that you can find your way around the three main areas of the Olympic site: the Village, the Sanctuary and the Sports Complex.

and wood; the tops are also often decorated with ivy, palm leaves, branches, birds and other ornaments, and come supplied with rod and cord to set them spinning. Hoops for rolling with the aid of a stick are manufactured in iron, bronze and, more commonly, wood, sometimes with small studs around the edge to make a clattering noise.

Most popular of all are dice and knucklebones. The former are a bit more expensive since they are manufactured to have six equal sides. The latter are cheap because they are simply the ankle-bones of sheep or goats. Since these have four sides and two rounded ends, and none of the surfaces is exactly the same size, games of knucklebones involve assigning different values to each surface, ranging from one (biggest surface) to six (smallest surface). Any local will be able to explain the rules.

Why, you may wonder, if the Greeks play both team games and ball games, are none included in the Olympic programme? Because they are collective and popular, whereas the 'true Olympic spirit', sad to say, is neither: it reflects the swaggering aristocratic ideal of heroic personal achievement.[61]

2 FINDING YOUR WAY AROUND

THE VILLAGE

The main permanent installations at Olympia are the Sanctuary, which is filled with temples, shrines, altars and statues, and the Sports Complex, which lies immediately east of it. But during the Games, much of the surrounding countryside, especially along the banks of the River Alpheios to the south, is occupied by a temporary Olympic Village.

The discomfort and lack of facilities in the Olympic Village have already been described (see pp. 18-20). Unless insulated by wealth, in which case you stay in a tented pavilion on a prime pitch attended by slaves, the combination of baking summer heat, lack of sanitation,

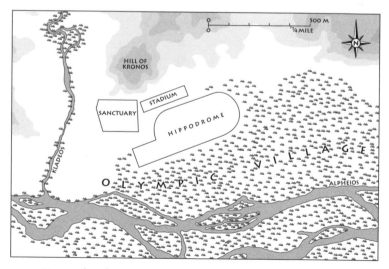

Map 3. The Olympic site, showing the relative locations of Sanctuary, Stadium, Hippodrome and Village.

rotting garbage and nighttime racket will make your visit an ordeal. Performing the most basic tasks, like washing or defecating, can involve a long sweaty slog through crowds, muck and swarms of flies, wasps and mosquitoes.

Under these conditions, tempers easily fray. With personal space at a premium and patience eroded by heat, tiredness and cheap wine, rows are common and sometimes degenerate into punch-ups. Little wonder that the police, hired for the festival to maintain order, are equipped with whips.[1]

Not much can be said about finding your way around, except that the River Alpheios, along whose banks the Village sprawls for about two miles, and the Hill of Kronos, which towers over the Sanctuary on its northern side, are the dominant natural features. Otherwise, the Village is an improvised shanty-town, with thousands of sheds, tents and awnings set up wherever people have found space. There is not – and could not be – any street map. You will have to create your own cognitive geography once you have pitched camp.

The only exceptions to this general picture of chaotic improvisation are a handful of buildings on the southern and western sides of the Sanctuary.

THE COUNCIL HOUSE (*BOULEUTERION*)

Located roughly midway along the southern wall of the Sanctuary, three separate buildings form a single complex. The matching buildings on the north and south wings each have a central colonnade and an apse at the front (western) end. Between them lies a square central chamber, and in front stands none other than Zeus *Horkios* ('god of oaths'), brandishing a thunderbolt in either hand, with his altar alongside.

This is the main office of the Elean Olympic Committee (EOC). Official meetings are held here, official records stored, and various ceremonies performed. It is here that the Judges (*Hellanodikai*) swear to judge fairly and keep certain information confidential, and it is here that athletes, their families and their trainers swear to obey the rules of the Games (see pp. 137ff). This is no light matter. The oaths are sworn before Zeus *Horkios* himself. Once the oath has been sworn, rule-breaking is not only punishable by a police flogging, but becomes a matter of sacrilege and divine retribution.

So the integrity of the Games – which is, as we shall see, in essence a holy rite of the utmost sanctity – is protected by both whip-bearing functionaries and a thunderbolt-armed deity.[2]

THE WORKSHOP OF PHEIDIAS

Just beyond the southwestern edge of the Sanctuary, you encounter a large rectangular workshop-studio built to resemble the main chamber of the Temple of Zeus. It was here, in the 430s BC, that the famed Athenian sculptor Pheidias crafted the gigantic gold and ivory ('chryselephantine') cult statue of Zeus which now sits in the Temple.[3]

Pheidias was the artistic genius who masterminded the decoration of the Parthenon on the Athenian Akropolis in the 440s BC, which is widely considered to be the greatest ensemble of artwork anywhere in the Greek world. His work included: two massive pediment sculptures portraying the birth of Athena (east end) and her struggle with Poseidon for the patronage of Athens (west end); four sets of stone panels ('metopes') on the four exterior sides of the Temple depicting myths concerned with the struggle between civilisation and barbarism; the great frieze on the exterior of the central chamber illustrating the Panathenaic procession with its parade of horsemen, charioteers, youths and gift-bearing maidens, all moving towards a pantheon of seated deities; and the colossal chryselephantine statue of Athena, eleven metres tall, wearing helmet and aegis, grasping spear and shield, her flesh made of ivory, her drapes, armour and armaments of gold.[4]

Pheidias was then hired to make a comparable statue of Zeus for the new Temple at Olympia (see pp. 50ff). In his on-site workshop, ivory was carved into face, torso, arms and feet, molten gold shaped into drapes and accoutrements in terracotta moulds, and the parts fixed into place on wooden beams. These were then transferred for final assembly in the central chamber of the Temple itself. The workshop has been preserved as a museum, where you can see tools, moulds, waste fragments, and even Pheidias's own drinking-cup on display.[5]

THE SWIMMING POOL AND BATHS

Very close to the Workshop of Pheidias is a swimming pool and some baths. The pool is open-air, 24m long by 16m wide and 1.6m deep, with steps leading down into it from either side. Swimming is not an Olympic event: the pool is for exercise, cooling off and unwinding, and its use is reserved for competitors. All you can do is look.

Likewise the baths. There are hip-baths, allowing athletes to sit in a pool of water that has been heated over a hearth, and also a steam bath, complete with changing room, boiler room and steam room. Water is first heated in bronze cauldrons, which are then plunged into the cold water of the steam-room pool to create the steam.

Again, these facilities are for the use of competitors only. (You may take comfort in a sense of virtue: Plato and others have condemned hot baths as wimpish.) On the other hand, this may be a good place to catch sight of some of the superstars up close, as they douse one another with pots of water to wash away the sand and sweat.[6]

THE SANCTUARY

The Sanctuary of Zeus at Olympia – or *Altis*, as it is known – is one of the holiest places in Greece. It is a rectangular enclosure surrounded by a low wall measuring approximately 200m east-west and 150m north-south. It nestles close to the Hill of Kronos on its northern side, with the floodplain of the River Alpheios to the south, and the River Kladeos flowing a short distance to the west.

It was on the Hill of Kronos, an even-sided, pine-encrusted conical eminence, that Zeus battled his father Kronos for control of the world (see p. 81). The Sanctuary beneath the hill marks the site of his victory. Its name is derived from the Greek word *alsos*, meaning 'grove': the *Altis* is a 'sacred grove'. Originally, it probably consisted of nothing but a crude wooden cult-statue, a simple altar, and a clutter of offerings and ornaments in a clearing in the woods. Over the centuries, it has been monumentalised by an accumulation of architecture and sculpture, such that what you see today is an interior jam-packed with

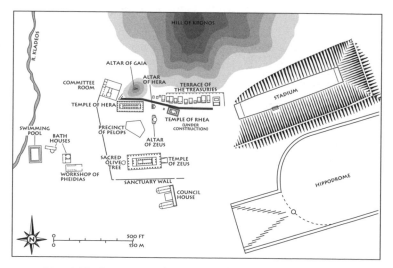

Map 4. The Sanctuary and Sports Complex at Olympia.

buildings, statues and altars, as well as the many remaining trees.

The monuments include the mighty Temple of Zeus, which dominates the enclosure and houses the massive chryselephantine statue of Zeus enthroned, the lesser temples of Hera and Rhea, the Precinct of Pelops, and the Terrace of the Treasuries. The spaces between the great buildings are filled with several major altars and countless minor ones, scores of statues set up by victorious athletes and horse-owners, and hundreds of dedications inscribed on stone. But sporting triumphs are far from being the only conquests commemorated.

Banish any notion that Olympia is a celebration of Greek amity. On the contrary, the monuments in the *Altis*, paid for by city-states, wealthy patrons and successful athletes, their dedicatory inscriptions a gloating record of triumph, stand testimony to the Greek city-states' long history of internecine bloodletting. The greatest of the monuments, the Temple of Zeus itself, was paid for out of war spoils, and celebrates Elis's victory over Pisa for control of the Sanctuary. Nearby, you can see an eight-metre-tall bronze statue of Zeus, also dedicated by the Eleans, this time paid for out of spoils taken in war against Arkadia. Inside the Temple there is a golden shield dedicated by the Spartans in thanks for victory over the Athenians at the Battle of Tanagra. Outside, by contrast, standing in silent testimony to Spartan defeat is the Winged Victory erected by the Messenians of Naupaktos after the Battle of Sphakteria. And so on, and so on – and this before we even consider the numerous other monuments boasting of mere athletic achievement.

So the *Altis* is much more than a religious sanctuary. It is an open-air museum of sports history, military history, mythology, and modern architecture and art. It merits at least one dedicated tour, or several more casual visits, during any week-long stay at the Games. One problem, given the relatively small size of the enclosure and the forest of trees, altars and statues that it contains, is moving around and getting a decent view amid the crush of other sightseers.

Another problem is knowing what to look out for as you walk around. This raises the perennial question of whether to hire a guide. There are always dozens of them touting for business at the Sanctuary. Most have their own quirky view of what you should and should not see. Some are straightforward charlatans. The best advice is probably not to use them, but to rely instead on this, your trusty guidebook.[7]

THE TEMPLE OF ZEUS

One of the largest temples in the Greek world, the Temple of Zeus at Olympia was designed by Libon of Elis, took more than ten years to build, and was completed around 456 BC. The colossal three-stepped platform on which the Temple stands measures 64m in length and 28m in width, making it only marginally smaller than the Parthenon in Athens. Rising from it and forming the outer colonnade are thirty-four fluted Doric columns, six at the front and back, thirteen down either side (we do not count the corner ones twice). Each column, built of huge drums piled one upon the other, measures 2.2m at the base and 10.4m in height. The entablature is equally massive, being virtually half the height of the columns again. The roof is tiled entirely in Pentelic marble from quarries near Athens, and over a hundred marble water-spouts in the form of lions' heads drain off rainwater.

Though constructed of low-grade shelly limestone, the bulk of the Temple has been coated with plaster and painted white to look like marble. The main exceptions are the garish friezes and pediments, to which the eye is drawn by the polychrome colour schemes used to finish their sculpted scenes. Gods and men, heroes and villains,

5. The Temple of Zeus at Olympia – one of the greatest monuments in Greece.

monsters and maidens can be seen high above in flashing red, blue and gold. Make sure you take these in before entering the Temple.[8]

On the east pediment, Zeus presides over preparations for the deadly chariot-race between Oinomaos and Pelops. King Oinomaos, a bearded tyrant, stands with his wife Sterope on Zeus's right. The challenger for the hand of the king's daughter, the young hero Pelops, stands with Hippodameia, the object of his affections, dressed for a wedding, on the left. The four-horse chariots stand ready either side, attended by servants, while two soothsayers look on, their faces filled with foreboding (see pp. 90-5).[9]

On the west side, Apollo stands alert and ready to impose punishment as a furious struggle between Lapiths and Centaurs rages at the wedding feast of King Peirithous. The Centaurs, half-man, half-horse, their lust aroused by booze and beauty, can be seen groping the breasts of Lapith women and attempting to carry them off, or biting, gouging and wrestling the Lapith men who have sprung to their women's defence.

The Centaurs – belching, bestial rapists – violate the sacred laws of guest-friendship and reveal themselves as embodiments of barbarism. Their offence symbolises the disorder that reigns without the protective power of Zeus, lord of the heavens, and his son Apollo, god of reason, civilisation and culture. The Lapiths, the outraged hosts, are champions of much more than endangered womanhood; they stand for the entire Hellenic moral order.[10]

Now return to the front of the Temple – the eastern side – and ascend the ramp up onto the platform. Pass around the central chamber to the western side, then look up. Inside the west porch, high up under the ceiling, are six panels representing six of the Twelve Labours of Herakles, the mythic founder of the Olympic Games (see pp. 53-64). Depicted here are the Nemean Lion, the Lernaian Hydra, the Stymphalian Birds, the Cretan Bull, the Keryneian Hind, and the Girdle of the Amazon. The remaining six labours are to be found in similar positions in the east porch when you return there: the Erymanthian Boar, the Mares of Diomedes, the Cattle of Geryon, the Burden of Atlas, the Taming of Kerberos, and the Cleansing of the Augeian Stables. These tales of brawny triumph form a fine gallery of athletic role models for today's generation of would-be sporting heroes.[11]

Pass now into the Temple itself. The interior is dominated by Pheidias's gold and ivory statue of Zeus. It stands at the west end, facing the entrance, wedged between the two-storey colonnades which divide the central chamber into a nave and two aisles. A staircase gives access to the upper floor of the aisles if you wish to get a close-up view of the statue. The god appears seated on his throne, gazing forwards, majestic, dominant, protective. So massive is the figure at thirteen metres high that, if the divinity were suddenly to stand up, his head would go through the roof.

On his head Zeus wears a golden wreath representing sprays of olive. In his right hand he holds a winged Victory, also gold and ivory, and in his left, a sceptre of power, wrought of many metals, surmounted by an eagle. A golden robe and sandals contrast with the gleaming white ivory of his flesh. The throne is painted and carved with figures, and adorned with gold, ivory, ebony and precious stones.

A shimmering image of the statue is reflected in a large rectangular pool filled with olive oil immediately in front of it. Among the temple staff are 'burnishers', whose job it is to make regular applications of oil to the ivory flesh to prevent it from cracking.[12]

Stand here for a while and ponder. It matters little whether or not you are a believer. Either way, the whole ensemble of towering symmetry, dazzling opulence, and magnificent immortality, overwhelms the senses and conveys an awesome sense of power. Most Greeks believe the power portrayed is divine. Even if you do not – even if you see in religion only the alienated powers of humanity itself – you still cannot help being awestruck by the scale and richness of this artistic masterpiece.

THE TWELVE LABOURS OF HERAKLES

The panels decorating the porches of the Temple of Zeus depict the labours imposed on the Greek hero Herakles in atonement for a monstrous crime. They appear here in part because Herakles was the mythic founder of the Games and a patron of athleticism and wrestling. But the stories have deeper significance.

Herakles, son of Zeus, the most famous of the mythic Greek heroes, is the subject of many great sagas. Brawny, bearded and shaggy-haired, clothed in a lion's skin and brandishing a wooden club, he relied on sheer brute strength rather than cunning and skill in his numerous encounters with men and monsters.

Thuggish he may have been, but he was a champion of civilisation nonetheless. At the dawn of time, when the wilderness was filled with dangerous beasts and settlements were preyed upon by barbarians and monsters, heroes had to be rugged, muscular and hard-living. Herakles was the greatest of them: he was both a creature of his primeval age and a precursor of the new Hellenic era to come.

Straddling two worlds like this, the old and the new, barbarism and civilisation, the contradiction between brutality and morality plagued the mind of Herakles and made of him a brooding, highly-strung, doom-laden figure of tragedy. Thus, he killed his own wife and daughter in a terrible fit of madness, and was then tormented by remorse and guilt. Seeking help from the Pythian Oracle at Delphi, he was advised to atone for his crime by placing himself in bondage to King Eurystheus of Tiryns. This was deep humiliation: Eurystheus was a weak king who had usurped the throne that Herakles himself should have occupied. He was to ask Eurystheus to impose ten trials of courage and strength. Only thus could the killer cleanse himself. And, if he succeeded, he would also regain the throne he had lost. He duly presented himself before his smirking — but somewhat anxious — rival.

To view the panels, begin on the west side, working from left to right. Note that the labours are not shown in the generally accepted chronological order. This is partly to ensure that the Cleansing of the Augeian Stables, the myth most closely associated with Olympia, comes at the end of the sequence.

Following pages: 6. The Twelve Labours of Herakles.

WEST SIDE

Panel 1 **First Labour: the Nemean Lion**

On this panel we see Herakles, exhausted by his exertions, standing over the corpse of the Nemean Lion.

Herakles' first labour was to bring back this monstrous lion's pelt. The roar of the beast, twice the size of any other lion, could be heard for miles around its cave. Herakles hurled a rock to draw it forth, then shot an arrow as it sprang, hitting it between the eyes.

But the arrow bounced straight off, as if the pelt were plate armour. Summoning the help of his father in Heaven, who promptly despatched the goddess Athena to the brawl, Herakles, courage restored, rolled a stone across one of the two cave entrances, advanced into the other, grabbed the giant beast around the neck, and choked the life out of it in his vice-like grip.

Panel 2 Second Labour: the Lernaian Hydra

Eurystheus, unnerved by Herakles' victory, next sent him to slay the Lernaian Hydra, half-sister of the Nemean Lion. Herakles appears on the second panel confronting the multi-headed monster.

She lived in a cave by a polluted pool, and into this Herakles shot fire arrows to goad her into the open. Out she came, a huge, scale-covered worm slithering forwards, sprouting two dozen writhing, hissing snake heads.

Herakles hacked at the heads, but two grew each time one was lopped off. The hero was driven back and cornered, and the Hydra was joined by her companion, Cancer the Crab, both moving in for the kill. Cancer snapped at Herakles' heels. Hydra's heads twisted and turned, fangs bared, dripping venom.

Herakles pulverised the crab with his foot, but to fight the Hydra he called on his charioteer Iolaos for help. The clever youth brought burning torches to cauterise the wounds and stop new heads growing as the hero hacked them off. Finally, only the Hydra's central head remained, and when he sliced through its neck and sent it splattering away, the monster collapsed lifeless.

Unfortunately, as Iolaos had helped Herakles kill the Hydra, Eurystheus refused to accept it as one of the labours.

Panel 3 Sixth Labour: the Stymphalian Birds

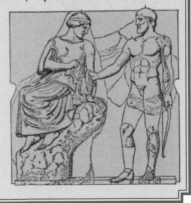

Depicted here is the goddess Athena equipping Herakles for his struggle against a flock of giant birds of prey, creatures with bronze beaks and talons for tearing human flesh. They lived around the stagnant marshes of Lake Stymphalos, but the ground was so treacherous, and the birds so numerous, that at first Herakles stood hesitant on the bank, unsure of how to proceed.

Athena supplied a pair of bronze castanets that Herakles clashed together, making such a racket that the birds rose shrieking from their roosts. Herakles was ready. His arrows were too few to slay them all, so instead he fired stones from a giant catapult. Amidst the whistle and thudding of the stones, pummelled birds dropped lifeless into the mire, one after the other. Those few that escaped never returned.

Panel 4 Seventh Labour: the Cretan Bull

Eurystheus ordered Herakles to capture the Cretan Bull, and we see him here, club upraised, leading the tethered beast – the once magnificent animal which Minos, King of Crete, had refused to sacrifice to Poseidon. In retaliation, the angry deity had afflicted Pasiphaë, Minos's wife, with an obsessive bestial lust for the bull. When the bull remained indifferent to her attempts at seduction, she asked Daedalus, the great inventor, to devise a solution.

Daedalus built a hollow wooden cow mounted on wheels. He covered this with the hide of a real cow to make it look and smell authentic. Pasiphaë was invited to climb inside and align her naked body with that of the wooden model. When the contraption was pushed into the field, the bull was aroused and impregnated both the contraption and its willing occupant.

The offspring of this unnatural union was a baby with the head of a bull: a 'Minotaur' (Minos-Bull). Pasiphaë enjoined Daedalus to build a labyrinth to contain and conceal her son – though one day, much later, Theseus penetrated the maze and slew the beast.

Herakles had perhaps an easier task. Minos offered assistance, no doubt eager to destroy the taurine object of his wife's infatuation, but the hero preferred to capture the bull single-handedly. Though it belched scorching flames, though it charged its tormentor many times, though it reared and twisted to escape capture through long hours of struggle, Herakles finally mastered the beast, roping it in and wrestling it to the ground.

Now tamed and compliant, the Cretan Bull was led back to Tiryns (though it later broke its tether and wandered across Greece).

Panel 5 Third Labour: the Keryneian Hind

The next panel shows Herakles wrestling to the ground a powerful, fleet-footed stag, one hand around the neck, the other wrenching back the antlers, the right knee pressing down on the animal's back. Eurystheus had ordered the hero to capture the fabulous, golden-horned and highly elusive Keryneian Hind. The animal was sacred to Artemis, goddess of wild nature, so Herakles could not risk doing it harm. It was a full year before he tracked it down at a watering hole, and there he trapped the animal in nets, forced it to the ground, bound it tightly, and dragged it back to Tiryns.

Panel 6 Ninth Labour: the Girdle of the Amazon

His ninth labour set Herakles on a course for the Black Sea and the land of a fabled race of warrior women. Eurystheus's daughter, Admete, had heard stories of a golden girdle studded with jewels worn by Hippolyte, Queen of the Amazons. This she craved, and this it was now Herakles' mission to recover.

At first, the task proved all too easy. Hippolyte was invited to a banquet aboard Herakles' ship. Charmed by the company of the rugged, bronze-limbed Greek hero, Hippolyte offered her girdle as a love gift.

The goddess Hera, ever-malevolent towards the offspring of her divine husband's illicit union with Herakles' mother, was irritated by the effortlessness of the mission. So she disguised herself as an Amazon and spread the rumour that Herakles planned to kidnap the queen.

The Amazons attacked the Greek ship and precipitated a furious battle. Herakles, convinced that Hippolyte's seductive wiles had been a trick to make him lower his guard, turned on her, brought her down and, when she refused to yield, smashed her to death with his club – the gruesome scene depicted on this panel.

The girdle, now battered and bloody, was taken from the body of the Amazon queen for delivery to a Greek princess.

EAST SIDE

Panel 7 **Fourth Labour: the Erymanthian Boar**

Eurystheus sent Herakles to the wild hills of Arkadia to capture the Erymanthian Boar, a huge beast that was feeding on flocks of sheep and terrorising local shepherds. He flushed the boar from its thicket with loud halloos, chased it up the mountainside into a deep snow-drift, and there, as it panted and reared on its stubby legs, threw himself on its back and wrapped it in chains.

Angry with his tormentor in Tiryns, Herakles heaved the boar onto his back and carried it all the way to the palace, where, as we see on this panel, he threatened to hurl it into the storage jar in which Eurystheus had taken refuge.

Panel 8 Eighth Labour: the Mares of Diomedes

For his eighth labour, Herakles was again sent overseas, this time to Thrace, to capture the four man-eating Mares of King Diomedes. The king kept the beasts tethered with iron chains to bronze mangers, and there he fed them on the remains of unsuspecting strangers.

Herakles went by ship to Thrace with Abderos, his new lover, and other comrades-in-arms. The hero's party managed to overpower Diomedes' grooms and secure the mares, but the alarm was raised and the king, at the head of his armed retainers, was soon in hot pursuit. Leaving Abderos to hold the mares, Herakles turned to fight.

He stunned Diomedes with his club and put the rest of the royal party to flight, but meanwhile the mares turned on Abderos and ate him. Racing back across the plain, they came upon the unconscious body of their master. And he, too, was devoured, awakening at the moment the meal began. His screams, as the living flesh was torn away, filled the air – until choked by gore and foam.

Herakles then noosed the mares, bloated with blood, led them to his ship, and stalled them in the hold. Before sailing back to Tiryns, he collected the bits of his lover, buried them with due ceremony, raised a mound over the site, and founded the city of Abdera as a permanent memorial.

The panel shows our hero leading one of the mares away, his sturdy club, as ever, brandished threateningly aloft.

Panel 9 Tenth Labour: the Cattle of Geryon

By the tenth labour, Eurystheus was beginning to panic. With only three labours to go, Herakles might survive them all and displace him on the throne of Tiryns. So he now sent the hero to the edge of the known world, to the far western limit of the Mediterranean, charged with stealing cattle from Geryon, a three-headed giant who ruled as king of the Phoenician city of Erytheia (Cadiz).

The journey was long, hard and dangerous; many wild beasts were encountered and slain on the way. Arriving at the straits that divide Europe from Africa, the Greek hero erected the Pillars of Herakles to narrow the passage and keep the monsters of the Atlantic out of the Mediterranean. Tired, thirsty and in bad temper after his exertions, Herakles leaned back against one of the pillars and let loose an arrow at the sun burning in the sky above.

Helios, charioteer of the sun, might have been angered. Instead, in admiration for the hero, he graced the *hubris* of the angry arrow with a smile, and offered his giant bronze drinking-cup as a vessel in which to complete the voyage to Erytheia.

Herakles soon spotted the cattle grazing on the slopes of Mount Abas, guarded by the herdsman Eurytion and his two-headed dog Orthos. As he leaped ashore, herdsman and dog attacked. The huge bone-crunching jaws of the dog's heads snarled and slobbered, but Herakles swung his club and smashed both skulls with a single blow. The herdsman was brained with a second blow before he could turn and run.

Herakles made off with the cattle, but had not gone far before Geryon and his troops caught up with him. As Herakles prepared to confront his pursuers, Geryon came on, a giant warrior armed with spear, sword and shield, his body protected by plate armour, a crested bronze helmet on each shaggy head, threats spitting from three mouths.

Herakles shot three arrows, one per head. As each barb bored through a face and penetrated a brain, the head slumped across the monster's chest. When the third hit home, the great hulk collapsed in a heap. The panel shows this final denouement.

Herakles herded the cattle overland all the way home to Tiryns, protecting them against numerous predators and rustlers, including Ligurian mountain tribesmen in the Alps and a cave-dwelling giant called Kakos near Rome.

Panel 10 **Eleventh Labour: the Golden Apples of Hera (and the Burden of Atlas)**

Among many fine gifts she received at her wedding, the goddess Hera's favourites were the golden-apple trees given by Gaia, Mother Earth. For his eleventh labour, Herakles was to find the trees, steal the forbidden fruit, and thus defy Hera, the Queen of Heaven herself.

Nereus, the Old Man of the Sea, knew where they grew. Herakles caught him napping by the ocean and, though he was a slippery creature who kept changing form and shape, held him fast in an unyielding vice-like grip until Nereus had told him all he knew.

Journeying through the Caucasus, Herakles encountered Prometheus, the Titan chained to a rock with a vulture pecking out his liver as punishment for stealing fire from the gods and giving it to men. Herakles killed the vulture and freed the Titan.

From the Caucasus he headed south, through Syria and Arabia, and thence came to Egypt. There he was taken captive by Pharaoh Busiris, who was in the habit of sacrificing foreigners to the gods in return for good harvests. Herakles broke his bonds and slaughtered Busiris and his priests, laying them over their own altar one by one, and splitting them open with the sacrificial axe.

Making his way along the North African coast, Herakles was challenged to a wrestling match by King Antaios of Libya, a muscular youth who had never been beaten and always fought to the death. Herakles accepted the challenge, but found his opponent far tougher than expected. As his own strength waned, that of his opponent seemed to increase. Each time Herakles pinned Antaios to the ground, he broke free with redoubled force. Sometimes, indeed, Antaios threw himself onto the ground, and then, muscles taut with fresh energy, leaped up again to renew the fight.

Antaios was the son of Gaia, Mother Earth, and as such drew strength from contact with her. Herakles, comprehending the source of his opponent's unflagging strength, lifted Antaios clear of the ground and held him suspended. The monster struggled ferociously at first, then slowly weakened, like a man drowning, until finally his limbs slumped. Herakles dropped the body onto his chest and held it in a giant bear-hug, squeezing Antaios's arms tight until his ribs snapped and his life-breath ceased in bubbles of bloody foam.

Herakles continued on his way for many days. At last, in the distance, he saw the Atlas Mountains. As he drew closer, he saw the massive form of the Titan holding up the sky outlined against the setting sun. Prometheus had advised Herakles to ask Atlas to collect the golden apples for him, which he now did, offering to shoulder the Titan's great burden while he carried out the mission. Atlas welcomed the break, so Herakles took the weight of the world on his back, and Atlas strode off westward.

Atlas pushed past the Daughters of Evening and entered the garden where the golden apples grew. Ladon, the serpent that guarded the apples, was twisted round the base of the tree, hissing hate from a hundred writhing heads. Atlas, undaunted, strangled each head in turn, and then gathered the apples.

Returning to Herakles, it occurred to the Titan that he might leave the hero holding up the sky and make off with the apples. Herakles had to think fast. The panel captures that critical moment of decision, showing Herakles still shouldering his burden, the gloating Titan holding out the apples before him. But Herakles asked Atlas to hold up the sky for a moment while he made himself more comfortable by rearranging the pillow on his shoulders. The Titan – gormless like most of his kind – agreed. Once Atlas had resumed his burden, Herakles picked up the apples and walked away laughing.

Back in Greece, no-one wanted the golden apples, for fear of Hera's wrath. Eurystheus dedicated them to Athena – but she promptly returned them to the Daughters of Evening.

Panel 11 **Twelfth Labour: the Taming of Kerberos**

When it came to the twelfth labour – or tenth, by Eurystheus's reckoning (see below) – the King of Tiryns, desperate to destroy his rival, had to come up with a truly lethal task. He decided to send Herakles into the Underworld to capture Kerberos and bring him to the surface. Kerberos, the guard dog of the nether regions, was a monstrous hound with three heads and a mane of snakes. Herakles had already killed Kerberos's brothers and sisters – the Nemean Lion, the Hydra and Orthos – so the dog harboured a vindictive hatred of the hero.

Herakles drugged Kerberos with opium-soaked cakes and passed through the gates of the Underworld. As he descended into the depths, ghostly forms appeared momentarily on either side, then flitted away into black mist. Sometimes he caught glimpses of fallen friends. Some, killed in their prime, he freed, forming a company of hell-breakers as he continued his descent. Reaching the deepest parts, he heard the creaking of instruments of torture, the cackles of demon guards, and the screams of the tormented. And here, in gloomy majesty, he met Hades, lord of the Underworld, most terrible of all the gods.

Hades, uneasy at the disturbance to his realm, agreed to allow Herakles to take Kerberos, but only if he did so without weapons or violence, and only if the beast was in due course returned. As shown here in the penultimate panel, Herakles tamed the beast though kindness, placed a chain round each of its three necks, and led it away to be shown in Tiryns.

Panel 12 **Fifth Labour: the Cleansing of the Augeian Stables**

The last panel shows Herakles working with a spade under the direction of Athena: it is a scene from the fifth labour, a story with a local theme.

The wealth of King Augeias of

Elis (the city that hosts the Games) depended on herds of cattle, but he owned so many that their dung lay too deep and heavy to be cleared, and the fields were left uncultivated beneath a solid blanket of manure.

Herakles' mission was to muck out the stables and clear the fields in a single day. This he did by breaking down an enclosure wall at a weak point identified by Athena, thus allowing the waters of the rivers Alpheios and Peneios to wash the land clean.

Herakles had demanded a fee for this service from the king. But when Augeias learned that this was a labour imposed to atone for murder, he withheld payment. And when Eurystheus heard that Herakles had sought financial compensation, he refused to count the labour as one of the ten.

Herakles had cleansed himself through trials of strength, but further ordeals lay ahead, and lasting happiness in life eluded him. A monster of physical strength, a killer-in-waiting tinged with madness, a semi-divine hero with a dark and dangerous past, he was never blessed with lasting love or a happy marriage, and the gods blighted an existence that repeatedly bordered on *hubris*.

Even so, such were his courage, strength, stoicism and record of achievement that the gods could not let him die. Escorted by Athena to Mount Olympos and presented to Zeus, he was granted immortality and joined the assembly of the gods.[13]

THE SACRED OLIVE TREE

Do not leave the vicinity of the Temple of Zeus without visiting the Sacred Olive Tree, which you will find behind the western wall. Legend has it that King Iphitos of Elis was told by the Delphic Oracle to seek out a wild olive tree 'now wrapped in the spider's fine net', and to take from this the leafy twigs to make Olympic victory-crowns. Another legend tells that Herakles, founder of the Games, begged the fabled Hyperboreans of the far north to give him a tree 'from the all-welcoming grove of Zeus, a tree to furnish shade for all, and to be a crown for deeds of prowess'. Either way, here it still stands, a gnarled and twisted giant of great antiquity, the holiest tree in the whole of Greece. From this tree, the grey-green foliage is cut to make the most prized of wreaths; cut, as the sacred rite requires, with a golden sickle by a boy whose parents are still living.[14]

THE ALTAR OF ZEUS

The Altar of Zeus does not lie in front of his Temple, as you would expect, but some distance to the north, far closer, in fact, to the Temple of Hera, his divine wife. This is easily explained. The Temple of Hera is older and was originally dedicated to both Hera *and* Zeus; the altar is located accordingly. Its appearance is wholly unexpected. Instead of a magnificent block of marble carved with images of sacrifice and dedications to the god, it is an immense cone of ash-paste several metres high that sits, squat and milky-grey, on a low stone pediment.

It marks the very spot, so legend has it, that was struck by Zeus's thunderbolt when he first laid claim to the Sanctuary. Here, at the midpoint of the Games, 100 oxen donated by the people of Elis are sacrificed, and when the portions offered to Zeus have been burnt, the ash is mixed into a paste with water from the Alpheios and plastered onto the altar (see pp. 220-2).

Four intervening winters wash much of this away, but enough survives of each new festive application for the monument slowly to grow, an incrementally swelling layer-cake of past devotions, its hidden innermost tiers a record of piety perhaps six centuries old.[15]

THE TEMPLE OF HERA

You are now close to the most ancient temple in the Sanctuary. The Temple of Hera, lying near the northwestern corner of the enclosure, is 150 years older than the Temple of Zeus. It looks it, being long, narrow and squat, its flat and heavy appearance contrasting with the soaring symmetry of its newer neighbour. In places, behind the crumbling plasterwork on some of the columns, the upper walls and the entablature, you can see, instead of stone, a superstructure of unbaked brick or wood. And if you study

7. The Temples of Hera (top) and Rhea (bottom), and the Terrace of Treasuries (right). Olympia was originally ruled by earth-mother goddesses.

them closely, you notice that the columns are not uniform, but subtly different, for they are being replaced one at a time, new stone ones being erected only when the original wooden ones have rotted beyond repair. Note the painted terracotta mouldings, fan-shaped sprays of geometric bands, at either end of the roof ridge.

This is the ancient Temple of Hera, dedicated to the mother goddess who reigned here in deep time, in a primeval matriarchal age, an age before wars, warriors and male domination. It seems she was displaced by Zeus from prime position centuries ago, perhaps when the Eleans defeated local tribes and took control of the Sanctuary: perhaps Zeus arrived as the conquering war god.

Today, inside the Temple, you will see colossal stone statues of Zeus and Hera, husband and wife, King and Queen of Heaven, the god standing bearded and helmeted, the goddess seated on her throne. The faces, plastered, painted and slightly grotesque, stare out at you, impassive and expressionless – except for that uncertain and somewhat disconcerting suggestion of a smile that seems to be worn by every statue around here.

Note also two items among the many treasures stored in the Temple. One is an ornamental couch that once belonged to Hippodameia, the local princess who became the wife of Pelops, the athlete-hero buried in the nearby Precinct of Pelops (see pp. 68-9). The other is the gold and ivory table for the olive wreaths of the victors in the Games. The table is stored in the Temple and is brought out for use only during the athletic contests.[16]

THE TEMPLE OF RHEA

Immediately in front of the Temple of Hera are two altars, one dedicated to Hera, the second to Rhea. Just beyond the latter, a new edifice is now under construction, the Temple of Rhea. It is unusual in two respects. First, there are very few temples dedicated to this particular goddess, or indeed to any other pre-Olympian deity, anywhere in Greece. Rhea was the wife of Kronos and the mother of Zeus. Kronos and Rhea were therefore the leading Titans or Giants, a generation of barbarous old gods overthrown by Zeus and his fellow Olympians at the dawn of time. The event – the Gigantomachy ('Battle against the Giants') – is often celebrated in Greek art and symbolises the triumph of civilisation (see p. 81).

Secondly, the new temple is back to front, facing west rather than east. The reason is simple. The Altar of Rhea is very ancient, its position hallowed by centuries of ritual observance, and it could not be moved. But immediately west of it lie the Altar and Temple of Hera. The Eleans, therefore, once they had decided to build Rhea a temple, had no choice but to locate it east of the existing altar.[17]

THE ALTAR OF GAIA

Near the foot of the Hill of Kronos, tucked away just beyond the edge of the Sanctuary, is another ash-mound altar, this one dedicated to Gaia or Mother Earth. A small chasm can be seen nearby, representing Chaos, the black hole from which Gaia sprang. Beside the mouth of the chasm is a second altar, to Themis, Gaia's daughter and goddess of Order, the polar opposite of the Chaos over which she stands guard. This place, now little regarded, is perhaps the most ancient cult-site in the whole of Olympia (see pp. 78-9).[18]

THE PRECINCT OF PELOPS (*PELOPEION*)

Just south of the Temple of Hera, you will see an earth tumulus covered by trees. It is surrounded by a low, irregular five-sided wall, and there is a monumental colonnaded entrance at the southwest corner. This is the burial place of none other than Pelops himself, the mythic athlete-hero who won a princess and a kingdom by victory in a chariot-race, and who gave his name to the Peloponnese. The great man's bones are kept in a special bronze chest. He is still honoured with regular sacrifices of a black ram, and, like Herakles, is revered by modern athletes as a role model, a mortal who achieved immortality through sporting prowess (see pp. 95-6).[19]

THE TERRACE OF THE TREASURIES

Along a terrace cut into the base of the Hill of Kronos and reached by monumental steps on the northern side of the Sanctuary is a row of what appear to be miniature temples. They are, in fact, treasuries, each built by a Greek city-state eager to advertise its status and achievement, and each packed with a hotchpotch of booty, votive offerings, *objets d'art* and antiquities (most of them fakes).

Myron, the tyrant of Sikyon, started the trend after victory in the chariot-race in 648 BC. Among the objects on display in the bronze-lined chamber of the Treasury of Sikyon today, you can see a fine statue of Apollo, three discuses used in pentathlon contests, a shield and a collection of armour dedicated as a victory offering, and a

8. A clutter of ancient decorated vessels of the kind you will see in many temples and treasuries at Olympia.

gold-handled ceremonial dagger said to have belonged to the legendary Pelops himself.

Similar displays can be seen in the other treasuries, these belonging to the city-states of Gela, Selinus and Syracuse in Sicily, Metapontion and Sybaris in southern Italy, Epidamnos in Northwestern Greece, Byzantion on the Bosphorus, Kyrene in Libya, and Megara on the Isthmus.

The treasuries' temple-like appearance is fitting: they do, after all, contain offerings to the gods. But they are more than that: the valuables within advertise historic victories, both military and sporting, while the rich decorative finish of the buildings themselves, with their gleaming white walls, fluted Doric columns, and painted terracotta panels and roof ornaments, proclaims the standing of the city among the Greeks.[20]

THE COMMITTEE ROOM (*PRYTANEION*)

In the far northwestern corner of the Sanctuary stands the Committee Room or *Prytaneion*, a large administrative building used for official EOC meetings and state banquets. Its functions overlap with those of the Council House, but while the latter is concerned with the everyday running of the athletic contests, the former is a more prestigious place concerned with the cult and the festival as a whole.

Here, in a special chamber, the sacred fire of Hestia, goddess of the hearth, is kept burning night and day. From here, too, ceremonial processions set out across the Sanctuary, often carrying a sacred flame of Hestia with which to light other fires. And in the main hall on the northern side of the building, great banquets are held during the festival for senior officials and champion athletes, while regular meals are served at other times, not only to officials, but also to visiting Olympic champions, for whom the right to eat in the Committee Room is a lifetime priovilege.[21]

MUST-SEE MONUMENTS

The Diagorids: an Olympic dynasty

The Sanctuary contains a forest of statues of athletes. It is easy to be overwhelmed by the abundance. But make time to see one especially important group. The Diagoras group of six statues represents a dynasty of Olympic champions.

Diagoras of Rhodes, the founder of the dynasty, won the boxing event in 464 BC. This was the culmination of his career, for he had previously won twice at both Delphi and Nemea, and four times at Isthmia. To commemorate his crowning victory, he commissioned an ode from Pindar and a statue from Kallikles (see pp. 187ff).

Diagoras's eldest son, Damagetos, won the *pankration* at Olympia in 452 BC and again at the next Olympiad, in 448 BC, when his brother Akousilaos won his father's event, the boxing. The two champions took a victory lap together carrying their proud father, there as a spectator, on their shoulders.

Diagoras's third son, Doreius, then won the *pankration* three times running (in 432, 428 and 424 BC). Dorieus was, in fact, a three-time *periodonikes* ('circuit winner': a champion at all four crown games), having, in addition to his three Olympic victories, a total of four at Delphi, seven at Nemea, and eight at Isthmia.

Then a third generation triumphed. Diagoras had two daughters, each of whom produced a son. Eukles won the boxing in 404 BC, while Peisirodos won the boys' boxing, also at Olympia, and probably in the same year.

The statues of the six champions, a father, three sons, and two grandsons, are grouped together in the Sanctuary, united in their achievement.[22]

The Winged Victory of the Messenians

As well as statues of athletes, the Sanctuary contains a clutter of victory monuments. One fine example is the spectacular Winged Victory of the Messenians.

Larger than most, it is hard to miss. Located around thirty metres east of the Temple of Zeus, this larger-than-life-size stone statue stands on top of a tapering triangular pillar some nine metres

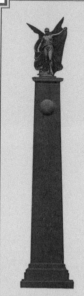

9. The Winged Victory of the Messenians.

high. The garish colour scheme is certainly eye-catching: the goddess's flowing garments are red, her hair black and bound with gold ribbon.

The event commemorated is recorded in the inscription on the base of the monument, but the whole message is unashamedly triumphalist. Swooping down from Mount Olympos on an eagle, representing Zeus, to crown the victors, the statue symbolises the gods' pleasure in, and the divine justice of, the Messenian victory over the Spartans in 425 BC.

In all Greece, there are no two enemies whose mutual hatred is greater. The Spartans conquered the Messenians centuries ago and made them serfs, ruthlessly crushing subsequent rebellions. Indeed, you can see the gloating Spartan monument to their latest repression in the Sanctuary.

But the Spartans do not always have it their own way. Their reputation for invincibility took some hard knocks in the long Peloponnesian War. Some time before the war, the Athenians had helped some diehard Messenian resistance fighters escape into exile and establish a new city at Naupaktos. These same Messenians then backed the Athenians during the war, helping them win a great victory on the island of Sphakteria, near Pylos, on the southwest coast of the Peloponnese. After 130 Spartans had been killed, the remaining 290 surrendered, of whom 120 were full citizens, members of a supposedly invincible blue-blooded military elite. Greece was stunned.[23]

For this special victory, the Messenians commissioned the sculptor Paionios of Mende to craft a mega-monument that would not go unnoticed. His work was in demand. Look closely at the inscription on the base of the monument. It refers to Paionios's success in winning the contract to make the roof ornaments that decorate the nearby Temple of Zeus. He was clearly the man for the job – and not too modest to let us know it.[24]

THE SPORTS COMPLEX

THE STADIUM

The running track at Olympia is 192m long, this distance being a *stadion* (though note that the precise length of a *stadion* varies across Greece: see p. 8). Apparently, it was Herakles who fixed the distance; one story has it that he measured it out by putting one foot in front of another 600 times, another that it was the furthest he could run before drawing breath.

The starting line is at the far, eastern side of the site, the finishing line close to the Altar of Zeus – an effective reminder that all athletic contests are performed in honour of the supreme deity. At each end of the track is a stone starting line (the *balbis*) with a single groove cut into it behind which the athletes start their races. Either end of the track can also be fitted with a turning-post (the *kampter*) to regulate the laps run in the longer races. The track itself is formed of beaten earth.

There is an area on the bank set aside for the Judges (*Hellanodikai*). They are instantly recognisable by their purple robes and the rods they carry with which to punish athletes who break the rules. Look out, too, for the Priestess of Demeter *Chamune*, almost certainly the only woman in the entire place, a privilege she owes to the great antiquity of the earth-mother cult she serves. She has a special seat which doubles as an altar opposite the Judges.

Any other woman trying to sneak a view takes an enormous risk. The EOC has a rule that any woman discovered inside the Sanctuary or Sports Complex during the festival – or even simply on the northern side of the Alpheios – is to be thrown off the cliffs of nearby Mount Typhaion.

So much for the track. What about spectator facilities? If the lack of amenities in the Olympic Village can be a shock to first-time visitors, experience of the Sports Complex can be equally alarming. There has been some discussion about a new stadium, but there are no plans at present, and the existing Stadium offers spectators nothing more than low earth-banks. With huge increases in the numbers attending the Games, matters are now at crisis point.

The existing seating-banks can accommodate perhaps 40,000 or so. But up to 100,000 can now be expected, so most spectators struggle to find a place with a decent view – or, indeed, any view. Many find themselves sitting on the lower slopes of the Hill of Kronos; it is some distance from the action, but it does afford some relief from the merciless crush further down.

There are no seats anywhere. You can sit on the grass between events, but you have to stand during them if you want to see anything, because that is what everyone else does. (*Stadion* probably derives from the Greek word meaning 'to stand', so it might be translated, entirely accurately, as 'the stands'.)

Nor is there any shade. The Games take place in high summer, when temperatures can soar to 35°C and above. You will need a hat, olive oil sun-block, and plenty to drink. You are bound to need to take a break now and then, but making your way out will be an ordeal, and the risk is that you will lose your place unless someone guards it for you.

Most spectators belong to organised groups. They will either have travelled to Olympia together or will have met up with people from the same city after arriving. On the stands, they form visible and, more especially, audible fan clubs, cheering on athletes from their hometowns.[25]

THE HIPPODROME

The Stadium is the setting not only for the four foot-races, but also for the pentathlon, the boxing, the wrestling and the *pankration*. The equestrian events, two chariot-races and a horse-race, take place in the Hippodrome, which lies immediately south of, and parallel to, the Stadium.

The track is roughly 600m in length (slightly over a third of a mile) – three *stadia* – and 250m wide, sufficient room for a line of no fewer than twenty chariots. Two pillars, one at either end of the track, mark the turning-points. There is a wooden barrier around the edge of the track to protect spectators from bolting horses and crashing chariots – of which there can be many.

The elaborate starting-gates, designed by Kleoitas of Athens in the mid-fifth century BC, have the waiting horses and chariots arranged like the prow of a ship pointing down the track. At the point of the prow is a bronze dolphin on a pole. Behind the point is a plastered mud-brick altar surmounted by a bronze eagle with spread wings. When the starter of the race sets the machinery in motion, the eagle rises, the dolphin falls, and the gates begin to open.

The gates are controlled by a sequential release mechanism operated by ropes that staggers the start to equalise the distance. The result is spectacular, with the horses or chariots on the outermost edge of the track bursting out of their stalls first, and then a series of succeeding pairs on either side until those at the centre of the field finally dash off. The *aphesis* (as the entire apparatus is called in Greek) is a much admired example of Athenian engineering.

The reverse slope of the southern embankment of the Stadium provides the main spectator accommodation, though there is also a low bank on the far side. The Judges' seats are on the north side of the Hippodrome, towards the western end, near the Sanctuary.[26]

THE GHOST OF THE HIPPODROME

The Olympic Hippodrome appears to be haunted. To one side of the track stands an ancient mound and a circular altar to Taraxippos ('Horse-frightener'). Jockeys and charioteers make offerings here in an effort to placate this angry spirit. For it is commonly the case that, when racing horses reach this spot, they are suddenly, for no apparent reason, seized with fear. Races have been lost as horses rear and throw their riders, or chariots career sideways and crash into their opponents.

But who is the Horse-frightener? No-one is sure, but most think it the malevolent spirit of either Oinomaos or Myrtilos. Both were killed by Pelops, the former in a chariot smash after a linchpin was replaced with a stick of wax, the latter when he was jettisoned from a cliff-top onto the rocks below (see pp. 92–3). Both died with bitter grudges on their lips (see p. 94), and either might be the unquiet spirit that still haunts Olympia's equestrian events.[27]

There is so much to see all around the Olympic site. To get the most out of your visit, and to make sense of the rich variety of architecture, art and antiquities on display, you are going to need to know the popular stories behind the many images and inscriptions. We turn now to the myths of Olympia.

3 MYTHS

You cannot understand the Olympics without knowledge of the myths that lie behind them. The Games are, from start to finish, a *religious* festival – in fact, the greatest religious festival in the entire Greek world. Everything that happens is suffused with mythological associations and ritual meanings.

Disentangling the evidence is far from straightforward. Greek mythology is a hopeless muddle. The same story can be told in a hundred different versions, the details changing over time, and varying from one city to another. The same site can be re-dedicated to a succession of different deities as the centuries roll on. Rituals performed in honour of one god can later be redirected to another.

If this seems bizarre, keep in mind that myths exist largely to explain holy rites and cultural norms. Thousands of years ago, magic – imitating something you want in order to make it happen – was performed by music, dancing, artwork and dressing up. Religion – appealing to a higher power for something you want – was a somewhat later development which depended upon offering up entreaties (prayers) or bribes (offerings). But the new religious rituals contained many 'fossils' from the old magic-making, so the early myth-stories about the gods accumulated around an established repertoire of ritual practice.

Then, as society developed further, myths were not only recycled, but also changed to fit new realities. The revisions, however, were simply tacked onto an existing corpus. Instead of discarding an old story that has been updated, the Greeks retain the original version alongside the new, often in a modified form. The result is a web of myths of bewildering complexity and contradiction.

Olympia offers countless examples. The Sanctuary is now dedicated primarily to Zeus, in whose honour the famous Games are celebrated, but a bewildering array of other deities (and heroes) is also worshipped within its precincts. Especially notable is the gaggle of earth-mother deities venerated at Olympia – perhaps more so here than at any other Panhellenic shrine. And there is strong evidence to show that long ago, when Greek religion was first evolving out of primitive fertility rite, it was these female deities who were paramount.

EARTH MOTHERS

One of Greece's darkest secrets is the war of the sexes waged at the dawn of time. The oldest cults at Olympia are those of the earth-mother goddesses, Gaia, Rhea, Hera and Demeter. But these mother goddesses were displaced by the power-god Zeus in a patriarchal coup centuries ago. No-one talks openly about this, and most are quite ignorant of the truth, but a good look at the evidence seems to leave little room for doubt. The clues are all over the site.

One thing that starts to become clear is that, in a dim and distant past, instead of fanatical Zeus-worship once every four years, Olympia played host to an annual pattern of festivals built around fertility rites and agricultural thanksgiving, held in honour of the primeval earth mothers. The date of the Games provides a special clue. The Olympics always take place at the second or third full moon after the summer solstice. Not only does the time of year prove that by origin it is a harvest festival (why else hold it at the hottest time of year?), but its synchronisation with the phases of the moon also links it to the menstrual cycle and female fertility.

Zeus is a usurper. Olympia, by origin, is a monument to mother-right.[1]

GAIA

The Greek creation myth runs like this. First, there was Chaos, a black hole of nothingness, a void without form, substance or light. From it, somehow, emerged Gaia, broad-breasted Mother Earth, along with Nyx (Night), Erebos (Underworld), Tartaros (Hell) and Eros (Sexual Passion). Of these, naturally enough, it was Gaia who, in the course of time, offered a place for gods and mortals to live, breed and prosper. And therefore, long ago, it was Gaia that men and women worshipped – for her fertility, her bounty and her warm benevolence.

You will see the chasm at the foot of the Hill of Kronos – where the Altar of Gaia still stands (see p. 68) – which was imagined to be her birthplace. So here, in a sacred grove, ancient fertility rites were celebrated, and the goddess rewarded the faithful with oracles – prophecies of the future – as guides to action in an otherwise unpredictable and hazardous world.

Here, too, guarding the mouth of the chasm, you can see a second altar, this to Themis, daughter of Gaia and goddess of order. She is here partly to keep Chaos in check, partly because she inherited Gaia's power of prophecy. Interestingly, the story goes that Themis later passed on this power to Apollo – or perhaps had it taken from her by force after the patriarchal coup, for he, of course, was a male god of the third generation led by Zeus.[2]

RHEA

Gaia and Themis are by no means the only earth mothers worshipped at Olympia. There is also Rhea, another of Gaia's daughters. Both Themis and Rhea therefore represent a second generation, the so-called 'Titans' or 'Giants'. They were all conceived through the incestuous union of Gaia with her own son, Uranus (Heaven).

It was a far from happy affair. Monstrous union spawned monstrous offspring. Some of the creatures emerging from Gaia's womb were born with a hundred hands and fifty heads. Uranus loathed the sight of them, and his disgust mingled with fear that his many children would conspire to overthrow him. So he stuffed the offspring back inside Gaia's cavernous womb as they appeared, leaving her screaming and writhing in an agony of perpetual birth pangs.

Gaia sought the assistance of her unborn children. She forged a huge scythe of grey adamant and passed it to her son Kronos. With it, in a single stroke, he sliced off his father's genitals. As great torrents of blood and semen splattered across land and sea, Uranus shrivelled into oblivion, and the children of Gaia, the race of Titans, were born.

Kronos, now master of the universe in place of his father, mated with his sister Rhea, and from this union sprang the Olympians, the third generation of gods. Rhea, then, is the mother of Zeus, god of the sky, Poseidon, god of the sea, and Hades, god of the Underworld, and also of Hera, Queen of Heaven, Demeter, goddess of the harvest, and Hestia, goddess of the hearth.

But again, incestuous union begat unnatural crime. Kronos, polluted by the blood of his own father, was warned by Gaia that his children would rise against him in their turn. To save himself, as they emerged from Rhea's womb he devoured them: a father-cannibal, eating his own children, laying crime upon crime, wading ever deeper into a moral mire of gore and guilt. And like Uranus, he was outwitted by the woman most deeply wronged by his crimes. Just as Gaia had engineered the destruction of her son-husband, the womb-stuffing Uranus, so now Rhea contrived the ruin of her son-husband, the child-eating Kronos.

Fat with her sixth child, Rhea, following the advice of her mother, went to Crete to give birth secretly in a hidden cave. Returning to Kronos, she handed him a stone wrapped in swaddling clothes, which he promptly swallowed, convinced that his latest child had been destroyed.

Zeus – for the baby was he – grew to adulthood among the Cretan shepherds, his true identity unknown. Then, impelled by divine instinct, he set out on his momentous mission to overthrow the old order. Anarchy, barbarism and mother-right were to be replaced by order, civilisation and patriarchy.

First he persuaded his mother to secure him an appointment as Kronos's cup-bearer, and used the opportunity to slip his father an emetic potion. Kronos, having drunk deep, suddenly lurched forwards and spewed out a great river of vomit. There, amid the surge of half-digested morsels and foaming wine, were Zeus's brothers and sisters, along with the stone-substitute that his mother had supplied in place of himself.

The young gods fled the palace of Kronos on Mount Othrys and established a new home on nearby Mount Olympos. From there, Zeus launched his war of liberation.

It lasted ten years, and war-weariness and a sense of hopelessness had set in before the final campaign. Zeus sought the advice of Gaia, his grandmother, and she proposed that the Olympians seek reinforcements among the god-beasts that Kronos had confined in Tartaros. Zeus broke into the prison and released its inmates, the monsters of the abyss, who rose in vengeance and violence against their oppressors.

In the final battle, Kronos and the Titans were thus defeated by an unholy alliance of the primeval and the new. And when it was over, most of the Titans were hurled into Tartaros and held there, chained to its torments for all eternity. The Titanesses, though, were spared, especially Rhea, who was honoured as the mother of the gods and an essential ally in the War of the Giants.[3]

For this reason, she, like Gaia, is worshipped at Olympia, and you will see that a new Temple of Rhea is being constructed in the Sanctuary right now (see pp. 67-8).

DEMETER

If Gaia represents the first generation of gods and Rhea the second, Demeter belongs to the third generation dominated by male power-deities – but not devoid of earth mothers. The worship of two is of particular importance at Olympia. Demeter is the goddess of agriculture, known at Olympia by the epithet Demeter *Chamune*, Demeter 'of the Earth-Bed'. Double-edged and highly charged, this interesting Greek word conflates the crop-bearing earth with the lovers' bed. And sure enough, Demeter has a dual role, being the divine equivalent of both farm manager and sex tutor.

Her sanctuary lies beside the Hippodrome. It is said to mark the very spot where the Earth gaped open to receive the chariot of Hades and instantly closed up again after the divine vehicle had passed. What lies behind this is a powerful story of rape and vengeance which, rather more prosaically, provides today's Greek farmer with his understanding of the seasons and the agricultural cycle, so it is worth recounting in full.

Hades, the gloomy lord of the Underworld, had become besotted with Demeter's daughter Persephone. Seeing her picking flowers in a meadow, he hardened with lust, swept down in his chariot and lifted her up and away, gripping tightly as she struggled and screamed.

Demeter had incestuously conceived Persephone with her brother Zeus. Unmarried and usually chaste, Demeter's impregnation by Zeus symbolised the subordination of ancient mother-right to patriarchal power. The abduction and rape of her virgin daughter by Hades, her own and Zeus's brother, had similar significance. Now, though, came a further twist in the cosmic struggle of the sexes, for the earth-mothers' collective retained their power over nature, and this power was now deployed to awesome effect.

Persephone herself, plunged into the darkness and depression of the Underworld, imprisoned there as a sex-slave, refused to eat and wasted away – to the despair of her would-be lover. Meanwhile, her mother searched for her on the surface. Hecate, another of the ancient earth mothers and the mysterious goddess of sorcery, ghosts and the black arts, was the first to break the terrible news. The young herdsman Triptolemos also told them that a giant chariot had been seen, its four black horses racing with thudding hooves and frothing mouths, the driver with reins in one hand and a beautiful girl in the other; as suddenly as it had appeared, it had plunged downwards into the depths of the Earth through a great chasm.

Immediately, Demeter knew: Hades – brother, kidnapper, rapist – had taken her daughter into the nether world. Why had Zeus allowed it? Why did the other gods do nothing? Demeter, in anger and vengeance, wandered the Earth blighting her bounty. The sun dimmed, the summer froze into winter, the crops growing in the fields shrivelled into blackened stalks of rot and stink. As last year's food-stores gave out, the spectre of famine spread its shadow over the Earth.

Zeus was panicked into action by this unexpected demonstration of matriarchal power. He ordered Hades to release the captive on condition that she had not 'eaten the food of the dead'. But she had. Not much – seven seeds from a pomegranate she had picked in an orchard – but enough to compromise the deal. Hades, gloating and lecherous, stood by his rights: seven seeds (symbolising seven rapes) were grounds enough to demand that Persephone should spend six months of every year with him in the Underworld as his queen; Demeter could have her for the remaining six.

But Demeter was not finished. The divine matriarch had a final shaft to launch. Henceforward, she decreed, the sun would shine and the crops grow whenever she and her daughter walked the Earth together. Triptolemos, the young herdsman who had delivered vital intelligence, was supplied with corn seed and a wooden plough, and then sent forth in a chariot drawn by serpents – another symbol of fertile earth – to spread knowledge of agriculture across the world.

But when the time came for Persephone to descend again into Hades's black domain, back to a filthy union between grunting lust and innocent beauty, summer would end and winter begin, lasting the whole six months until she was returned to her mother. And so the cycle was to continue, for all eternity.

That is why Demeter is worshipped across the whole of Greece: she is the sensitive goddess upon whom the return of summer, fertility and new growth depends.

It is clear that the rites of Demeter once had great significance at Olympia, for, you will recall, the Priestess of Demeter *Chamune* is the only married woman permitted to be present at the Games. That special seat and altar of hers in the Stadium are the fossils of once elaborate holy rites (see p. 73).[4]

HERA

Of all the earth-mother cults at Olympia, that of Hera is the one whose rituals survive most strongly in contemporary practice. Wife of Zeus, Queen of Heaven, goddess of marriage and family life, she is honoured with the most ancient temple on the site (see pp. 66-7), is the recipient of regular sacrifice and offerings, and, once every four years, in a festival separate to Zeus's Olympics, she is the focus of special ceremonies and games known as the *Heraia*.

The *Heraia* is shrouded in mystery. Men are not allowed to participate or spectate. Women are sworn to secrecy about the mysteries of the cult. What we know is this. The *Heraia* is the occasion when a newly-woven robe, or *peplos*, is offered up to Hera and used to redress the sacred statue in her temple. Sixteen local married women are charged with weaving this robe, and it is these women who organise and judge the games. They have a special meeting-house in the

10. A bronze figurine of a girl runner. With one breast exposed and bare feet in contact with Mother Earth, she is probably participating in the *Heraia*, the ancient fertility rites performed at Olympia in honour of Hera.

marketplace at Elis. Their mythic mentor is Hippodameia, who assembled the original sixteen matrons to dance in honour of Hera as a thanks-offering for her marriage to Pelops, and whose shrine is maintained by their successors in the Sanctuary (see pp. 91ff).

The girl-athletes, all maidens, run three foot-races according to age groups, always of the same length, one *stadion* minus a sixth (probably because a *stadion* is 600ft, and a woman's pace is smaller than a man's). The girls do not compete naked – they wear a short dress – but their female power is nonetheless displayed and transmitted in what is, without question, an ancient fertility ritual, and perhaps, in part at least, a prenuptial rite of passage. As they run, their long hair flies loose, their dresses are unhitched at the right shoulder to expose a single breast, and their bare feet pound the track in direct contact with Mother Earth. The energy of their young bodies symbolises the dynamism of life.

The fact that the *Heraia* is an exclusively female event is undoubtedly significant. The girls are carriers of the fertility with which the soil must be recharged. They are also between states, in transition from maidenhood to marriage, a moral muddle of ambiguity and uncertainty. Because of this, the girl-athletes are taboo as long as the festival lasts. Men must stay away, both to protect the girls' fecundity from contamination, and to protect themselves from the power and danger of girls in such volatile condition.

Like male athletes at Zeus's games, the female champions of the *Heraia* are also awarded olive wreaths, enjoy a sacrificial feast of beef, and have the right to erect victory monuments. No less telling of the hidden origins of the men's games is the fact that the gold-and-ivory table for the olive wreaths is stored in the Temple of Hera, not that of Zeus: it is the goddess, not the god, who crowns the victors.[5]

POWER-GODS AND SUPERHEROES

The old religion, with its mother goddesses and fertility rituals, was displaced but not destroyed by the rise of the power-gods. Gaia and Rhea are still sometimes honoured – at Olympia especially – but more often their cults have morphed into those of third-generation goddesses: as well as Hera and Demeter, there is also Artemis, goddess of wild nature, Aphrodite, goddess of beauty and love, and Athena, goddess of war, wisdom and the crafts.

None of this alters the basic truth that Greek myth has come to represent a new world of patriarchal power. The mother goddesses continue their eternal work of fertilising the cornfields, olive groves and vineyards of Greek farmers. But, for better or worse, it is the boys who now run the cosmos.

ZEUS

Zeus dominates Greece today. He is King of Heaven, lord of the skies, supreme arbiter and judge. He is also a conservative defender of the status quo, a divine strongman who upholds order, patriarchy and property. Those who violate city laws, religious taboos, or such norms of social life as guest-friendship and hospitality to strangers risk his terrible wrath.

This is a heavy workload. Zeus is always in demand for advice, on-the-spot decisions, and righting wrongs, real and imagined. It is Zeus this, Zeus that, Zeus another thing. With his work cut out, he needs to delegate and compartmentalise. So he specialises in different branches of his multiple, overlapping responsibilites in different places. At Olympia, we encounter Zeus in two distinct roles. Here, above all, he is Zeus the military oracle, and Zeus the Panhellenic arbitration service.

Oracles are a central feature of Greek life. Do not assume that they are simply exercises in fortune-telling for the gullible and simple-minded. Everyone takes oracles very seriously indeed, and they are consulted for all sorts of reasons by individuals and families, politicians and generals, cities and confederations of cities. Nature is fickle. Neighbours are hostile. The world is full of risk and uncertainty. Getting some advance notice of what is coming your way is no light matter in Greece.

The gods, of course, can see ahead, and some of them are specialists in foresight and prophecy. The best-known of these is Apollo, who operates mainly out of Delphi (in Central Greece), which is the most famous oracular sanctuary of all. But Zeus is also an oracle-god. His main centre is at Dodona in Epiros (in northwest Greece), but he has various secondary bases in other parts of Greece, including one at Olympia.

It seems likely that, in this as in so many other things, Zeus has usurped a function once performed by the original divine residents of the site. The ancient tradition, as we have noted, is that Gaia was a source of oracles, that she passed her power to her daughter Themis, and that Themis then passed it on to Apollo (see p. 79). More likely, the power was seized. Then, at some point later, the franchise passed to Zeus, under whom the Olympic oracle has become renowned mainly for its military prophecies.

The oracular procedure is for the applicant to make an offering in anticipation of the service to be performed and then to submit his question to the attendant priests. The deity is consulted, the seer, functioning like a divine voice box, receives a reply, and an interpreter writes down the meaning of the message, which is then delivered to the client. The seer is highly learned in the mysterious and secret art of communicating with the divine. Knowledge of the art is passed down through two or three select family lines. If you seek a prophecy at Olympia, it will be delivered by a member of the Iamidai ('the sons of Iamos'), the Klutiadai ('the sons of Klutios') or the Telliadai ('the sons of Tellios') (see p. 89).

Such is the reputation of the Olympic oracle that many generals consult it, and many take Olympian seers with them on campaign to provide regular assistance with operational decision-making. The results seem to be impressive. By right, Zeus gets a tithe (one-tenth) of the spoils for the victories with which he is credited, and Olympia is packed with victory monuments and trophies of captured hardware.[6]

Zeus's performance record in his other major Olympian role – as Panhellenic peacemaker – is less impressive. At any one time, there will be several revolutions and local wars raging in different parts of Greece, and every few years there will be a major war between leading states and their allies. Over the last 120 years or so Athens, for example, has experienced three revolutions, a fifty-year war against the Persians, a thirty-year war against the Spartans, and numerous other local wars. Zeus the peacemaker is not much in evidence in contemporary Greece.

IAMOS THE OLYMPIC SEER

Iamos was the son of Apollo, god of prophecy, and the Arkadian nymph Evadne. In an effort to conceal her illicit love with the god, Evadne had given birth in the wilderness and abandoned her infant in a bed of gold and purple flowers at the foot of the Hill of Kronos at Olympia.

Apollo sent two snakes to nurture his offspring with the honey of bees, so the infant survived. When grown to young manhood, Iamos, a creature of nature seeking a role among men, waded into the River Alpheios and prayed for guidance to both his father, Apollo, and his grandfather, Poseidon.

'Arise, my son,' answered Apollo, 'and accompany my voice to a land which everyone may share.' Apollo led his son, who had since wandered far, back to his birthplace at Olympia. There, he taught Iamos the art of prophecy, and told him that one day, when Olympia had become the place of a great festival thronged with men,

he should set up an oracle at the very top of the Altar of Zeus (see p. 65).

This, in time, he did. Atop a heap of ash and cindered bone, Iamos used to read the omens in a sacrifice made upon the altar fire. If the flame soared, the gods approved and the news was good. But if there was no flame, if the fire merely smouldered and spluttered, and fat oozed from the flesh and dribbled into the ashes, then the omens were bad, and Iamos delivered the supplicant a black report of pending doom.

The descendants of Iamos — the Iamidai clan — maintain the oracle and practise the secret art to this day.[7]

So, regarding any little worries — about the honesty of your business partner, the fidelity of your spouse, the quality of last night's fish, or the future of the planet — pop down to the Altar of Zeus for a quick consultation. The Iamidai brothers have a direct line to god.

HERAKLES – BUT NOT *THAT* HERAKLES . . .

Remember the point about Greek myths being a terrible muddle, even for the Greeks themselves? This applies especially to the foundation of the Olympic Games, for which there are three separate mythological traditions, two of which, to compound the confusion, concern different heroes of the same name.

We begin with Herakles – but not the primeval superman who wasted barbarians and hunted down monsters at the dawn of time to make the world safe for civilisation; not, that is, the Herakles associated especially with Olympia and depicted performing his Twelve Labours on the decorative panels of the Temple of Zeus in the Sanctuary (see pp. 53-64).

We are concerned first with an earlier Herakles, one of five brothers appointed by Rhea to guard the infant Zeus on Mount Ida in Crete. (She had hidden Zeus there to prevent him being eaten by his father, Kronos: see pp. 80-1.) This Herakles – sometimes called 'Cretan Herakles' – used to run races with his brothers on Mount Olympos (in northern Greece) where victors would be crowned with wreaths of wild olive. The Olympian gods – for whom, of course, Mount Olympos was home – also engaged in running, jumping and wrestling events. This, in a sense, was the First Age of the Olympics – one that long predates the use of the present site.

PELOPS

Our second myth concerns Pelops – he of the *Pelopeion*, the hero-shrine that you can see in the Sanctuary (see pp. 68-9) – but the tale begins with his grandfather.

King Tantalos was mortal but of divine parentage and an intimate of the gods. Having invited his Olympian

11. The myth of Pelops as depicted on the east pediment of the Temple of Zeus at Olympia. Zeus presides in the centre of the scene. On his left stand King Oinomaos and Queen Sterope, on his right Pelops and Hippodameia. On the far sides, the chariots of the two rivals are being prepared for the race.

friends to a banquet one day, he decided – for reasons which remain obscure – to serve them a stew containing the dismembered remains of his own son. Demeter had tucked into the left shoulder before she and the other gods realised and recoiled in horror.

Tantalos was condemned to an eternal torment of hunger and thirst. Bound forever to a fruit tree overhanging a lake, he could never reach either the refreshing water at his feet or the abundance of apples, figs, pears and pomegranates dangling from the branches above.

Meanwhile, having collected the pieces and boiled them up in a magic cauldron, the gods reassembled Tantalos's son and restored him to life. Demeter thoughtfully provided a new left shoulder-blade of ivory. Thus was Pelops (or 'Muddy-Face') reborn.

Such was the beauty of Pelops, who was not only resurrected but also much improved, that Poseidon fell in love with him, and made him gifts of horses, chariots and riding skills.

Pelops inherited his father's realm, but he was unable to defend it against rivals, so he set off with his followers to win a new kingdom elsewhere. He sailed from western Asia to the Peloponnese, and from the east coast headed inland until he reached the territory of King Oinomaos ('Heavy-drinker') of Elis and Pisa. Here, he caught sight of the king's stunningly beautiful daughter, Hippodameia ('Horse-tamer'), and was immediately determined to have her as his wife – together with her father's kingdom.

But Oinomaos was a black-hearted man, a gloomy sexual monster tormented by incestuous desire. His wife, Sterope, was rumoured to be his mother. His lust for his daughter could be assuaged only in the oblivion of his cups. In a mind poisoned by perversion and jealousy, he devised a murderous scheme to destroy all would-be suitors. Any who wished to sue for Hippodameia's hand he would challenge to a long chariot-race across the width of the Peloponnese from Pisa to the Isthmus of Corinth – a race with a terrible hidden catch. Though the young man would be accompanied by Hippodameia herself and would be given a head-start, if Oinomaos caught up, having taken time to sacrifice a ram to Zeus at Olympia, he was entitled to spear the challenger in the back. The penalty for a failed suit, in short, was death.

The king, in this way, destroyed one rival for his daughter after another, since he possessed the finest racehorses in Greece. A dozen or so skulls of young men lined the lintel of the palace as trophies. When Pelops swaggered onto the scene, Oinomaos was confident of another victory, and his opponent was soon made aware that he faced a mortal challange.

But Hippodameia, who hated her father and burned for Pelops, devised a plan for Oinomaos's destruction. She persuaded Myrtilos, the king's chariot-master, to swap one of the bronze linchpins that secured the chariot wheels to the axle for a replica of wax. 'For my sake,' she answered seductively when Myrtilos enquired as to why he should scheme against his master: a false promise of sexual favour.

All went according to plan. Pelops set off first, the king following soon after, but as the latter gained on his opponent and raised his spear to strike, one of his wheels suddenly flew off. Oinomaos was thrown, dragged and trampled to death in a high-speed crash.

Later, to atone for the crime, Pelops, Hippodameia and Myrtilos journeyed to the sea together to make sacrifice and purify themselves. But there, the crime was compounded. Myrtilos claimed Hippodameia's favours as his reward for murder, and Pelops kicked him over a cliff to drown in the sea. He died cursing all the descendants of Pelops and Hippodameia (see p. 94).[8]

What has all this got to do with the Olympic Games? The story goes that Pelops founded Zeus's games in gratitude for his victory over Oinomaos in the deadly chariot-race. At the same time, his new wife Hippodameia founded complementary games for Hera in thanks for her deliverance from her father.

That is why the Elean Olympic Committee honours

THE PELOPS HERITAGE TRAIL

There are plenty of Pelops-related sites and memorabilia scattered around Olympia and its environs. If you have a day to spare, why not spend it paying tribute to one of the mythological forefathers of the Games?

Begin at the Sanctuary and the *Pelopeion* (the tomb and shrine of Pelops), where you will also be able to marvel at the ivory shoulder-blade given to him by Demeter, and a surviving wooden pillar from Oinomaos's palace. Hippodameia's couch – on which she and Pelops may or may not have celebrated his victory – can be found in the Temple of Hera.

Moving on to the Terrace of the Treasuries, Pelops's ceremonial dagger can be viewed in the Treasury of the Sikyonians. And at the Hippodrome, you might like to join the horse-riders and chariot-racers in making an offering at the trackside altar to the 'Horse-frightener' – possibly the ghost of one of Pelops's victims.

Slightly further afield you can contemplate the path of death and destruction with the memorial of Myrtilos, Oinomaos's grave, and the Mound of the Suitors, all to be found around Olympia. The boney remains of Pelops himself are kept in a bronze chest at the Sanctuary of Artemis *Kordax* at Pisa nearby.[10]

THE CURSE OF MYRTILOS

Myrtilos's curse on all the descendants of Pelops and Hippodameia, which he made as he sank beneath the waves, was no impotent gurgle. He was well connected, being the mortal son of Hermes, head of communications on Mount Olympos, and the gods respected Myrtilos's dying wish. The results were awesome.

Pelops and Hippodameia assuaged their blood-guilt and lived long and happy lives. Not so their progeny. Remember Tantalos, the father of Pelops, who had made his own son into a stew and served it to the gods? Pelops himself, restored to life by the good grace of the unenthusiastic banqueters, seems to have avoided the family-eating disorder of his father. Unfortunately, the habit merely skipped a generation and resumed.

A bitter row erupted between Atreus and Thyestes, two of the many sons of Pelops and Hippodameia. Both sought the throne of Mycenae and the bed of Europe. Atreus, backed by Zeus, was the victor on both counts, but his triumph was dashed by the discovery that Thyestes had nonetheless slept with his new wife. No doubt drawing inspiration from Grandpa Tantalos, he got his revenge by serving up his brother's children at a feast where Thyestes was the guest of honour.

But there was a glitch. Thyestes's son by his illicit union with Europe had escaped the stew. Aigisthos ('Goat-strength') had been exposed on a hillside at birth, rescued by goatherds, and suckled by a she-goat.

Atreus's son Agamemnon had meanwhile inherited his father's crown and taken Klytemnestra as his wife. While he was away for ten years fighting the Trojan War – as well as rescuing the Greek fleet from a curse put upon it by the goddess Artemis, and sacrificing his own daughter Iphigeneia in the process – the crafty Aigisthos seduced Klytemnestra and moved into Agamemnon's palace. When the king returned from the war, Aigisthos murdered him and usurped his throne.

The surviving children of Agamemnon, Orestes and Elektra, honour-bound to avenge the death of their father, duly murdered their mother and her lover.

All in all, a rather effective curse, you might say.[11]

Pelops above even Herakles. Zeus and Pelops are the joint recipients of parallel sacrifices. Bulls are sacrificed to Zeus and the offering is burnt and rises from the ash-altar as smoke. Black rams are sacrificed to Pelops and the blood and guts tipped into a ritual pit.[9]

HERAKLES: ANOTHER FOUNDER OF THE GAMES

Among the victims of the curse of Myrtilos was Herakles. A great-grandson of Pelops, he was afflicted with madness and his life was a domestic disaster. He murdered his first wife and children, and was in turn accidentally murdered by his last wife. Like so many others, he laboured – in his case, literally – under the curse of Myrtilos.

Let us recall Herakles' Fifth Labour, the Cleansing of the Augeian Stables, which involved shovelling up history's biggest ever pile of poo (see pp. 63-4). King Augeias, whose cattle were responsible for the mess, was ruler of Elis. Within his territory lay the site of Olympia. The story goes that Herakles, on successfully accomplishing his mission by using the waters of the Alpheios to wash away the muck, decided to give thanks by dedicating a shrine to his divine father.

Herakles named the Hill of Kronos, fenced off the Sanctuary, marked out the area of the Olympic Village, consecrated the site with divine images and altars, and founded the four-yearly Games with an inaugural festival.[12]

Hold on a minute! Surely the Games were already up and running, having been founded three generations earlier by this Herakles's great-grandfather Pelops? The problem, to repeat, is that myths are ancient stories that become increasingly muddled over time – like a dozen balls of wool that have unravelled and become hopelessly tangled. The fact is that two distinct foundation myths concerning two different heroes are both offered as explanations for the origin of the Games. The best way to reconcile them is to think of it this way: Pelops organised occasional local games at Olympia, but it was Herakles who turned them into a regular Panhellenic festival. But keep in mind that this is simply an *ex post facto* rationalisation of what were originally quite separate stories.

What sort of games were these, the 'revival' games inaugurated by Herakles? Our word 'labour' is a rather poor translation of the Greek word *athloi*, meaning 'contests'. Herakles was emphatically *not* a 'labourer': he was an 'athlete'. The Greek word for manual labour – the work of peasants, artisans and general labourers – is *ergon*. Aristocrats do not do *ergon*: it is a degrading activity performed only by those unable to live off the income of their estates. Above all, aristocrats do not do *ergon* for which they are paid: this is doubly degrading, for it is one thing to work on your own land, quite another to be so poor that you are forced to work on another's in return for wages.

The myth of the Cleansing of the Augeian Stables makes the distinction explicit. Herakles demanded payment from the King of Elis for his work, thereby transforming it from *athlos* into *ergon*. The king, aware of its true nature, refused payment. Eurystheus, Herakles' malevolent taskmaster, knowing that payment had been sought, refused to recognise it as a true 'labour'. Herakles was a semi-divine aristocratic hero: he could not perform paid manual labour without losing caste. The games he founded were clearly not 'labours' – they were a series of 'contests' designed to display the excellence and supremacy of social superiors. Thus, the original Olympics were profoundly elitist – and this very much set the tone for all that was to follow.[13]

OLYMPIC AGES

In the mythological tradition, Cretan Herakles gives us what might be called the First Age of the Olympics, and Pelops and Theban Herakles the Second Age. This means that the historical Olympics belong to a 'Third Age', the assumption being that these began in 776 BC and were founded by the semi-legendary King Iphitos of Elis.

Since the Olympics are central to Greek conceptions of the past – which is a potent mix of myth and history – this table should help you get to grips with their place in the mythological past.[14]

Greek epoch	Olympic epoch	Founder	Character of the Games
Age of Obscurity	First Age of the Olympics	Cretan Herakles	Games on Mount Olympos
Age of Fable 1	Second Age of the Olympics I	Pelops	Occasional local festival at Olympia
Age of Fable 2	Second Age of the Olympics II	Herakles	Regular Panhellenic festival at Olympia
Age of History (begins 776 BC)	Third Age of the Olympics	King Iphitos of Elis	Revival of regular Panhellenic festival at Olympia

WHAT THE MYTHS *REALLY* MEAN

Virtually the entire complex of Greek myth is threaded together at Olympia and celebrated in stories told, rituals enacted, and scenes depicted. Olympia reaffirms its status as the premier Panhellenic shrine with a massive panorama of classical myths.

But it is all fabrication.

You would not dare say so – except perhaps in the privacy of a select symposium attended only by Athenian intellectuals. To question the existence of the gods, to deny the historicity of the heroes, to imply that Olympia's most revered ancient rites are mere mumbo-jumbo, especially if you are a visiting barbarian, is at best highly offensive, at worst, positively dangerous.

Let us not forget the recent case of Socrates. The leading intellectual of the most liberal-minded city in Greece he may have been: it did not save him. Some say he was asking for trouble, mixing with a clique of hard-core reactionaries, many of whom had supported a right-wing coup in 404 BC. But democracy had been restored the following year, and the supporters of the ousted dictators amnestied. Not until 399 BC was Socrates put on trial, and the charge was not treason, but, as the official court record states, 'That Socrates does not recognise the gods the city recognises, but introduces other and new deities; also, that he corrupts the young. Penalty demanded: death.'

And so it was. The old man was condemned and, spurning the chance of flight and exile, accepted the ultimate sentence. Surrounded by friends, and in accordance with the Athenian method of execution, he drank a miniature cup of hemlock in the state prison.[15]

You have been warned: things can turn very nasty in Greece if you make light of religion.

But between ourselves, it is all made up. What no-one can admit is that the rituals came first, and then gods, heroes and fables were invented to give them greater meaning and significance. The real question to be answered is this: what is the symbolism at work in the sacred ceremonies and athletic contests that make up the Olympics? Or to put it another way: what exactly do the Games *mean*?[16]

HUNTING MAGIC?

There are certainly incidental features of the Games that may be throwbacks to primitive hunting magic. The nakedness of athletes is reminiscent of hunters, who sometimes discard much of their clothing to reduce scent.

The crowning of victors with vegetal crowns is perhaps suggestive of hunters' camouflage. The main events obviously replicate the methods of the hunt.

Nor has the decline in the economic importance of hunting, due to the development of farming, necessarily reduced its social significance. It remains a pastime symbolic of aristocracy, leadership, warfare and male prowess. Babylonians, Egyptians and Persians have long regarded hunting as the sport of kings. Mycenaean Greek kings mixed hunting and sport in the late Bronze Age. Greek heroes like Herakles were both hunters and athletes, and in numerous Greek myths the hunt is the setting for deeds of skill, stamina, courage and derring-do.

What are the Olympic foot-race and horse-race if not mimes of the hunt in the manner of primitive magic? Are the discus and javelin not missiles cast to bring down prey? Does Herakles not wrestle to submission the Erymanthian Boar? Does he not choke the Nemean Lion like a mighty pankratiast? So the links are there, and they are many.[17]

DEATH RITUAL?

How did Achilles celebrate the funeral rites of his lover Patroklos, slain in battle by the Trojan hero Hektor? He built him a pyre 100-feet square, and placed the body on a bier at the summit. He made offerings of honey and oil, sacrificed numerous sheep and cattle, and then slaughtered two dogs, four horses and twelve Trojan warrior-nobles.

Achilles was fulfilling a vow. 'Fare you well, Patroklos, even in the House of Hades,' he proclaimed. 'See, I am fulfilling now all that I promised you before, to drag Hektor's body here and give it to the dogs to eat raw, and cut the throats of twelve splendid Trojan children at your pyre, in my anger for your killing.'

The fire burned through the night. When the flames died away the following morning, the cremated bones of

Patroklos were collected and placed in a golden jar. Then the site of the pyre was marked with a circle of stones, the jar was placed within, and a mound of earth was raised over it: the Tomb of Patroklos.

But this was not the end, for 'Achilles kept the people there, and sat them down in a broad gathering, and brought from his ships prizes for the games – cauldrons and tripods, horses, mules, strong heads of cattle, fine-girdled women, and grey iron.'

The funeral games that followed were on a grand scale and keenly contested. As well as a chariot-race, a boxing match, a wrestling contest and a foot-race, there were discus, javelin and archery competitions. Much blood was spilt among contestants, and bitter rows among the spectators almost brought them to blows. Most violent of all was the armed duel.

Setting down a spear, a shield and a helmet, Achilles announced: 'We want two men, the best among you, to fight for these prizes. They are to put on their armour, take up spears of cutting bronze, and fight a duel here in front of the crowd. The first to make a hit in the other's fine body, and reach his innards through his armour and his dark blood, will receive from me this sword with its silver-nailed hilt, a beautiful piece of Thracian work, which I took from Asteropaios. And both contestants can take this armour and share it: and we will give them both a fine feast in my hut.'[18]

What is the connection here between death and sport? Like the beasts and men sacrificed on the pyre, the exertions of the athletes are an offering to the shade of the deceased, and a symbolic register of his rank, status and identity. But also, coming after the grim holocaust of the night, the games complete the rite of passage of the deceased with an energetic assertion of the continuity of life: the dynamism of sport, where the mind pushes the body to the limits of physical possibility, is the ultimate negation of death.[19]

BLOOD SACRIFICE?

Perhaps there is something deeper still. Death means the loss of blood, as it drains from the fallen warrior's wounds, and as it coagulates in the pale and waxy corpse.

To shed blood in return for blood shed is to exact vengeance: when Achilles slays Hektor and sacrifices twelve young Trojans, he tells the dead Patroklos that it is 'in my anger for your killing'. Achilles here is a protagonist of a primitive blood-feud.

But this bloodletting is more than mere atonement. The blood of Hektor, the twelve Trojans, and the many sheep, cattle, horses and dogs sacrificed around the funeral pyre represent a power-potion for the regeneration of life. Just as the menstrual blood of women, flowing in synch with the waxing and waning of the moon, can re-fertilise the Earth, so sacrificial blood can reanimate a corpse and enable the deceased to take his place among the ancestral spirits of the Underworld.

Without the ritual, the spirit is lost in the void. When the ghost of Patroklos visits Achilles to remind him of his obligation, what does it say? 'Bury me as quickly as can be, so I can pass through the Gates of Hades. The ghosts, the phantoms of the dead, are keeping me away. They will not let me cross the river to join their number, but I am left wandering in vain along the broad-gated House of Hades. And give me your hand, I beg you with my tears – as I shall never again return from Hades, once you have given me my due rite of burning.'

Blood, burning and burial: without these, the spirit of the deceased is consigned to oblivion, condemned to float in emptiness forever. Blood is required for the resurrection of the spirit, burning to release it from its physical shell, and burial to despatch it from this life to the next.[20]

What has this got to do with sport? The Olympic festival is an inextricable tangle of myth, ritual and contests, and through that tangle runs a thick red thread – the obsessive symbolism of blood and blood sacrifice for ordinary Greeks preoccupied with the eternal cycles of life and death.

UNITY CULT?

Some commentators see the Games as an expression of Panhellenic unity and identity. Of these, many are content to attribute the intention that it should be so to Pelops, when the first Games were inaugurated at Olympia, or, more often, to Herakles, when they were re-established on a grander and more permanent basis (see pp. 90ff). Others – dissatisfied perhaps by the rather poor record of both Pelops and Herakles in the Panhellenic goodwill department – have advanced the case for King Iphitos of Elis, a rather more convincing standard-bearer for the cause.

Iphitos came to a sad end: he was thrown from the walls of Tiryns by Herakles for harbouring a justifiable suspicion that the hero was guilty of theft. Fortunately, before this happened, he had made time to re-found the Olympic Games after a period of lapse. An important feature of the 'Iphitan revival' was the emphasis on the Sacred Truce (see pp. 149-51). The story goes that, with Greece racked with war and pestilence, Iphitos sought advice from the Delphic Oracle. He was specifically told, in an uncharacteristically clear and concise set of recommendations, that he should restore both the festival *and* the truce.

This he did. And the proof is there. You can still see Iphitos's commemorative discus at Olympia, with the words of the truce inscribed in a circle around the top.[21]

So much for the myths. But what do we know about the *real* history of the Games? Let us now take a closer look at that 'Age of History' which began – or may have begun! – in 776 BC.

4 HISTORY

IN THE BEGINNING ⋅ ⋅ ⋅

The Greeks have definite ideas about the origins of the Olympics. But those ideas turn out to be a set of 'invented traditions' – essentially myths and rituals rooted in a primeval past. What do we know of the *actual* history of the Games?

The traditional view is that they began in 776 BC. There is a list of Olympic victors extending back to that year, when one Koroibos of Elis is recorded as the winner of the sprint (or *stadion*) race. This list, which provides a complete record of every sprint winner from 776 BC to the present day, was compiled by one Hippias of Elis a few years ago. Inevitably – since the Greeks are probably the most disputatious people in the ancient world no sooner was the list published than its reliability was challenged. There are a good few who take issue with Hippias, not least because he is an Elean, with a patriotic interest in promoting the antiquity of the Games held under the auspices of his own city.

The evidence is contradictory and the question vexed. Far be it from us to weigh in with an attempt at definitive judgement. Suffice it to say, some extremists think the Olympics may be no older than 604 BC, making the official 'record' a shocking travesty. Rather more favour a date around 725 or 700 BC. But the majority nail their traditionalist colours to the mast and agree with Hippias. Ask any Greek standing next to you in the Stadium when the Games began and he is almost sure to answer, 'When Koroibos of Elis won the sprint.'[1]

Whenever they started, we can distinguish two distinct

phases in the development of the historical Games. For convenience, we can dub these the Archaic (or Aristocratic) Games and the Classical (or Citizen) Games.

THE ARCHAIC (OR ARISTOCRATIC) GAMES

In the early days, the Olympics seem to have been an informal local festival with only aristocratic contestants. Athletes competed not so much as representatives of their cities – many of which were little more than villages, or at best hilltop strongholds – but on their own accounts, to prove their superiority over their peers, and to win honour, fame and prizes.

Prizes? These seem so alien to 'the Olympic tradition', yet it seems near certain they were once awarded. Today, athletes appear to compete for honour and fame alone; it is enough to win, to be crowned with the wild-olive wreath, to be known throughout Greece as Olympic champion. Is that not so?

Well, not exactly. After all, you will never meet a poor sports-star. The sturdy peasant-farmer who takes time off to win glory at Olympia and then returns dutifully to his plough is the stuff of fable. The reality is that athletes: (a) need patronage to get to the top in the first place; (b) can expect to be richly rewarded by a grateful home city if they win; and (c) find their star status will thereafter make them a welcome addition to the programme at countless prize-giving games across Greece (see pp. 124ff)

Nonetheless, a basic point remains: the EOC emphatically does *not* award prizes at the modern Games. It is the home city that sometimes provides the financial backing and rich rewards of its athletes. Only cities hosting 'money games' offer celebrity-level prizes to attract the best athletes to its festivals.

But things did not work that way 350 years ago. What

was the incentive then, when city-states were mud villages, and the Olympic Games only a local festival? Why should anyone bother to compete?

Archaic Greece was a very different place. It was ruled by gangs of rowdy nobles, each in control of a walled hilltop redoubt, from which they dominated and ruled a few square miles of farmland. A true 'band of brothers' who would stand four-square together in a bust-up with their neighbours, they were also egotistical, highly competitive, and given to boasting and brawling among themselves.

What held this fractious society together were strict rules of conduct in relation to kinsmen and guest-friends. A stranger was always entitled to food, drink and shelter, and once granted, he became a guest-friend, one with whom permanent reciprocal social obligations as binding as those attaching to kinsmen had been established.

What made these social connections especially durable and effective was the universal practice of gift exchange. Aristocratic social networks were kept connected by the endless circulation within them of 'prestige goods'. Hosts would send their guests away laden with presents. The higher the status of donor and recipient, the greater the value of the gifts. The greatest lords accumulated huge reserves of prestige goods: arms and armour, highly crafted bronzes, fine horses and chariots, pretty slave-girls, expensive fabrics, jars of wine, oil and honey. These reserves became measures of a man's rank and status. Prestige goods were the currency of social power.

Treasure, then, was honourable. How could other men judge accurately one's 'excellence' (*arete*) without this measure of worth? To be excellent and for other men to know it: that was the thing.

Homer is our source for this period. His two great poems, the *Iliad* and the *Odyssey*, were first written down in the eighth century BC, around the time the Olympic Games were founded. Though they represent an oral poetic tradition which had been developing since the

12. Homer, the blind bard of the distant age when the Olympics were founded.

twelfth century BC, the poems as we have them do tell us much of Homer's own social world – that of the boisterous warrior-nobles of the early Archaic Age, among whom he lived and worked as an entertainer.

Homer was successful because he gave his audience what it wanted. You do not offend your patrons. You tell it as they like to hear it. *Arete* is central to the aristocratic value-system Homer describes, and by it he means not just 'excellence' in a general sense, but the excellence to which the men who were his listeners aspired: manly beauty, physical prowess and staying-power, courage and endurance in battle. Homer's nobles were neither patriots nor democrats. They did not fight for a cause. They were bragging, bickering individualists out for personal glory. That is why they needed prizes: not for their own sake, but as measures of achievement.

What does Achilles offer as prizes at the funeral games of Patroklos (see p. 100)? For the charioteers, 'A woman skilled in excellent handcraft, and a tripod with handles holding twenty-two measures, for the winner to take. For the second, the prize he set out was a mare six-years-old and unbroken, pregnant with a mule foal. For the third, he put down a beautiful cauldron holding four measures, untouched by the fire and with its new brightness still on it. For the fourth, he put down two talents of gold, and for the fifth, a two-handled bowl untouched by the fire.'

There was a prize for everyone (there were only five entries), but, of course, the value of the prize reflected the 'excellence' of the recipient. This was also the pattern for other contests. The winner of the boxing was given a mule and the loser a two-handled cup. When Achilles displayed the prizes for the wrestling, the relative values were precisely estimated: 'For the winner, a great tripod to stand over the fire, which the Achaians [Greeks] among themselves valued at twelve oxen's worth; and as the prize for the beaten man, he brought a woman into the centre, one skilled in the range of handcraft, and they valued her at four oxen.' For the foot-race, a silver mixing-bowl, a great ox, and half a talent of gold were the prizes. There were arms and armour for the duellists, a five-years' supply of pig iron for the discus-throwers and the archers, and a spear and a cauldron for the javelin-throwers.[2]

Now, of course, these are only stories. Whatever germs of historical truth about events long ago Homer's poems may contain, they have become encrusted with centuries of legend and fable. But the *Iliad* is not a fantasy. Characters may be invented, but they inhabit a social world that would have been recognisable to Archaic-Age Greeks. And the evidence is there at Olympia for you to see. The Sanctuary is a museum of expensive antiques, its temples and treasuries piled high with *objets d'art*, many surviving from the 'heroic age' of the Games, when they were, at some point, dedicated as votive offerings.

Much of what you see is junk. There are discarded ceramic libation jugs, chipped and cracked; fragments of hammered metal sheet, long since detached from the objects they once decorated; countless dress pins, brooches and other items of jewellery; and thousands of terracotta and bronze miniatures of deities, warriors, charioteers, athletes, bulls, horses, stags, goats, even beetles.

But there are also many objects of extraordinary richness of material, handicraft and artistry: cups of gold and basins of silver; polished tables, beautifully carved bedsteads, and couches inlaid with silver and ivory; purple blankets and mantles, and rich, glistening embroideries; necklaces strung with gold and amber. Above all, there are many fine bronze tripod cauldrons.

The greatest of these was valued by Homer's Achaians

13 and 14. A bronze tripod cauldron and a mounting in the form of a griffon – the temples and treasuries at Olympia are rammed full of such objects.

at twelve oxen, and many of the examples you will see at Olympia are in this league. They are phenomenal prestige goods, designed not for use but for display and donation. Some stand a metre high. The three tripod legs and the two handles, together with the attachments for each, are often highly decorated. Geometric designs and scenes of sacrifice and combat have been hammered into the bronze sheets covering the legs, while horses, lions, winged figures and fearsome griffon-heads adorn the wholly impractical handles.[3]

Admittedly, this Olympic museum of antiquities does not actually prove that prizes were awarded in the Archaic Games; every object on display in the Sanctuary today was originally placed there as a votive offering. But Hesiod, a poet more or less contemporary with Homer, tells us that when he won 'a tripod with ring-handles' in the poetry contest at the funeral games of Amphidamas in Chalkis, he 'dedicated it to the Muses of Helikon in the original place where they set me on the path of fine singing'. This statement, the number of ancient votives at Olympia, and Homer's generic descriptions of games in which precisely such objects are offered as prizes, combine to make a strong case.[4]

So the Olympics began in 776 BC, or somewhat later, perhaps around 700 BC, and it was originally a local festival in which aristocratic athletes competed for prizes. What else do we know? In Homer's descriptions in the *Iliad* and the *Odyssey*, all the classes of contest included in the modern programme are mentioned, except for the horse-race, the *pankration* and the race in armour. But does this mean that all the others were part of the programme from the outset? Not necessarily. The (sadly incomplete) record of Olympic champions gives the year in which a winner is first recorded for each event, and from this we may hazard a guess at the date of its introduction to the programme.

THE FIRST OLYMPIC CHAMPIONS

Event	Date of introduction	Winner
Stadion foot-race (600ft)	776 BC	Elis
Diaulos foot-race (1,200ft)	724 BC	Elis
Dolichos foot-race (12,000ft)	720 BC	Sparta
Pentathlon	708 BC	Sparta
Wrestling	708 BC	Sparta
Boxing	688 BC	Smyrna
Tethrippon chariot-race (four horse)	680 BC	Thebes
Horse-race	648 BC	Krannon (Thessaly)
Pankration	648 BC	Syracuse
Boys' *stadion*	632 BC	Elis
Boys' wrestling	632 BC	Sparta
Boys' boxing	616 BC	Sybaris
Race in armour	520 BC	Heraia (Arkadia)
Sunoris chariot-race (two horse)	408 BC	Winner uncertain [5]

The Games seem to have started with fewer events, and the programme has gradually evolved over the last three and a half centuries. Along the way, there were a couple of false starts. The record shows there was a boys' pentathlon only once, in 628 BC, and a mule-cart race only between 500 and 444 BC. The latter was a bizarre anomaly. Expensive because it required a pair of mules, a racing cart and a skilled (seated) driver, it can hardly have been a dignified sport for an equestrian aristocrat. Little wonder that it was dropped from the programme.[6]

Where did the ideas for the different events come from? None seems to have been an Olympic invention: there are older precedents for every one. None even seems to have been peculiarly Greek: search the sculptures and paintings of the Babylonians, the Egyptians, the Assyrians, the Hittites and the Minoans, and you will probably find some kind of precedent for every Olympic event.

The Mycenaean Greeks (c. 1600–1200 BC) were well connected – as both traders and pirates – with the peoples of the wider Eastern Mediterranean world. They were voracious culture vultures, absorbing the different ways of life they encountered, and importing foreign exotica back home to Greece. The Mycenaeans were into chariot-racing, running, boxing, wrestling and possibly armed combat; and if they did not invent these sports themselves, they could easily have discovered them abroad.[7]

This gives us a link with the Homeric tradition. The Trojan War – the real-life event on which the myths of the *Iliad* and the *Odyssey* are based – took place in the twelfth century BC. Homer's Achaian heroes were the last of the Mycenaean Greeks, distant ancestors of the Dark Age warlords of the tenth century and the Archaic Age aristocrats of the eighth, whose feasting halls (*megara*) were the conduits through which the poems were transmitted (and transformed) over some four centuries. The importance of sport in the lives of Homer's heroes, and its centrality to their festive occasions, suggests an unbroken line of development from the Mycenaean Age.[8]

THE CRETAN CONNECTION: THESEUS AND THE MINOTAUR

The connections forged by those enterprising Mycenaean Greeks have even come down to us in myth. One of the most famous concerns a bloody and fraught relationship between Mycenaean Athens and Minoan Crete.

Every nine years, seven boys and seven girls were to be delivered up to the slaughter: that was the appalling tribute levied on Athens by King Minos of Crete. The children were to be fed to the monstrous abomination entombed in a labyrinth beneath his palace: the Minotaur, a creature with the head of a bull and the body of a man, the unnatural offspring of the union of Queen Pasiphaë and the Cretan Bull.

When the third tribute was due, Prince Theseus – the acknowledged son of King Aigeus of Athens, though in fact secretly sired by Poseidon – insisted on being included among the victims, for he was determined to slay the Minotaur. So it was that he sailed with the others to Crete in King Minos's black-sailed ship at the appointed time.

On the night before the Athenians were due to be fed to

15. The Athenian hero Theseus battling the Minotaur in the Labyrinth of Knossos on Crete.

the Minotaur, Minos hosted a banquet in his palace at Knossos There, admiring his beautiful face, superbly muscled body, and calmly commanding demeanour through the flickering light of the feasting hall, Princess Ariadne fell in love with the Athenian hero.

The House of Minos was charged with explosive sexual tensions. It was Poseidon's affliction of Queen Pasiphaë with bestial lust for the Cretan Bull that had produced the monster in the labyrinth. Little wonder, perhaps, that Minos sought satisfaction elsewhere. But his numerous infidelities eventually provoked retaliation. Pasiphaë put a spell upon him, and henceforth, whenever the old man lay with another woman, he discharged not seed, but a stream of serpents, scorpions and millipedes that devoured his partner's private parts.

Poor Ariadne. Her mother was a bestial witch and her father a serial seducer with a malignant organ. Theseus, as well as being a prime catch, offered an escape route from hated parents. So Ariadne offered to help Theseus kill her half-brother if he agreed to take her back to Athens as his wife.

The deal done, Ariadne gave Theseus a secret plan of the labyrinth, a ball of magic string, and a fine, shining, razor-sharp sword. These had been supplied to her long before by Daedalus, King Minos's master architect and artisan, who had harboured an understandable aversion to his royal master. These vital aids spelled the Minotaur's doom.

As Theseus advanced into the darkness of the tunnels, he soon lost all sense of direction amidst the endless twists and turns. But the plan showed the way, the magic string marked it out, and the bellowing of the beast grew louder and louder.

He found the Minotaur in a great hall at the centre of the maze. The air was heavy with the stink of rotting entrails. The broken bones of children crunched underfoot. As soon as the beast saw an armed opponent at the entrance to the hall, it let out a great roar and charged with levelled horns. But Theseus dodged, swung round, grabbed its neck, twisted it up, and plunged his sword into the Minotaur's flesh.

The great beast collapsed, the death-spasms stilled in seconds amid gushing torrents of black bull-blood.

Theseus set sail for home with Ariadne and his thirteen young companions. But he betrayed Ariadne, abandoning her on the beach at Naxos where the ship had stopped to take on water. In her grief, she came close to hanging herself, but was rescued by Dionysos, god of wine, and became his consort.

Theseus's callous ingratitude earned a bitter reward: forgetting to hoist a white sail as he approached the harbour of Athens – the agreed signal that all was well – old King Aigeus, assuming that his son had perished, jumped from the Acropolis to his death.

Thus, Theseus, having liberated his country from tutelage to Minoan Crete, was crowned king of a newly independent city.[9]

What is the origin of this bloody legend? It is surely a record – in the fossilised form of myth – of a tributary economic relationship, and therefore a cultural conduit, between Minoan Crete and some of the Mycenaean cities. In this way, the sporting traditions of Crete, formed in part by contact with the East, reached Mainland Greece.

FIGHTING, HOMER-STYLE

Is sport simply war without the shooting? Warriors routinely exercise and train, and all the sporting events of the Greeks seem to be tests of fitness for the battlefield. The Olympics measure the power and accuracy of the spear-cast, the speed and skill of the charioteer, the strength and endurance of the hand-to-hand fighter. The Greeks are both warlike and sports-mad, and it is perhaps no accident that their athletic contests are exceptionally gruelling and bloody.

The Archaic Games correspond with a style of warfare described in Homer, but one that was fast passing away when the poems were written down. The protagonists were small warlord retinues, probably never more than a few hundred strong, their membership drawn from a social and military elite.

The richest were conveyed across the battlefield in chariots. All were equipped with crested helmets and broad shields, and many with cuirasses and other body-armour. The principal weapons were the bow and the spear, though swords were also used, and some warriors were renowned for their swordsmanship. The spear could be cast as a javelin or wielded close-quarters as a pike; either way, the preference was to keep the enemy at a distance. The raid, the ambush and the skirmish dominated strategy, and the tactics of combat were tentative, more hit-and-run than pitched battle, more chaotic swirl of rival champions than the organised collision of formed masses.[10]

This, as far as we can tell, was the way of war for the men who first competed for Olympic olive-wreaths some three centuries ago – men for whom those early contests were exercises in mock-battle appropriate to their rank and status.

THE CLASSICAL (OR CITIZEN) GAMES

If we accept that the Olympic Games began as early as 776 BC, they must at first have been no more than a local festival dominated by aristocratic athletes from Elis. By around 700 BC, they seem to have developed into a major Peloponnesian festival, with participation by citizens of many local cities, and even a few from other parts of Greece. But not until around 600 BC did the Olympics become a truly Panhellenic festival regularly attracting competitors from all over the Greek world. In other words, we should probably think less in terms of a single act of creation at a specific date, and more in terms of a process of evolution over almost two centuries.

Coincident with this – assuming it is correct – was the transformation of the Games from a socially exclusive event for upper-class hearties into a popular sports festival able to attract the biggest crowds in Greece. And this was because Greece itself was undergoing radical change.

The swaggering lords and masters of the Homeric Age were toppled between around 650–500 BC. A new power was rising: a middle class of prosperous farmers and small businessmen. There were various reasons for this. First, land ownership has always been much more equal in Greece than in many other parts of the world, and the better-off peasants always fight hard to protect their family plots. Second, no Greek is ever far from the sea, and seafaring and overseas trade are economically important; consequently, land and inherited wealth are less central to social and political dominance than elsewhere. Third, since early in the Archaic Age (c. 750–500 BC), ordinary citizens have been empowered by the general obligation to undertake military service; in Greece today, war is not the preserve of a professional elite, but the common undertaking of all. Finally, the Greeks have an unparalleled tradition of bloody-minded resistance to the pretensions of their upper classes.

Travel almost anywhere in the vast Persian Empire that stretches from Egypt to India, from the Caucasus to Arabia, and you are in a world dominated by civil servants, landlords and priests. The common people are cowed and sullen; after taxes, rents and tithes are paid, enough is left to support only a minimal existence – but any dissent, any whisper of protest, never mind actual revolt, is ruthlessly crushed. The Greeks regard the Persian emperor as an 'oriental despot' and his people mere 'slaves'.

Travel around Greece and the impression is quite different. There are exceptions. Messenia, in the south-western Peloponnese, is a miserable place. Centuries ago, the Messenians were conquered and subjugated by the Spartans, and now they work as serfs (or 'helots') on the estates of the Spartan military elite (but see p. 72). Messenia, though, is notorious. For Greeks to be slaves, and for other Greeks to hold them as slaves, is widely considered to be an abomination. Personal freedom is supremely important to the Greeks. The ideal is to have your own farm or business, so that you are of independent means. To be compelled to sell your labour to another, to be dependent on an employer for a livelihood, is considered bad enough. To be any sort of bondsman is the very negation of citizenship and manhood.

The villages and small towns of Greece that you see on your way to the Olympics will give a very different impression than similar places abroad. Everywhere you pass, you will meet comfortable, well-fed, somewhat self-important local citizens – men eager to impress, keen to talk and share news, men who look you straight in the eye, ask direct questions, and give confident answers. The Greek middle class is of a distinctive type. What is not so immediately apparent – what is in fact rather surprising – is that these men are some of the toughest soldiers, and some of the most red-blooded revolutionaries, in the world.

Soldiers and revolutionaries are usually on opposite sides. Not in Greece. The Old Greece of self-styled Homeric 'heroes' was brought down by a wave of revolutions powered by deep-rooted changes in military affairs. It is the division of Greece into a thousand bickering city-states, such that at any particular time there is always somewhere in the world where Greeks are trying to kill Greeks, that makes the entire race exceptionally warlike. As the cities grew richer and more populated, swelling from villages and strongholds of a hundred or so into metropolises of thousands, warfare was transformed from a matter of warlord retinues into one of massed citizen militias. This is when the middle class came into its own.

The new Greek armies are based on a 'phalanx' of 'hoplites'. The phalanx is a closely-packed formation of spearmen standing shoulder-to-shoulder, eight or more ranks deep, the shields of the men forming the front rank overlapping to form a shield wall, their spears levelled along the top to present to the enemy a hedge of razor-sharp blades. Each soldier – or 'hoplite' – supplies his own equipment, including a crested helmet, a cuirass, a large round shield, a long thrusting-spear and a sword.

Now this is expensive kit: only around one in three citizens can afford it. The result? The hoplite phalanx is a middle-class bloc. And once dominant on the battlefield, it was soon dominant in the politics of the city. Aristocratic

16 and 17. A hoplite and a bronze hoplite helmet of Corinthian style. Militia service is an obligation on all adult male Greek citizens. The better-off citizens serve as heavy-infantry hoplites in the phalanx.

chariots disappeared from war, and aristocratic govern-ments succumbed to a wave of 'hoplite revolutions'.

Almost everywhere, new councils and popular assemblies replaced hereditary regimes of 'the best' (*aristoi*) and 'the well-born' (*eupatridai*). Farmers, merchants and master-craftsmen, even dockers, fishermen and market-traders, now rub shoulders with the gilded elite in the highest echelons of state power. Hardened reactionaries still denounce 'democracy' (*demokratia*: the rule of the citizen-body) in their cups. Some even plot counter-revolution. But most of the rich have adapted. More than a few have even made new political careers as 'champions of the people'.

Without this background, it is impossible to get a handle on the nature of the Olympic Games today. There is a real sense in which hoplites, gymnasia and games go together. Coincident with the transformation of the Olympics into a mass Panhellenic games around 600 BC is both the emergence (or recasting) of the other crown games

– the Pythian, Isthmian and Nemean (see p. 124) – and the earliest appearance of the gymnasium in Greek life.[11]

THE GYMNASIUM

If you are seriously rich, you do not need a state-funded gymnasium in which to exercise and train. You have ample space at home or on the estate. If, on the other hand, you are of modest means but have sporting ambition, or even if you just want to indulge the popular passion for exercise, athletics and the body-beautiful, you need public facilities.

All well-appointed modern cities, therefore, in addition to their marketplaces, council chambers and temples, have at least one gymnasium (*gumnasion*). Typically, there is an open-air running track (*stadion*), an open-air 'wrestling ground' or exercise square (*palaistra*), and at least one covered colonnade as shelter from sun and rain (*stoa*). In the more elaborate complexes, the *palaistra* may have covered colonnades on all four sides, and there may also be a covered running track (*xystos*), either as part of the *palaistra* or alongside it. Running surfaces are formed of raked earth, and a sand-pit (*skamma*) is provided for practising combat sports. There are usually baths and basins for the essential ablutions. The largest gymnasia have specific rooms set aside within the courtyard colonnades as changing rooms, oiling rooms, punch-bag rooms, dusting-powder storage rooms, and so on.[12]

These are not simply sports complexes. The Greek gymnasium is a multifaceted cultural phenomenon, one in which the state has an urgent interest, and to which all citizens are deeply committed. Because the army is a citizen militia, the fitness of all its young men is a matter of state security: no-one is going to win a war fielding an army of fatties.

The Greeks also have a strong sense that a healthy body, while it may not guarantee it, certainly contributes to a healthy mind. They speak of *kalokagathia*, which means something like 'fine appearance and conduct', and will often describe a young man as *kalos kai agathos*, 'beautiful and good'. Admittedly, much of this talk has a distinctly homoerotic undertone, and the local gymnasium is a well-trodden hang-out and pick-up joint for middle-aged pederasts (see pp. 33ff). But the prejudice against ugliness goes further: it is equated, in an ill-defined but persistent way, with wickedness.[13]

Consequently, the Greeks do not make any sharp distinction between physical and intellectual education, and the two are commonly combined in the gymnasium. Teachers can often be seen instructing students, either sitting on benches or on the ground in shady areas of the gymnasium, even as others exercise nearby. Perhaps the best-known example in Greece today is that of the famous Athenian philosopher Plato, who has just set up a new school in a gymnasium located a short distance northwest of the city. The gymnasium is beside a grove – extra shade is always desirable – and a sanctuary dedicated to the Attic hero Hekademos; because of this, Plato's school is known as 'the Academy'.[14]

The equal emphasis on both sports and intellectual education reflects the dual role of the citizen in modern city-states. Fighting in the phalanx, he must be fit and healthy. Voting in the popular assembly, he must be well-informed and clear-thinking. The state requires citizens who are both physical and political. The gymnasium supplies both.

Crown games festivals are the epicentres of this entire gymnasium-based cult of citizenship, fitness and physical perfection. For the Greeks, victory in Panhellenic contests has become the ultimate expression of cultural achievement.

CLASS, VIRTUE AND BEAUTY: THE CASE OF THERSITES

The cult of the body-beautiful is a pervasive reactionary obsession that has infected the otherwise democratic spirit of modern Greece. It has roots in the aristocratic culture of the Archaic Age. Homer describes a scene early in the *Iliad* in which a common soldier has the temerity to voice his opinions before his social superiors during a council of war. The poet's characterisation of this plebeian upstart is withering:

> One man still railed on, the loose-tongued Thersites. His head was full of vulgar abuse, reckless insubordinate attacks on the kings, with anything said that he thought might raise a laugh among the Argives [Greeks]. He was the ugliest man that went to Ilios [Troy]. He was bandy-legged and lame in one foot; his humped shoulders were bent inwards over his chest; above, his head rose to a point, sprouting thin wisps of wool.

After denouncing Agamemnon, the Greek leader, for waging a rich man's war, Thersites is rebuked by Odysseus, who threatens to strip him of cloak and tunic to expose his hideousness, and then assaults him with a royal sceptre. Homer is warm in his enthusiasm for this robust reaffirmation of the social order:

> Thersites writhed, and a heavy tear fell from him, and a bloody weal sprang up on his back under the gold-studded sceptre. He sat down frightened and in pain, and with a helpless look wiped away the tears. For all their disaffection, the men laughed happily at him, and one would glance at his neighbour and say: 'Oh yes, Odysseus has done thousands of fine things before now, proposing good plans and leading in battle. But this now is far the best thing he has done among the Argives, putting a stop to this horror's rantings in assembly. I doubt that his proud heart will ever again impel him to taunt the kings with insults.

So there we have it: class, virtue and beauty — a nasty little nexus of snobbery and prejudice.[15]

KEEPING THE POLITICS IN SPORT

OLIGARCHS v DEMOCRATS

Some city-states are democracies, others oligarchies. In democracies, the key decisions are made by popular assemblies that all adult male citizens are entitled to attend. In oligarchies, power is in the hands of smaller councils of wealthy property-owners. The conflict between democrats and oligarchs tends to be embittered and endemic.

Indeed, the almost continuous internal wars that rage throughout Greece are usually a matter of city-state rivalry – over such things as borders, trading rights and national security – or political conflicts between oligarchs and democrats. The latter may be internal civil wars, or inter-state wars between opposing confederations. The greatest of all wars among the Greeks – the thirty-year cycle of conflict known as the Peloponnesian War (431–404 BC) – was both a struggle to preserve the balance of power between Athens and Sparta, and also a battle between democracy and oligarchy.

Do not be surprised if you often hear right-wingers committed to oligarchy banging on about *homonoia* ('unanimity') and panhellenism at the Olympics: this premier sporting event is saturated with politics. Most Greeks view the internecine wars as at best, regrettable, and at worst, disastrous. But the conservative faction has an ulterior motive for promoting peace across the Greek empire. The underlying idea is that Greeks have common interests, should not be fighting each other, and instead need to unite against foreign enemies. In fact, one enemy in particular: Persia. A vast Asian empire ruled by a despotic militarist, Persia is ideal for the role of *bête noire*, having twice attempted to conquer Free Greece in the twin invasions of 490 and 480–79 BC.

Homonoia, Panhellenism, anti-Persianism: this is the characteristic ideological cocktail of Greek conservatives. Nowhere is it more on display than at Olympia. Herodotus, for example, the historian of the Persian Wars, chose the Olympic Games to offer recitations from his work. Plato, in his *Republic*, has written of the role of such festivals in bringing Greeks together and fostering their ethnic identity. And Gorgias, the Sicilian philosopher, delivered a speech at Olympia in 408 BC in which he urged his fellow Greeks not to consider one another's cities as spoils of war, but to direct their military aggression against foreign 'barbarians'.[16] The common message? Killing foreigners abroad is to be preferred over redistributing wealth at home.

PATRIOTISM, PRESTIGE AND PROPAGANDA

Remember that Greece is comprised of some one thousand city-states, and many of them have 'a history'. The military insecurity inherent in Greece's extreme political fragmentation has put a premium on patriotism and a strong sense of collective identity inside each city-state.

The solidarity of the citizens, their loyalty to one another, is a matter of national survival. Hellenism – the overarching culture of language, myth and religion shared by all Greeks, which sets them apart from other ancient peoples like the Persians or the Egyptians – is all very well, but it tends to operate at the rather rarefied level of inter-state summits (and sports festivals, of course). Sadly, the animosity that divides Athenian and Theban, or Spartan and Argive, is rather more tangible than Panhellenic theory. The prestige of the city-state and the patriotism of its citizens are therefore paramount. Intense civic pride – embodied in monumental architecture, works of art, richly endowed sanctuaries, edifying myths, and a calendar of processions, sacrifices and festivals – is *de rigueur*.

Inter-state sport is one of the supreme expressions of this contradiction between Panhellenic ideology and city-state rivalry at the very heart of Greek politics. Panhellenic festivals dedicated to harmony become major opportunities to proclaim independence, wealth, and power vis-à-vis other Greeks.

However contradictory, both elements in the ideological brew – Panhellenism and city-patriotism – are active ingredients. This is especially so in relation to the colonies. Remember that 'Greece' does not just mean the mainland and the islands. It includes all the colonies of Eastern Greece (those around the Black Sea and on the northern and eastern coasts of the Aegean), of Western Greece (on the coasts of southern Italy and Sicily), and others further afield, including settlements on the coasts of Libya, southern France and northeastern Spain (see Map 1).

All of this is 'Greece' (or *Hellas* as the Greeks themselves know it), not in a narrow geopolitical sense – there is no Greek 'empire' – but in the wider sense that all these cities are linguistically and culturally Hellenic, being populated by direct descendants of Greek colonists, even where they exist surrounded by far more numerous native people with very different traditions. The 'colonials' tend to be especially keen to assert their Greekness by participating in the big inter-state festivals. This is hardly surprising: where cultural identity is less secure, keeping it up requires more effort.

So sport in Greece is at once competitive, political and professional. Because major sports festivals provide opportunities to showcase the city, public money is freely expended on gymnasia, prizes at local games, and rewards and honours for returning Panhellenic heroes. In terms of prestige and propaganda, this is money well spent. The result, of course, is the professionalisation of sport (see pp. 160ff).[17]

RIVAL GAMES

The Olympic Games is the paramount athletic festival in Greece. But it is one of many, the pinnacle of a steadily swelling hierarchy of events. There is, in fact, an apparently unstoppable multiplication of games festivals.

There are, to start with, three other 'crown' or 'sacred' games – top Panhellenic events which offer only wreaths as prizes. All athletes aspire to qualify for them, and if a crown of Olympic wild-olive represents the supreme athletic achievement, one of Pythian laurel, Isthmian pine-branch, or Nemean wild celery is a close second.

The Pythian Games at Delphi (in honour of Apollo) are quadrennial like the Olympics, while the Isthmian at Corinth (in honour of Poseidon) and the Nemean at Nemea (in honour of Zeus) are biennial. Matters are so arranged that at least one crown games is held each year; sometimes, of course, there are two. These four festivals constitute 'the circuit' (*periodos*). All top athletes aspire to compete at every one. Those that win at all four rank as *periodonikes* ('grand-slam champions').

In addition to the four crown games, there are about fifty other festivals of sufficient standing to attract significant numbers of 'foreign' athletes – that is, athletes travelling from other city-states to participate. The incentive to do so is the prizes offered. The Greeks draw a sharp distinction between the four 'stephanitic' games (*stephane*: wreath or crown) and the many other 'chrematitic' games (*chremata*: money).

The incentive for the city or sanctuary hosting a money festival to offer big prizes is, of course, the crowd-pulling, prestige-raising, revenue-earning effect of celebrity appearances. That said, as we have seen, the practice goes back a very long way: Homer's heroes competed for prizes (see pp. 104-8). Among the most popular of the money games are the Asklepieian Games at Epidavros (in honour of Asklepios) and the Greater Panathenaic Games at Athens (in honour of Athena).[18]

In addition to the crown games and prize games of Panhellenic stature, there is a third category of exclusively local games, in which only citizens of the city can participate, and of which there are certainly hundreds, and probably thousands. Among the better known are the Lesser Panathenaic at Athens (in honour of Athena), the Karneian at Sparta (in honour of Apollo), and the Eleutherian at Larissa in Thessaly (in honour of Zeus). Athens alone has no fewer than nineteen major festivals and a total of 144 festival days each year. Not all festivals involve games and competitions, but many do, and each of these has its own individual programme.[19]

Some offer athletic events not in the Olympic schedule, like the middle-distance *hippios*, a four-*stadia* foot-race (2,400ft), which is included at the Isthmian and the Nemean. Some offer mixed athletic-equestrian events, like mounted javelin-throwing (at the Panathenaic) or a rodeo competition that involves leaping off a horse to grapple a bull (at the Eleutherian). Some include such exotica as the *lampededromia*, a relay race with a torch as a baton. Many include, in addition to their athletic and equestrian programmes (*gumnikos agon* and *hippikos agon* respectively), a musical programme (*musikos agon*) as well. At the Greater Panathenaic, for example, there are four such events: lyre (*kithara*)-playing, pipe (*aulos*)-playing, lyre-singing and pipe-singing. Delphi, in addition to the lyre and the pipes, offers poetic recitation.

Especially noteworthy at the Lenaia and the Dionysia festivals at Athens are the drama competitions, where new plays are performed for the first time. Every play written by the great Attic bards – Aeschylus, Sophocles, Euripides and Aristophanes – was first seen at the Theatre of Dionysos during one of these two festivals.

It is worth pausing to take full account of the economic value of the prizes on offer, especially those at the

Panhellenic events open to all. Take the men's lyre-singing competition at the Greater Panathenaic Games. The prizes are as follows: first, a gold crown worth 1,000 drachmas and 500 drachmas in cash; second, 1,200 drachmas; third, 600 drachmas; fourth, 400 drachmas; and fifth, 300 drachmas. Now, given that you can live comfortably on a drachma a day in Greece, this being a typical skilled artisan's daily rate, even the fifth prize represents a year's earnings, while the first amounts to the eye-watering equivalent of five years' income.

Or take the boys' *stadion* race. Here, the winner gets fifty *amphorae* of olive oil, with a market value of around 1,000 drachmas; and the runner-up ten *amphorae*, worth around 200 drachmas. The total value of the prizes offered for the athletic events alone at the Greater Panathenaic Games is around 50,000 drachmas.[20]

Admittedly, this is as good as it gets: Athens is the richest city in Greece, and the Greater Panathenaic, held only once every four years, is her greatest festival. But even given the far less generous prizes usually awarded elsewhere, there are so many festivals that it is easy to see how hundreds of professional athletes can make a living in Greece. So forget the spin. There are no 'amateurs' at Olympia.

OLYMPICS ON TOP

A century ago, in an ode dedicated to a chariot-racing champion, the poet Pindar described the Olympics as 'the greatest of games'. The stars always list their Olympic victories first, usually followed (in order) by the Pythian, the Isthmian and the Nemean. The other three crown games seem to have developed in the shadow of Olympia, owing their rise to Panhellenic status in part to the fact that, alongside the lead event, they constitute a circuit offering a major festival at least once a year.

It does not matter that Olympia's venue is by far the hardest to reach; that, indeed, seems merely to enhance its status. They all come: not just the champions and the fans, but politicians, generals, philosophers, historians, poets, musicians and artists. They come not just to win sporting glory or, in far greater numbers, to see it won; they come to build a political network, secure a commission, launch a new book, or simply find an audience.

It is not simply that the effort of getting there imparts to the venue a certain cachet. Because Elis is a small and remote city-state, it is no threat to any of the great powers. Olympia is free to flourish beyond the constraints of *realpolitik*. The same cannot be said for any of the other crown venues. Nemea, ostensibly run by the small neighbouring town of Kleonai, is in fact controlled by Argos, one of the three major powers of the Peloponnese. Isthmia is controlled by Corinth, another of the major Peloponnesian powers (the third being Sparta). Delphi is such a hot potato – with its central location and its premier oracle in addition to the prestigious Pythian Games – that it is run by a board of twelve representatives, the Amphiktyonic Council, drawn from different tribes in Thessaly and Central Greece. Twice, first around 590 BC and again in 448 BC, so-called 'Sacred Wars' have been fought for control of Delphi.

Nor does it matter that Olympia is exclusively athletic and equestrian; that there is no arts festival, no *mousikos agon* with its programme of pipe-playing, lyre-singing and poetry recital. Again, perhaps this merely redounds to Olympia's credit. Olympia is not for wimps, but for real men, so there is no insipid aestheticism and no dodgy subjective victories 'on points'. Winning is clear-cut – you compete directly with your opponent – and it is all about speed, strength, stamina and sheer physical excellence. The glory is undiluted: Olympic honours are not shared with bald poets and perfumed lyre-players.[21]

Quite simply, the Olympic Games are the living centre

of a nexus of myth, ritual and ideology that amounts to the very essence of Greekness. When, during Olympia's great quadrennial congregations, tens of thousands come together to celebrate holy rites and cheer the athletic excellence of their champions, they express the solidarity and identity of an entire people.

5 MANAGEMENT

THE EOC

The Olympic Games are managed by the Elean Olympic Committee, a board of nine *Hellanodikai* ('Judges of the Greeks'), all of whom are citizens of the local city-state of Elis. A small state ruled by an oligarchy (like virtually all the Peloponnesian city-states), Elis's selection procedure involves the election by popular vote of a group of respectable property-owners, the citizens voting tribe by tribe. All the names are then inscribed on potsherds (*ostraka*) and placed in a large ceramic vessel. A final choice of nine is made by drawing lots.

This may seem an odd procedure, but it is an almost universal Greek practice, in both oligarchies and democracies. The lot reduces the influence of patronage and possible bribery in the electoral process, and it allows the gods to have their say. In democracies, it has the additional advantage of making elections less of a popularity contest and widening participation in the highest levels of government.

The EOC members combine the roles of management committee, supervisory officials, and the judges and umpires at actual events. Although the nine work as a tight-knit group, there is a division of labour among them, with subcommittees of three responsible for the equestrian events, the combat sports, and the foot-races and pentathlon.

The *Hellanodikai* are instantly recognisable. They wear purple robes – the royal colour in Greece – and carry forked sticks, making them a highly visible presence at all the

18. One of the nine *Hellanodikai* who form the Elean Olympic Committee which runs the Games.

programme's many processions, rituals and contests. You will see them watching the events from elevated seats in the Stadium and the Hippodrome.

Their duties extend beyond the festival itself. During the ten months prior to the Games, they reside in special living-quarters (*Hellanodikaion*) in the centre of Elis and operate as a forward-planning team while simultaneously undergoing a crash in-service training course. They receive instruction from the *Nomophylakes* ('Guardians of the Rules'), a special commission of the city-state of Elis responsible for maintaining, amending and implementing the detailed protocols and rules governing the conduct of the Games. If the Judges are elected amateurs, the Guardians are the 'civil service' experts who advise them. During the final month, when all athletes hoping to compete at the Games must be in residence at Elis, they adjudicate on applications, supervise final training, and organise qualifying heats.

The honesty and impartiality of the *Hellanodikai* are renowned; rarely in the history of the Olympics has any suspicion arisen regarding this. Were it not so, of course, Elis's exclusive control of the Games would immediately be open to question, so the city-state authorities have a deep-rooted interest in maintaining the Judges' highest standards of public service. Some responsibilities are especially sensitive.

The *Hellanodikai* have to judge who is entitled to compete in different events. They must ensure that athletes are Greeks of free birth and men without any taint of homicide in their past. This is easier said than done, since Greeks do not carry ID cards, passports, or any other official documents that identify them. Greece is a face-to-face society with minimal bureaucracy, where almost everything, from a business deal to a marriage contract, depends on word-of-mouth exchanges, with all important matters sealed by oath. And Greeks, of course, share cities, houses and beds with non-Greeks.

Establishing paternity – and the all-important rights of citizenship and inheritance that go with it – is what keeps half the courts in Greece in session. The Olympic Judges can do no more than accept the decision of the local city-state: anyone enrolled as the citizen of a Greek city-state somewhere qualifies to compete. The real problem is that the only written record of the fact is that held in the home city's archives. No-one has a birth certificate they can carry around with them.

Consider the Judges' particular problem in allocating competitors to age categories for the separate boys' and men's events (see p. 143). Many Greeks are hazy about how old they are. The better-organised states do keep records of the citizens born each year – so an Athenian or a Spartan could check his age in the state archive if he was unsure – but the calendar varies from city to city. There is vast potential here for disputes over age categorisation which can be resolved only with the aid of an abacus. The Judges responsible for making these fine decisions have to swear a special oath that they will judge without accepting bribes and will keep all information they receive about the athletes confidential.

Particularly sensitive is the Judges' responsibility to uphold the quality and integrity of the Games by rooting out anyone below-par or of dubious morals. The EOC's final injunction to the athletes before setting off from Elis on the journey to Olympia sums up the intention: 'If you have worked so as to be worthy of going to Olympia, if you have done nothing indolent or ignoble, then take heart and march on; but those who have not so trained may leave and go wherever they like.'

Having spoken thus, the *Hellanodikai* lead the procession of officials, athletes, trainers, ambassadors and spectators on the two-day trek to Olympia. Once there, they manage the actual contests, enforce the rules, present the victory wreaths, and preside over the festival's final celebratory feast. Though appeals to the Olympic Council, with its fifty aristocratic members, against the Judges' decisions are technically possible, they are exceptionally rare and almost bound to fail. In practice, the Judges' decisions are absolute and irrevocable, and they have the power to fine, scourge, disqualify or expel athletes guilty of lying, cheating or any other infringement.[1]

HERALDS

The *Hellanodikai* are merely the most visible pinnacle of the administrative infrastructure. Also of real importance are the Heralds (*Spondophoroi*), whose duties, like those of the *Hellanodikai*, commence long before the Games begin. The Heralds travel across Greece, visiting as many city-states as they can, to announce the upcoming festival, to invite participation, and to proclaim the Sacred Truce.

Sadly, as we have seen (see pp. 2ff), the Sacred Truce is not a comprehensive armistice. It is merely a declaration that athletes and spectators travelling to the Olympics are religious pilgrims under the protection of Zeus. It as good as guarantees safe passage there and back, but it does not prevent other Greeks trying to kill each other in the meantime.

In each city, the Heralds are received by one, two or three specially appointed local officials, the *Theorodokoi* ('Envoy-receivers'). Their job is to host the visitors, facilitate their work, and then organise the participation in the Games of athletes, trainers and VIPs from their own city.

One of the Heralds also has a key role during the Games. Functioning as both timetable and results service, he announces each event and its outcome by trumpet blast and acclamation. Standard practice when announcing victors, by the way, is to give name, patronymic and city.[2]

WHIP-BEARERS

Then – a surprising class of official to modern eyes – there are the Whip-bearers (*Mastigophoroi*). These are the *Hellanodikai*'s official enforcers, the Olympic police corps, whose responsibilities include directing crowds, keeping order, cracking down on pedlars and prostitutes, and imposing summary punishment on rule-breakers and disturbers of the peace (see pp. 152-5). Because of the numbers attending the Games and the real danger of matters slipping out of control, the Whip-bearers proper are assisted by a lesser category of security guards known as *alutai*, who also carry whips.[3]

OTHER OFFICIALS

In addition to Judges, Guardians, Heralds and Whip-bearers, the Olympic staff includes many other officials. Those who belong to the permanent staff can be divided into two categories, the secular administrators and ancillaries on the one hand, and the religious functionaries on the other. The former include five bailiffs responsible for the grounds and its many treasures, a secretary who maintains the official archive, an official tourist guide, a woodsman who provides fuel for sacrifices, and a butcher-cook who prepares feasts. The latter include a sacrificial priest, three sacred attendants, two prophets, a piper, a libation-pourer and three ritual dancers. Needless to say, the numbers of both secular and religious staff increase greatly during the actual Games.[4]

GROUNDSMEN

A small army of part-time groundsmen reinforces the permanent staff in the immediate run-up to the Games. The Stadium and Hippodrome are let out to local farmers between festivals, so the grass must be cut and the seating banks smoothed out before the festival. The running track has to be dug up with hand-picks, sprinkled with water, and then levelled with rollers to create an even, compacted surface. The lanes are then marked out with white lime. The starting mechanisms in both the Stadium and the Hippodrome have to be set up. The equipment, in storage for four years, needs to be checked over and repaired where necessary, and then the entire mechanisms must be tested, and tested again, after installation to ensure perfect functioning. Sand pits have to be prepared for the pentathletes and wrestlers. Many buildings will also require repairs and repainting. The whitewashed exteriors, stained and peeling in places after four winters, must shine again like marble.[5]

FUNDING

The job of EOC members is time-consuming, stressful, and subject to intense and often critical public scrutiny. You might expect them to be well paid. They are not. On the contrary, they are expected to contribute personally to the considerable costs of laying on the Games.

Regular taxes on property or income are almost unknown in Greece except during wartime emergencies. The only major state expenditures are those on the armed forces, public buildings and city festivals. Otherwise, the Greek state is a minimal one, with education, health, housing and welfare all essentially the responsibility of families and, to some degree, wider networks of kinship, guest-friendship and private patronage.

In fact, even the cost of war is borne largely by the individual citizen, who supplies his own equipment and serves on a voluntary basis; only the richest city-states can afford to pay their own soldiers or hire mercenaries. In many cities – those with democratic governments – the rich are required to make extraordinary contributions. Athens runs its navy as a compulsory public-private partnership, with the state paying to build the ships, but with individual aristocrats paying for their maintenance, crewing and training. Each *trierarchos* ('trireme-master') is ostensibly performing a *leitourgia* ('liturgy'), a voluntary contribution to the community; in reality, he is paying a compulsory wealth tax.

The same public-private principle applies to other essential state functions. The state usually pays for the construction, refurbishment and decoration of public buildings, but wealthy private citizens often bear the costs of the numerous festivals, with their heavy consumption of sacrificial animals, fuel and incense, food and wine. Athens imposes around a hundred festival liturgies each year, including those of *choregoi* ('chorus-leaders' or 'impresarios'), whose obligation it is to fund costumes, stage props and rehearsals in drama competitions.

The underlying problem is that the state has only modest income. The treasuries of some of the major powers are subsidised by war booty, reparations and tribute. Sparta, top dog since the surrender of Athens at the end of the Peloponnesian War in 404 BC, has recently mounted a series of very lucrative military campaigns in Asia Minor (Turkey), bringing back shiploads of Persian loot. A few cities, like Athens, are blessed with their own bullion mines or some equivalent golden goose. The great majority, however, have to rely on the income from various rents and charges on city property, and on tolls and customs charged in the city's markets and ports.

The Olympics, of course, are one of the most expensive festivals in Greece, and Elis is a small and relatively poor city-state. Though no prizes are awarded and facilities in the Olympic Village are minimal to non-existent, the maintenance of the Sanctuary, with its numerous temples, treasuries, shrines, altars and statues, demands the year-round work of permanent groundsmen. This regular cost the city bears. But expenses soar during the festival itself, with many additional staff, massive oil consumption, numerous sacrifices, much official wining and dining, and all sorts of other incidentals. Downsizing, even cutting corners here and there, is not really an option. If anything goes wrong, or if anything is substandard and compares poorly with other festivals, Elis, the EOC and the individual Judges are in disgrace, their fitness to run the Games immediately in question. The people of Elis get their big moment only once every four years, and everything must go well. To ensure that it does, and in return for the great honour their city bestows upon them in electing them to the office, the *Hellanodikai* are expected to contribute substantially.

That said, Olympia is a nice little earner. It receives a trickle of pilgrims and tourists throughout most of every year, and the payments and donations made, including portions of sacrificial animals, go to the support of the permanent staff. During the main festival, of course, the trickle turns into a torrent, and revenue pours into the Sanctuary. What is not clear is whether this is sufficient to earn the Eleans (or some of them) a profit, enable them to more or less break even, or leave them (or at least the *Hellanodikai*) with a shortfall. It is perfectly possible that the Games do in fact lose money, but that the honour and prestige they bring to Elis and its leading men are sufficient reward to make it all worthwhile. Needless to say, there are neither accurate records nor published accounts.[6]

THE EOC RULES

Eligibility to compete at the Olympic Games is precisely defined and closely monitored by EOC officials. The criteria are as follows:

1. COMPETITORS MUST BE GREEK

Though the precise definition of a Greek may vary somewhat from city to city, it generally means one born of two married parents of citizen lineage and status.

There is, of course, no such thing as 'Greek citizenship'. All Greeks are citizens of particular city-states. Competitors are listed by their own names, their father's family name, and their city-state. There is no such thing as a Greek without a city. This is one of the reasons exile is considered such a grievous matter: statelessness is a form of social, political and cultural extinction.

But potential ambiguity remains. With around a thousand city-states and Greeks scattered over the entire length of the Mediterranean, is there not a grey area, especially in more distant regions, where loosely Greek settlements grade into what are essentially native towns which happen to contain some Greek residents? In theory, the distinction is clear: colonies founded by Greeks and populated by their descendants remain Greek. The reality can be equally clear, where the residents speak the Greek language, worship Greek gods, and can trace their family lines back through a solidly Greek genealogy. But it is not always so straightforward. What, for example, about the Macedonians?

Geographically, the Kingdom of Macedonia lies between Greece and the rest of the Balkans, and the name *Makedones* actually means 'highlanders'. By ethnic origin, the population is a mix of Dorian Greeks with Thracians and Illyrians. Society is dominated by a horse-riding feudal aristocracy notorious for drunken boorishness and perpetual feuding. The king is weak, and the court's Hellenism is a thin cultural veneer. True, the dominant language is Greek, but the northern accent is sufficiently thick to cause many city-state Greeks difficulty, and even educated Macedonians will sometimes lapse into local dialect, which is virtually incomprehensible.

Purity of language is an especially sensitive matter. Greeks make fun of the accents even of other Greeks and certainly of foreigners, among whom, in the trading ports of the eastern Mediterranean, Greek is a *lingua franca*. The Greek word for a foreigner – *barbaros* – literally means a speaker of an incomprehensible 'bar-bar-bar' language. Does this include northern highlanders speaking in dialect?

The 'Macedonian Question' came to a head when King Alexander I arrived at an Olympic Games in the early fifth century BC with the intention of competing in the short sprint. Other competitors protested that he could not because he was *barbaros*. Interestingly, the argument turned on Alexander's claimed descent from Herakles and a family in the solidly Greek city-state of Argos; on this basis – and, it seems, on this basis alone – he was allowed to run. However, though he finished in equal first place, his name does not appear in the official victory lists. Retrospectively deemed 'non-Greek' – for reasons not recorded – Alexander of Macedonia has been erased from Olympic history.[7]

2. COMPETITORS MUST BE FREE-BORN

As rigid as the cultural distinction between Greeks and *barbaroi* is the social distinction between free men and slaves. It is not that slaves are not physically present at the Games; rather, it is that they are socially invisible.

The Olympic Judges, Priests and bailiffs all have slave workers on their staff. Most athletes and trainers have slave attendants. The equestrians have entire gangs of them to look after horses and chariots. Since slave jockeys and charioteers are known, you may even see them at the reins on the Hippodrome track. That may seem strange, but in ancient Greece it is the *owner* who is the competitor in the equestrian events, not the jockey or charioteer, and the owner is free to employ whomever he wishes to ride his horse or drive his chariot – even a slave – and therefore quite likely a foreign 'barabarian'.

The better-off spectators turn up at the Games with anything from one to an entire troupe of household slaves to wait upon their every need during the five-day festival. Many of the privatised service-providers in the Olympic Village – the wine-sellers, pastry-cooks, fishmongers and pimps – employ slave labour. For the sociologically minded, the Olympic experience offers a complete cross-section of the whole of Greek society, from Sicilian tyrants and Athenian celebrities to the slave groundsmen who shovel the proverbial.

Slaves are numerous and busy wherever you go in Greece, yet they are 'non-persons', existing in a kind of limbo outside the society of the city-state. Only a kind of limbo, mind, for all slaves 'belong' to a master, whether an institutional authority like a city or a temple, or an individual such as an industrial contractor or the head of a household. By definition, slaves are not 'free' labourers; they are always slaves *of* something or someone. In particular, household slaves, including those who labour on family farms, are considered full members of the *oikos* (a Greek word that embraces the home, the family, and their estate or property in a single concept). But who are they? Where have they come from?

Breeding slaves is expensive. A slave woman who is breast-feeding or child-minding is of little use to her master, and the child will not be capable of work until many years have elapsed. Of course, slave women often find themselves pregnant (in both domestic and commercial contexts), but a combination of contraception, abortion, infanticide and neglect usually ensures that no children result. The slave families that do exist are highly unusual. So, since slave reproduction has so much stacked against it, and makes no economic sense to the slave-owners, you can assume that relatively few of the slaves you see were born into slavery.

In fact, most are war-captives. Many of them will be prisoners of war – men actually taken in battle. But many more will be civilians rounded up in a captured city or conquered territory in the aftermath of victory. Recent Spartan campaigns in Asia Minor, for example, have yielded rich hauls of captives. The standard practice is for the soldiers to sell their captives to the slave-dealers who are to be found among the camp-followers of all ancient armies. The dealers then sort the slaves into batches, transport them to city markets, and organise a sale. Generally speaking, because they have been relocated to a geographically and culturally alien place, and because they are less likely to have experienced a wide measure of personal freedom in the past, foreign slaves tend to be easier to manage than Greek ones. There are also moral barriers to the enslavement of Greeks. Civilians are often left unmolested during Greek-on-Greek fighting, and even combatants taken prisoner may be promptly released at the conclusion of hostilities. If and when Greeks are offered for sale, public disapproval can be strong.

Nonetheless, because Greek warfare is so chronic and intensive, and because it can sometimes be so embittered and savage, there are in fact large numbers of ethnic Greeks among the slave population. Neither their masters nor the authorities would permit these Greeks to compete in the Games. The same is true of serfs like the Messenian helots of the southwestern Peloponnese, and equally of the debt-bondsmen one encounters in many parts of Greece, poor men who have had to sell themselves into servitude to a creditor in order to work off their debts. Slaves, serfs and debt-bondsmen are all disqualified. For Greeks, athletics and freedom are inseparable; the reek of sweat, sand and the oil of the gymnasium is the smell of a free man.[8]

3. COMPETITORS MUST BE MALE

No woman can compete in the Olympic Games. No married citizen-woman may even attend the Games, and no unmarried citizen-girl is likely to be allowed anywhere near them by her father. Except for the Priestess of Demeter *Chamune*, who for traditional ritual reasons has a seat of honour at all contests (see p. 82), the only women you are likely to see during the five-day festival will be the socially marginal – entertainers, prostitutes, slaves and tinkers.

The sense that the gymnasium and sporting contests belong firmly to the world of men runs deep. The Greeks associate manhood with larger, stronger, more muscular bodies, bronzed by the sun, glistening with oil. The realm of women, by contrast, is that of the home, where they manage the household, look after children, and work at their looms. Gender roles are sharply defined and rigorously enforced by family, community and state. Sexist images abound in the media.

Take a close look at some of those prestigious painted pots you see everywhere, whether as votive offerings, prize trophies, or the best tableware at a posh symposium. The men, tanned and naked, appear fighting, running or carousing. The active women are goddesses, monsters or whores. But it is the women you see sitting at their looms, their white flesh symbolic of housebound respectability, who represent the citizen-wives of Greek men.

Scroll through any of the classics and you will find numerous literary examples. In Homer's *Odyssey*, when

Penelope, wife of the wandering Odysseus, attempts to participate in a grown-up discussion, she is firmly rebuked by her teenage son Telemachos: 'Go back in the house, and take up your own work, the loom and the distaff, and see to it that your handmaidens ply their work also. The men must see to the discussion, all men, but I most of all. For mine is the power in this household.' Or consider the words attributed to the captive princess Andromache in Euripides' play *Trojan Women*: 'As Hektor's wife, I strictly set myself to attain all womanly perfections, every sober grace. Since a woman, however high her reputation, draws slander on herself by being seen abroad, I renounced restlessness, stayed in my own house, and refused to open my door to gossip in the manner of other wives. Having by nature a sound mind to school me, I was sufficient to myself. I kept before my husband a quiet tongue, a modest eye. I knew in what matters it was for me to rule, and where in turn I should yield him authority.'

Comic playwright Aristophanes reinforces traditional roles by making a mockery of their reversal. When, during a scene in *The Poet and the Women*, one of the male characters appears on stage in drag, the absurdity of it all provokes a stream of ribald comment: 'Tell me, why this perturbation of nature? A lute, a yellow gown? A lyre and a hair-net, a woman's girdle and a wrestler's oil-flask? A sword and a hand-mirror? It doesn't make sense. What are you – a man? Then where's your cloak? Where are your shoes? And what have you done with your tool? But if you're a woman, what's happened to your bosom?'

So ancient Greece is deeply chauvinist: men do war, sport and debate; women do housework, childcare and weaving. Hera's games at Olympia may be for girls, but that is for ancient ritual reasons (see pp. 84ff). The main games, Zeus's games, are exclusively male and a reflection of the dominant patriarchal order.

The simple fact is that Greek men both love women and hate them. They desire them, but at the same time fear them. Specifically, they fear the destructive power of female infidelity, with its potential to blast the *oikos* apart by creating illegitimate offspring with claims on property. Greek citizen-women are therefore segregated and secluded so that their sexuality can be controlled and the paternity of progeny guaranteed: this is the deepest root of patriarchy in a society of small property-owners.

But those who oppress others can never themselves be truly free. Judging by the myths they tell, the minds of Greek citizen-men are filled with nightmare images of adulteresses and child-killers, witches and warrior-women, and emasculating medusas with heads of hissing snakes.[9]

4. COMPETITORS MUST BE CORRECTLY CLASSIFIED AS MAN OR BOY

When do boys (*paides*) become men (*andres*)? The Greeks are not sure. Some festival organisers, notably those at Isthmia and Nemea, deal with the uncertainty by creating an intermediate category, *ageneioi*, 'beardless youth', running separate contests for the three different age-groups. But this merely relocates and doubles the problem, for instead of having to make only one set of arbitrary decisions, distinguishing *paides* and *andres*, you now have to make two, distinguishing *paides*, *ageneioi* and *andres*. The Olympic authorities, like the Pythian, cannot be bothered. There are no *ageneioi* at Olympia; you are either a boy or a man, and you make the transition from one to the other in a single leap. But when? And how can we measure it?

The EOC specifies seventeen as the upper age-limit for boys. Anyone who turns eighteen during the year in question is obliged to compete as a man (even if still only seventeen at the time of the actual Games). What is decisive, then, is an approximate chronological age. Poor record-keeping, differences between city-state calendars, and an absence of portable documents preclude precision. Indeed, they make outright fraud possible. How is this prevented?

The Judges have been known to reject an age claim on the basis of the size and physique of the athlete. When the burly and hairy Pythagoras of Samos turned up in 588 BC, dressed in a purple robe and wearing his hair long to make himself look more youthful, he was ridiculed for seeking admission to the boys' boxing contest. Allowed to enter the men's competition, he won the crown. You can see his victory statue in the Sanctuary with its curious epigram: 'Wayfarer, if you recall a certain Pythagoras, long-haired, far-sung boxer of Samos, here I am. Go ask some Elean about my deed, though nothing he says will you believe.'

In this last cryptic comment, is Pythagoras perhaps still professing the innocence of his claim to have been but a boy in 588 BC? Who can tell now whether he was a cheat or simply over-developed for his age? But perhaps that is the point: it did not matter, since it would not have been fair for him to have been classed as a 'boy' and pitted against others much smaller. Whatever the truth, no lasting opprobrium seems to have attached itself to Pythagoras, who became a sporting superstar credited with being 'the first scientific boxer'.

Were a fraud successfully perpetrated, there is the always the risk of subsequent exposure and disgrace. The Judges, remember, have the power to fine, scourge, disqualify and expel errant athletes. The shame of the cheat – shame shared by family, friends and city-state community – is extreme.

The other check on honesty is divine. At regular intervals, during both training and festival, prayers are offered, sacrifices made, and oaths sworn before fearsome images of vengeful deities. Athletes who lie and cheat – or those who do so on their behalf, since boy athletes are usually represented by their fathers – risk penalties far more terrible than anything a Whip-bearer could threaten.

I The gold-and-ivory statue of Zeus inside the Temple of Zeus at Olympia.

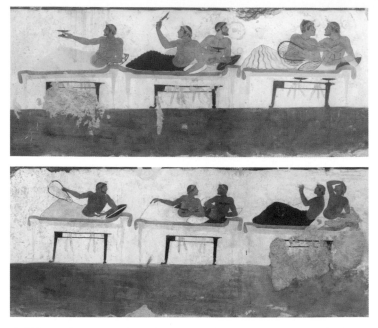

II This tomb painting from the inside of a stone sarcophagus depicts a Greek symposium in full swing. We see singing, pipe-playing, lyre-playing, games (the aimed flicking of wine drops), intimate conversation, and open gay flirtation.

III How not to behave at a symposium. Greeks drink their wine diluted with water and in occasional sips. Getting drunk is not generally approved of. Puking up on your host's couch will put you beyond the pale.

IV Demeter (right), the earth-mother goddess of the harvest, wearing a royal crown and holding a royal sceptre. Opposite is her daughter Persephone, also a fertility deity, shown holding a torch and pouring a libation. The torch allows her to light her way in the Underworld. The story goes that the land is blighted by winter during the six months of every year that Demeter's daughter is condemned to spend in the gloomy company of Hades.

V The sort of routine religious procession you will see all over Greece, involving libations, animal sacrifice, and the musical accompaniment of pipes and lyre. The main difference at Olympia is that women play almost no role.

VI Olympia in 388 BC, showing the Sanctuary (top centre), the
Stadium (top right), the Hippodrome (bottom right), and the edge of

the sprawling Olympic Village (bottom left). Compare with the plan on p. 44.

VII A black-figure vase-painting of a charioteer preparing to race. He is attended by two grooms, one controlling the horses already harnessed, the other escorting the trace horses. The older, bearded man is the owner.

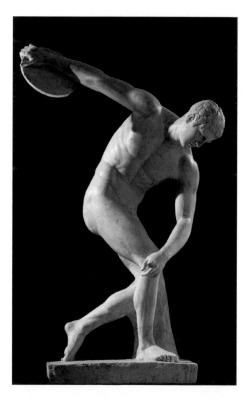

VIII The *Diskobolos* ('Discus-thrower') of Myron. The sculptor has captured a split second in time, with the athlete, having swung his arm back, about to hurl himself forwards for the cast.

IX A black-figure vase-painting showing two boxers. Note the leather thongs on the hands, the characteristic punching to the head, and the profuse nosebleed of the boxer on the left.

X The head of a life-size bronze statue of a boxer, with cauliflower ears, broken nose, heavy brows, and numerous cuts.

XI A black-figure vase-painting of the *pankration*. The upright figure is poised to punch, but the kneeling figure is offering his submission by raising a finger. Note the judge, with rod of office, watching closely on the left.

Two further age-related eligibility issues arise. The first is the youngest age at which a boy is permitted to compete. This has been set at twelve, though the Olympic authorities reserve the right to ban any older youngster whose physical development they deem insufficient. The Olympic champion Pherias of Aigina, for example, who won the boys' wrestling in 464 BC, had been banned from participating four years previously for being under age. Anthropologically, of course, what defines 'boys' as opposed to 'children' is puberty. Olympic 'boys' are not children but adolescents, and that is why it is right for them to compete. Whether we regard the Olympics as hunting magic, mock warfare or Panhellenic unity cult, it is appropriate that Greece's men-in-the-making should participate fully in one of the key cultural activities – organised sport – by which manhood is defined.

What of the upper age limit? None is stipulated: the matter is settled by experience. Those too old to compete will either exclude themselves or be weeded out by the *Hellanodikai* during the month's training and trials at Elis before the festival begins. This brings us neatly to the fifth eligibility criterion.[10]

5. COMPETITORS MUST BE IN PEAK CONDITION AND AT THE TOP OF THEIR SPORT

Athletes swear an oath that they have been in training during the whole of the ten months prior to the Games, and of the last of these there can be no doubt, for they are required to spend it at Elis itself under the direct supervision of the EOC. The Judges lay down a strict regime of exercise, diet and discipline during this final month. Athletes and their personal trainers are likely to appeal in vain against any aspect of it, and evasion of its requirements could result in exclusion from the Games.

The month's training and trials at Elis provide an opportunity for the Judges to weed out below-par athletes. The hopeful competitors, meanwhile, have an opportunity to weigh up their opponents and, until the official opening of the Games, to exercise a right to withdraw. Victories without opposition in the Olympic boxing, wrestling and *pankration* – victories 'without dust', as they say – are fairly common.[11]

6. COMPETITORS MUST BE RITUALLY PURE, MORALLY UPRIGHT AND OF HONEST INTENT

Behind a veneer of sweet reason, Greeks are deeply superstitious. They inhabit a dichotomous world of symbols in which everything is either clean or dirty, pure or polluted, permissible or tabooed. This obsession is summed up in the word *miasma* – that which is defiled and in need of purification. You cannot see it, hear it or touch it, yet a hundred different strains of this deadly disease are all around us. It is, moreover, highly infectious, transmitting its noxiousness through physical contact, such that an entire community may quickly become contaminated.

An alarming range of everyday events gives rise to *miasma* and an immediate need for ritual purification, including menstruation, sex, giving birth, and contact with those in a transitional state like puberty, marriage or death. It can sometimes happen accidentally. Get muddled saying a prayer, use the wrong knife on a sacrificial chicken, or discover that your libation jug is a secondhand piss-pot, and you can expect a squadron of winged furies to ascend from the depths. Or so most Greeks seem to believe.

Miasma is a matter of degree. That arising from bodily functions and minor slip-ups is much less serious than that due to deliberate sacrilege or to voluntary or involuntary homicide. The famous 'Desecration of the Herms' in Athens in 415 BC is a case in point. Herms are square-cut pillars surmounted by sculpted heads of divinities and graced with erect phalluses in the appropriate position as symbols of fertility. You see them all over Greece, especially at street corners and in sanctuaries, marketplaces and the porches of private houses. They are traditionally used to mark boundaries and distances, which is why they are associated with Hermes, head of communications on Mount Olympos (thus the name *hermaioi*), but nowadays other deities are often also represented.

One night, nearly all the herms in Athens had their faces disfigured and the phalluses knocked off. The following morning, the city was in uproar. The state immediately offered large rewards for information, and passed a decree guaranteeing immunity to anyone who came forward – citizen, foreigner or slave – with information. The result was a veritable witch-hunt. Right-wing conspirators were assumed to be plotting against the democracy, and on the basis of information supplied by informers there was a series of arrests. Some of the prisoners were later tried and executed.

Executed. For defacing a statue. That is how serious it was. The fear was that the wrath of the gods would descend on the city – a city at war – unless the polluted were discovered and eliminated. To save itself, the city-state of Athens required a blood sacrifice to restore its ritual purity and the peace of the heavens.

The EOC are equally obsessive about the ritual purity of the Olympic Games. Any serious taint of *miasma* is likely to kill an Olympic career stone-dead. It is bad enough to break an administrative norm, never mind a religious taboo. The great Theagenes of Thasos was lucky not be disqualified altogether in 480 BC when he entered an event 'merely in order to spite an opponent'. This was deemed dishonest intent, out of keeping with the true Olympic spirit. He wore himself out defeating former champion Euthymos of Lokri in the boxing, so that he was forced to withdraw from his own event, the *pankration*, leaving his opponent victor without a contest. This went down like a stone with the crowd (the blood-spattered *pankration* is always a favourite), and the EOC imposed a massive 12,000-drachma fine, half to be paid to Zeus, half to Euthymos. This was an astronomical sum, even for a top celebrity – and a lifetime's income for an ordinary Greek.

The message? Do not mess with the EOC. Do not bring the Games into disrepute. And above all, do not come to Olympia harbouring filthy secrets.[12]

The EOC's eligibility rules amount to a robust reaffirmation of the traditional social order. The Olympics define Greek citizen-manhood by rejecting various categories of culturally and socially inferior others – foreigners, slaves, women, boys and criminals. Olympic athletes belong to an elite that is ethnically Greek, free-born, patriarchal and morally upright. Cultural identity and social status are expressed through participation in the Games. Potential threats to both are excluded at the outset: no foreigner, slave or woman ever gets a chance to challenge the supremacy of the Hellenic master-race.[13]

KEEPING TO THE RULES

DO NOT DO AS THE GODS DO

The Greek gods can seem all too human and immoral. Numerous myths record them being petty, spiteful, vindictive, deceitful and greedy. Adultery, kidnapping, rape, and the murder of innocents seem to be everyday events among the residents of Mount Olympos. At least 120 women known to us by name have been seduced by Zeus, who often disguises himself as the husband in order to get into the wife's bed. He even brags about his casual affairs when demanding sex from his own long-suffering wife Hera, apparently on the basis that telling her she is the best of the lot will make her amenable. In less happy moments, he is the perpetrator of shocking domestic violence: 'I am not sure,' he threatens his wife, 'you may not soon be the first to feel the benefit of your troublesome mischief, when I flog you with blows of the whip. Or do you not remember when you were strung up high, and I hung two anvils from your feet and fastened a golden rope round your hands that could not be broken? You hung there in the sky and the clouds, and the gods throughout high Olympos were distraught.'

Do not be misled. The behaviour of the gods is no licence to be like them. The gods can get away with being outrageous because they are immortal and all-powerful. Not so mortals, who live their lives in the coils of the divinely-sanctioned social and religious order in which they find themselves. That said, the gods are not greatly concerned with routine crime. Lying, cheating, theft, assault, rape, even murder seem, in and of themselves, of surprisingly little concern. The gods turn out not to be the all-purpose guardians of public morality one might expect. That is, unless they are specifically invoked: and there lies the rub.[14]

THE SACRED TRUCE

Two things drive the gods to murderous fury: impiety and perjury. Those guilty of these offences display *hubris* – a degree of pride and arrogance inappropriate in a mere mortal and therefore deserving of divine punishment.

To deny the gods, to refuse them sacrifice, to exclude them from a share of the spoils, to desecrate their images or steal from their temples, all these things threaten their majesty and invite swift and consummate retribution: they are, literally, 'impious'. The month-long Sacred

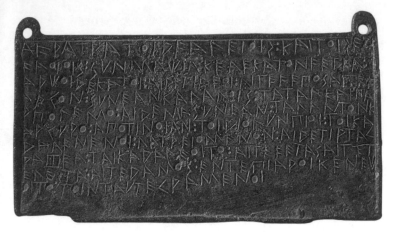

19. A bronze tablet recording an alliance between the Eleans and the Herarians of Arcadia. The pre-eminence of the Olympic festival depended upon Elis's neutrality in most inter-Greek conflicts.

Truce falls into this category. It is not, to repeat, a general peace (*eirene*), only an armistice (*ekecheiria*) of limited application and duration. But in so far as it goes, it is a potent religious injunction, symbolised by the Statue of Ekecheiria that stands in the front hall of the Temple of Zeus in the Sanctuary.

The Olympic Games are a religious festival – the most important in Greece, indeed – and the truce which casts a mantle of protection over all participants is sacred. It turns those participants into pilgrims and puts them under the care of Zeus. To kill a man on his way to a sports festival is homicide: that is one thing. To kill a pilgrim on his way to a religious festival is impiety: much worse. And the Sacred Truce extends, of course, to Olympia itself. Whatever else may be happening in Greece, however many the wars raging, open warfare by or against Elis during the holy month is taboo.

The Sacred Truce is effective. During the worst of the Greeks' many civil wars – the Peloponnesian War of 431–404 BC – the Olympic Games were held on schedule. Athenians and Spartans, democrats and oligarchs, bitter enemies separated by a river of blood, continued to pitch up at Olympia every four years to do nothing worse to each other than to cheer on their own man in the short sprint or the chariot-race. True, there was a nasty row between Elis and Sparta after the EOC imposed a fine on the Peloponnesian superpower for supposedly breaking the Sacred Truce. What is interesting is that although Sparta indignantly denied the charge and refused to pay the fine, and were therefore banned from 420 BC onwards, they made no attempt to interfere with the continuation of the Games from which they were excluded (see pp. 156-7). All the Spartans ever wanted was to take part again. Happily for them, the dispute was resolved and they returned to the Games ten years ago.[15]

OATHS

Divine anger at impiety is easily understood. But perjury? In Greece, this is not a civil matter, but a religious one. Whenever other Greeks need a guarantee of honesty, they insist that an oath be sworn before one of the gods, usually Zeus, one of whose many roles is the punishment of oath-breakers. To cheat after swearing an oath is to lie to a god. The offence can be hidden from other mortals, but not from Zeus, the all-seeing and all-knowing, who finds himself mocked and diminished.

So the EOC demands that athletes, trainers and guardians swear a series of oaths: that the ten-month regime of training before the Games has been followed; that the ages claimed for boys are true; and that they will obey the rules, play fair, and do no harm to the Games. These oaths are sworn before an image of Zeus *Horkios* ('god of oaths'), who stands before his altar brandishing a thunderbolt in each hand. Awesome in their power, terrible in their implications for violators, the Olympic oaths are not merely the EOC's main defence against cheating. They are also an anti-pollution device – a protection

20. A silver ring depicting Zeus *Horkios*, who appears standing beside his altar brandishing thunderbolts as a warning to rule-breakers at the Olympics.

against the *miasma* that might contaminate the entire Games if a wicked man, tainted by homicide or impiety, were to gain admission.[16]

OFFICIAL ENFORCERS

Even without the help of the gods, the EOC infrastructure for enforcing the Olympic rules is impressive enough, with its hierarchy of Judges, Guardians, Heralds and Whip-bearers, backed by bailiffs, security-men, and various groundsmen and other ancillaries who can be called upon in an emergency (see pp. 129ff). These functionaries deploy three main sanctions.[17]

FLOGGINGS

When the Greek council of war met before the Battle of Salamis in 480 BC, the Athenian admiral Themistokles was rebuked for speaking before his turn: 'At the Games, Themistokles, those who start too soon are flogged.' In other words, whipping is the routine penalty at the Games for all kinds of minor misdemeanours. In fact, the whip has become a symbol of authority. It is wielded primarily by either the official Whip-bearers (*Mastigophoroi*) or the seedier class of security goons who provide the heavyweight back-up (*alutai*). It is often used casually in both refereeing and crowd control (you have been warned), but where formal flogging as punishment occurs, its application must be ordered by the Judges. That is why you will see Judges accompanied by ceremonial rod-bearers (*rabdouchoi*): the power of the EOC is symbolised by the right of the Judge to inflict corporal punishment.

The rod (*rabdos*) is sometimes the weapon used. It is essentially a switch cut from a willow tree, and it can produce painful red welts. More fearsome, however, is the true whip (*mastix*), the leather scourge carried by the Whip-bearers, which is more likely to be employed in formal punishment. A famous case occurred in 420 BC, when Lichas of Sparta entered the chariot-race under a false, Theban name. Lichas belonged to a top, horsey, sporting family – his father had two Olympic chariot victories to his credit – and he was determined to continue the tradition. The problem was that Sparta was banned from the Games that year because she was formally at war with Elis. When

21. In this scene, while two boxers spar on the left, two pankratiasts are breaking the rules by gouging at one another's eyes – two fouls that attract a flogging from the trainer or judge depicted on the right.

his team won, and a Theban victory was duly announced, Lichas stepped forward to crown his charioteer with a ribbon and thereby revealed the champion's true identity. The outraged EOC imposed a flogging – though with the rod, not the whip, perhaps out of deference to Lichas's age and noble status – and, for good measure, reaffirmed a Theban win. (But see pp. 156-7.)

Flogging seems an exceptionally degrading punishment for any free-born Greek, let alone a celebrity superstar or an ancient aristocrat. It is a punishment usually reserved for slaves. What are we to make of this curious practice? Perhaps there is a partial parallel in the strange Spartan custom of toughening up teenage boys by encouraging them to steal and then flogging them if they get caught. Sparta, of course, is hardly ever representative

DISQUALIFICATION: THE STRANGE CASE OF KLEOMEDES OF ASTYPALAIA

In the Games of 496 or 492 BC, Kleomedes of Astypalaia was disqualified by the EOC after he killed his opponent in the boxing. The case illustrates important principles of Olympic governance.

The EOC decision was based on the fact that Kleomedes had violated boxing rules, used illegal tactics, and thereby caused the death of Ikkos of Epidavros. Exactly what happened is disputed. One version of events has Kleomedes quite literally tearing open his opponent's ribcage. Whatever the exact nature of the foul, the EOC response was decisive. Kleomedes not only lost his crown, but was fined the huge sum of 24,000 drachmas.

Now there is more to this than meets the eye. Kleomedes had not only broken the rules; by committing a homicide, he had polluted the Games with *miasma*, making purificatory rites essential. Kleomedes' fine was, in a sense, blood-money paid to Zeus as compensation for the killing, while his disqualification amounted to a ritual purgative – the expulsion of a bloodstained, contaminated presence.

of Greece as a whole: it is notorious for its austere and brutal militarism. But this particular custom, whatever its value in the socialisation of Spartan youth, bears the hallmarks of ritual practice. In seeking the favour of the gods, blood is a sacrifice, and pain both a test of virtue and an atonement for wickedness. Olympic flogging is perhaps a contribution to the eternal struggle against *miasma* and the furies it can unleash.[18]

FINES

More serious offences are punished by fines. This intermediate penalty may be additional to both flogging and disqualification. Fines are likely to be imposed in

---

The story has an ambiguous ending, and Kleomedes' true character remains in doubt. He did not accept the EOC's judgement with good grace, maintaining that he had been unjustly treated. Weighed on the divine scales of justice, failure to atone doubles the offence, and some of the gods at least seem to have taken this view. They drove the apparently unrepentant sinner mad with grief, so that when Kleomedes returned to his home city, he pulled down the roof of a school and killed many of the children within.

Other gods appear to have interpreted the matter differently.

Stoned by a mob of angry citizens, Kleomedes fled to a temple for refuge, climbed inside a chest and pulled the lid shut on top of him. When the citizens opened the chest, he had gone. Mystified and frightened, they sent an embassy to the Delphic Oracle, and were told 'Kleomedes of Astypalaia is the last of heroes. Honour with sacrifices him who is no longer mortal.'

This the worthy citizens of Astypalaia duly did: Kleomedes – seemingly killer-boxer, insane child-murderer, and disgraced Olympic cheat – is worshipped to this day as a sporting superstar in his home town.[20]

WAR AGAINST THE EOC

Between 420 and 397 BC, relations between Elis and Sparta were in crisis. The trouble began during the Peloponnesian War. The two states were on different sides and therefore formally at war with each other. Elis accused Sparta of making an attack on her territory during the Sacred Truce, and imposed a huge fine of 200,000 drachmas, which the Spartans refused to pay.

The EOC then banned the Spartans from Olympia and denied them the right to make sacrifice in the Sanctuary or compete in the Games. This was taken very badly. The Spartans had established an extraordinary pre-eminence in chariot-racing, with an almost unbroken string of victories since 448 BC. Their record was now threatened.

This was the context for Lichas's application to compete under a false name and his subsequent exposure and flogging (see pp. 153–4). If the EOC was outraged by Lichas's affrontery, the Spartans were equally outraged by the brutal treatment of one of their most high-born and respected senior citizens. Fearing retaliation, the Eleans, with the support of contingents from Athens, Argos and Mantineia, posted guards around the Games as additional security.

In the short run, the Spartans did nothing. But the ban, the

the following cases: giving false information in order to gain admission to the Games as a competitor; attempting to bribe opponents into allowing themselves to be beaten; and breaking competition rules in ways that seriously disadvantage or even endanger other athletes.

Fines may be imposed on the athletes themselves or on their trainers or guardians, depending on circumstances. The fines imposed can be substantial, and athletes have been known to refuse to pay them, but an unpaid fine does, of course, preclude participation in future festivals.

Fines can also be imposed on city-states, and the crisis in relations between Elis and Sparta, which caused Sparta treatment of Lichas, and a subsequent refusal (in c. 414 BC) to permit King Agis to sacrifice and pray for victory at Olympia, kept Elean-Spartan relations in a state of cold war for two decades. The Spartan mood was not improved by a spectacular Athenian victory in the chariot-race in 416 BC. The Spartans themselves were not to win again until 396 BC.

The tensions finally erupted in the Elean-Spartan War of 399–97 BC. King Agis led an army into Elean territory, attacking both Olympia and Elis itself, and ravaging the Elean countryside. There was little his enemy could do to defend itself, but Agis's aims were limited to securing Sparta's right to sacrifice and compete at Olympia. This done, peace was made, and the Spartan army withdrew.

Because Sparta was a major power, had it attempted to take control of Olympia it would have destroyed the integrity of the Games. A Panhellenic boycott would have been a real possibility. The very thing the Spartans were fighting for – readmission to the Olympics – might have burst like a bubble in their hands. It was convenient to all, including the Spartans, that Elis, an otherwise second-rate state that was no serious threat to anyone, should remain guardian of the Games. Sparta's chariots were back in the race: that was what really mattered.[21]

to be banned from the Games and Lichas to have to make a false declaration in order to be admitted, was triggered by an unpaid fine (see p. 156).[19]

We turn now to the athletes themselves. What sort of men are these Panhellenic sporting superstars that you will see and cheer during your week at Olympia?

6 THE ATHLETES

The real reason that you and tens of thousands of others have trekked hundreds of miles to this jam-packed, foul-smelling, insect-infested, sun-scorched valley is, of course, to see the greatest sporting superstars in Greece perform. This section introduces you to the lives and careers of the athletes. What sort of men are they, and how have they reached this dizzy summit of success? Let us begin with a famous example.

THE LONG ROAD TO OLYMPIC GLORY

Theagenes of Thasos was one of the all-time greats. And like many another sporting hero, he has attracted numerous legends since his death a couple of generations ago. One story is that he was a secret son of Herakles, who is supposed to have lain with his mother disguised as her husband. Another is that, aged nine, he picked up a bronze statue of a god in the marketplace and carried it home over one shoulder. He was lucky to escape a death sentence for such sacrilege, but the offended Thasians satisfied themselves with ordering the child to carry it back to its proper place.

Theagenes' own statue, also mounted in proud Thasos's marketplace after his death, was itself the focus of athletic attention: an embittered former rival used to beat it nightly. Eventually the statue, fed up with mistreatment, toppled over and fatally crushed its assailant. The sons of the deceased then prosecuted the statue for murder, and the Thasian court decided in their favour, passing a sentence of death. The statue was therefore taken beyond the city boundary and 'drowned' in the sea. But the preposterous story does not end there.

Shortly afterwards, famine struck Thasos. As was usual in such cases, an official delegation was promptly despatched to the Delphic Oracle, the consultancy with the most direct hotline to Apollo. The advice was 'to take back the exiles'. Since no-one could work out what this meant, nothing was done, and the famine continued. A second delegation had to be sent for further clarification.

This time, the Pythian priestess was more explicit. Declaiming in her customary manner, she made it clear that it was one particular 'exile' who needed to be returned: 'You leave great Theagenes unremembered.' Not exactly cheering news, because the real Theagenes was a potful of burnt bone and the bronze Theagenes was at the bottom of the sea. Fortunately, soon afterwards the statue was brought up in the nets of Thasian fishermen and Theagenes was duly restored to his plinth in the marketplace, where he still stands, much honoured, today.

Theagenes was a remarkable athlete. Records for the early fifth century BC, his *floruit*, are full and accurate, and show that he won two Olympic crowns, for the boxing in 480 BC and the *pankration* in 476 BC, and no fewer than three at Delphi, ten at Isthmia and nine at Nemea. Equally remarkable is the fact that he was something of an all-rounder: not only did he win many crowns in both boxing and the *pankration*, but he also later took up long-distance running, winning the event at the minor games at Phthia in Thessaly.

We can be less confident about the total number of victories attributed to him. Whether the figure is 1,400, 1,300 or 1,200 crowns – the sources differ – this seems an incredible tally, even if Theagenes himself regarded 'most of them as rubbish'. To achieve this, he would have needed to win a prize roughly once a week throughout an exceptionally long sporting career of up to three decades.[1]

Perhaps he did. Many Greeks believe so. Either way, the key point is this: Theagenes was no amateur, but a full-time professional who became a celebrity superstar with earnings to match. In this, he was typical. The first thing you need to know about the Greek athletes you will see performing at Olympia is that they are all full-time professionals. No part-time sportsman will ever make it to the top. Why is this?

A PURSUIT FOR GENTLEMEN?

It is widely believed that almost any Greek male citizen, whatever his background, can reach the top level in sport if he has real talent. There are formal barriers to participation in the Olympics, but class is not one of them; the Games are, in this sense at least, democratic.

This 'open to all' ideal is supported by much anecdotal evidence. The Kynosarges gymnasium at Athens, for example, has a reputation as the hang-out of low-born athletes. The tradition seems to go back to Themistokles, the victor in the famous Salamis naval battle against the Persians in 480 BC, a man of humble birth who was a staunch democrat. It seems that Themistokles invited some of his posh friends to exercise with him at the Kynosarges as a way of breaking down class distinctions.

More recently, an anonymous right-wing pamphleteer (known simply as 'the Old Oligarch') has denounced the Athenian democracy for ruining the city's sport and culture by letting in the masses. The rich Athenian aristocrat Alkibiades has let it be known that he took up chariot-racing to avoid contact with ill-bred commoners in wrestling contests.

Presumably Alkibiades has in mind the likes of the following: Koroibos the butcher, who won the first Olympic short sprint in 776 BC; Polymnestor the goatherd, who won the boys' short sprint in 596 BC; Glaukos the ploughboy, who took the boxing crown in 520 BC; and Amesinas the cowherd, victorious in the wrestling in 460 BC. He must also have been worried, however, at the prospect that his avoidance strategy might have been frustrated by the deplorable practice, recorded from as long past as 672 BC, of poorer citizens banding together in sporting consortia to share the expenses of chariot-racing.

Do not be misled by all this upper-class ranting – for that is what it is. Despite the claims of snobs like Alkibiades, the Games have retained their deeply aristocratic character. Legends attach themselves to the Olympics like iron filings to a magnet, and the matter of the class origins of athletes is no exception. Was Koroibos actually a butcher – or a priest wielding the sacrificial knife? Were Polymnestor and Amesinas really humble herdsmen – or did their families just own a lot of pasture? Was Glaukos a *bona fide* ploughboy – or did he simply do a repair job on a plough (see p. 167)?

Even if we are being too cynical, even if a few low-born athletes do succeed in making it to the top, they are rare exceptions. And outbursts of oligarchic rancour about the supposed 'democratisation' of athletics reflect not so much social reality as the moral panic of the high and mighty. While it is true that no regulation excludes the low-born, and while it is also true that democracy and government-funded gymnasia have increased opportunities for working-class athletes in some cities like Athens, Greek sport is still dominated by the upper classes.

The simple fact is that top-level competition requires time and money. Most successful athletes are effectively full-time, with training, travelling and competing filling their year. To compete in the Olympics is to commit a year of one's life: ten months' full-time training in the run-up, a month's training in residence at Elis immediately before, and then attendance at the Games themselves. Little wonder that the Athenian philosopher Plato says that anyone who hopes to win at either Olympia or Delphi has no spare time for anything else.

It is not simply that aspiring athletes are prevented from earning a regular living. They also have to shell out on trainers' fees, travel costs, special diets, equipment and various incidentals. Athletics is an expensive profession. The rewards can be huge. But for every sporting celebrity, there are a hundred wannabes.

Most Greeks are working people with farms and businesses to run; they simply do not have the time to devote to sport. And in their less guarded moments, those who like to complain of the vulgarisation of the Games admit that there is little real evidence of it. When the leader of the chorus seeks to define 'solid citizens' in Aristophanes' play *Frogs*, he describes them as 'people we know to be well-born and decent men, people of justice, fine gentlemen, and nurtured in the *palaistrai*, in the choruses, and in music'. 'Solid citizens' turn out to be the idle rich: those who, because they do not need to work, have time for athletics, drama and recitals. In truth, lack of means is a very effective form of social exclusion in Greek athletics.

Little wonder that you are more likely to see a Panhellenic champion at a private symposium of upper-class intellectuals than at a downtown bar frequented by democratically-minded tradesmen. The group which brought down the Athenian democracy in a short-lived coup in 404 BC is said to have included politicians, intellectuals and athletes. Typical of the group was the welcome they gave to Autolykos after he won the Panathenaic *pankration* in 422 BC. His combination of high birth, good looks and athletic stardom – the right-wing historian Xenophon considered him 'beautiful and of good character' – made him an ideal addition to the symposia of the Athenian Right.[2]

Wealth matters: it is the invisible class barrier to mass participation in top-level sports. Private patronage may very occasionally provide the necessary lift. Rich men have been known to subsidise the sporting careers of good-looking young men from humble backgrounds for pederastic motives. More commonly, however, patronage – and pederasty – operates within, rather than between, classes.

Public facilities probably play a bigger role in helping poverty-stricken young athletes. The provision of a city gymnasium overcomes the problem that most people do not have access to private facilities. But it makes no difference to the fact that having the leisure to use the facility depends upon wealth. Very few city-states pay any sort of maintenance and training allowance to support promising youngsters.

The plebeian prodigy finds himself at an impasse: to attract the patronage (private or public) he requires to match the advantages enjoyed by the gilded elite, he would need to demonstrate in advance his ability to outshine them. The only alternative would be an indiscriminate shower of state liberality. The example of Kroton in southern Italy, the only city-state ever to have spent lavishly on sports training for a sustained period, is the exception that proves the rule: its athletes won the men's Olympic short sprint twelve times out of twenty-seven between 588 and 484 BC.[3]

One reason public support for lower-class athletes is not provided more often is right-wing opposition. This has got nothing to do with principled disapproval of the 'professionalisation' of sport. There is not – and never has been – anything 'amateur' about Greek sport. The Greeks do not even have a word for this. The closest they get is *idiotes*, a word used to describe a private person who lacks professional expertise; by extension, it then comes to mean someone who is unskilled, ignorant and commonplace. A close cousin of this word is *banausia*, which means the life and labour of those who work with their hands, and – by a similar process of extension as in the case of *idiotes* – boorishness, vulgarity and lack of culture. The authors of these neat linguistic conceits are, of course, the Greek upper-classes, whose contempt for anyone who has to work for a living is the stuff of a thousand drunken symposia. The prejudice against using public money to support athletic careers has nothing to do with a (non-existent) amateur tradition; it is about keeping the plebs out.

It is not even true that the 'professionalisation' of sport means the decline of the aristocratic all-rounder. The latter is an Homeric ideal, not a reality that we can substantiate. Odysseus, who rides chariots, races on foot, boxes and wrestles, hurls javelin and discus, might be like one of those very irritating boys we all knew at school who was good at every sport. But Odysseus is only make-believe. At the highest level of competitive sport, as everyone knows, you have to be a specialist. Even victories in more than one event *in the same sport* are exceptionally rare, as when the same runner won the 600ft, the 1200ft, and the race in armour in a single day at Olympia in 512 BC. To win in different Olympic sports is almost unheard of. We can safely say, on straightforward commonsense grounds, that success in top-level competitive sport must have required extreme specialisation since the earliest days of the historical Olympics, whether that was in the mid-eighth or the late sixth century BC.

The simple truth is this. With very few exceptions, only the rich have the time and leisure to become top athletes. Only those who start out rich are ever likely to become richer still by competing in prize games. For the great majority, Greek sport is spectator sport. And if a tiny few, through sheer talent and good fortune, do succeed in rising from the bottom to join the sporting glitterati, they do so by internalising the elitist values of the Games. They do not subvert the system: they are absorbed by it.

I hope that knowing all that does not spoil it for you. Try and focus on the sport and forget that the winning athletes, who are already very rich, will earn more in the next year than you will see in a lifetime.[4]

SPORTING DYNASTIES

Another key fact about the celebs is the importance of family connections. Greece's most famous sporting dynasty is the Diagorids of Rhodes. Between them, the father, three of his sons, and two of his grandsons won no less than nine Olympic crowns in the boxing and the *pankration* (see p. 71). Such was the strength of the family tradition that, as a popular story has it, one of Diagoras's daughters, Kallipateira, was discovered to have entered the Games in disguise in order to see her son compete (see p. 30).

The Diagorids are exceptional, but far from unique. Many have been the proud fathers, once champions themselves, who have stood in the Olympic Stadium to watch their sons win sporting glory in their turn. To found a dynasty and nurture new generations of sporting heroes can provide ageing athletes with a second calling.

After all, most sportsmen cannot remain at the top for long. Milon of Kroton may have won six or seven consecutive Olympic victories. Theagenes of Thasos may have been unbeaten in boxing for twenty-two years. But achievement like this is the property of a tiny handful of all-time greats. Most champions have far shorter careers.

Some retire to a life of ease. Some go into politics. But a good few remain active in sport. Supporting the family tradition is one option, but another is to switch to the equestrian events where age is no barrier, since there is no requirement at the modern Games for competitors to ride or drive their own horses; indeed, given the dangers, it is far more common to employ jockeys and charioteers (see pp. 201ff).

Homer, as so often, provides a suitable role model. The ageing Nestor gives detailed tactical advice to his son Antilochos in advance of the chariot-race in the funeral games for Patroklos (see p. 210). And after the race, Achilles pays homage to Nestor's achievements and prestige: 'I give you this prize simply as a gift. You will not fight a boxing-match now, or wrestle, or enter the spear-throw, or race with your legs. Old age has its cruel hold on you now.' The point is that, despite his age, Nestor's former athletic prowess qualifies him to be a mentor and role-model for the next generation.[5]

ELIS: CITY OF CHAMPIONS

Location matters. Here is another of the secrets of success.

However pre-eminent Olympia, for most Greeks it is hard to get to. Even since achieving Panhellenic status, Olympia has continued to attract a disproportionate number of local athletes. The Eleans, for example, still excel at their own festival, accounting for around ten per cent of men's champions and twenty per cent of boys' – more than any other Greek city. The Spartans, who are neighbours of the Eleans in the Peloponnese, produce almost twice as many Olympic champions as the Athenians, who have to travel from the far side of the Isthmos.

Noteworthy, too, is the greater propensity of adult athletes to travel the distance. The boys' events are less prestigious, and the effort of getting to Olympia in this case requires greater commitment, since a boy must be accompanied by his father or another older male relative. On the other hand, parents have sometimes been criticised for denying promising youngsters their opportunity to compete at Olympia.[6]

TRAINING

THE BODY-BEAUTIFUL

You will find the athletic celebrities easy to spot. Spectators come in all shapes and sizes, and tend to shuffle around in groups somewhat aimlessly, chatting, laughing, gazing at the sights. But the competitors are big, erect and muscular,

GLAUKOS OF KARYSTOS: A WORKING-CLASS HERO?

Glaukos was the greatest sporting hero in the history of Karystos. He was descended from the fishermen of Anthedon, a seaport on the Boiotian coast, but his family had migrated to Karystos on the island of Euboia. It was there that he was born, brought up, and eventually began working life as a farm-labourer alongside his father.

One day, when the iron share fell out of the wooden frame of the plough he was using, Glaukos hammered it back into place using his hand as a hammer. Demulos, his father, recognised his potential at once, and entered him for the boys' boxing contest at the next Olympic Games (in 520 BC).

He received a tremendous battering at the hands of gymnasium-trained opponents, but he made it to the final bout. At one stage, bruised and bloodied, he was on the brink of submission, but his father called out, 'Come on, son, the one for the plough', and Glaukos managed to land a sudden knock-out punch to take the wreath.

Glaukos's final victory tally included, in addition to his Olympic crown, two from Delphi, and eight each from Isthmia and Nemea. He later pursued a career in political administration in Sicily, but after his death his body was returned to Karystos where he was buried on a small offshore island that bears his name to this day.

So much for the legend, which would appear to prove, gratifyingly, that even simple men can become sporting superstars. Unfortunately, we simply do not know how much of it is true. There is no official record of Glaukos's lineage and rank. He bears the name of at least five characters from myth, including another Glaukos associated with Anthedon — a fisherman who ate a magic herb, dived into the water, and became an oracular god of the sea. Visit quaint old Anthedon today, wander along the fishermen's huts amid the seaweed on the foreshore, and the ancient denizens, red-eyed and broken-nailed from decades of diving and fishing, will tell you that they are all descendants of Glaukos . . .[7]

and you will see them striding purposefully about, carrying oil-scaper and oil-flask, trademarks of the athletic young man all over Greece. Often, if they are about to exercise or compete, or sometimes just to show off, you will see them wander by completely naked. Then you can often tell one from another, the lumpy-faced boxer from the runner with bulging thighs, the rock-like pankratiast from the more streamlined pentathlete.

All athletes aspire to conform to an ideal of the body beautiful. Gymnasium addicts are obsessive about cultivating a 'Polykleitian' appearance. Polykleitos was a famous Argive sculptor who wrote a treatise on how to represent the human body in bronze or stone according to a set of mathematical rules (believing that 'beauty comes about from many numbers'). Maths may or may not be necessary, but there is no doubt that the Greek maestros have created a fairly consistent model of male beauty. Such artistic masterpieces as the *Doryphoros* ('Spear-carrier'), the *Diskobolos* ('Discus-thrower') and the *Diadoumenos*

22. Young men at exercise in the gymnasium, displaying three distinct body-shapes: from left to right, lanky, fat and the athletic ideal. The depiction illustrates the Greek obsession with the body-beautiful.

('Crowned athlete') are exemplars of this aspirational perfect form.

In reality, everyone tends to be either ectomorphic (thin), endomorphic (big) or mesomorphic (in between). If you are lanky or fat, you are nothing. The Polykleitian ideal is the perfect mesomorph, with broad shoulders, muscular stomach, pert bum and heavy thighs.

The Greek body-beautiful cult, reinforced by the absurd notion that soundness of body implies soundness of mind, is nothing less than tyranny. It is powered by lust, of course. Greece is filled with images of naked men with perfect bodies because it is also filled with pederasts. But we digress. The point is that even Olympic athletes are rarely capable of conforming to the ideal – as you will see from the parade of them on show. In practice, specialisation and rigorous training routines tend to produce something more lop-sided than the Spear-carrier or the Discus-thrower.

You will think the athletes stranger still when oiled and dusted. The universal practice among Greek athletes is for them to anoint themselves with olive oil before practice or performance. You will see numerous rectangular stone tanks, often divided into compartments like two or three kitchen sinks ranged side by side, and provided with large bronze ladles. These are the oil tanks. Athletes give themselves a liberal all-over coating of the stuff, the oil serving both as sun-block and lubricant in the blazing summer heat. The wrestlers three classes of them, remember: the wrestlers *per se*, the pankratiasts and the pentathletes – also cover their bodies in dust to counteract the slipperiness of the oil; it is a strict requirement that they do so before competing. This gives them a bizarre appearance, like participants in a primeval ritual dance – which, perhaps, is what it really is.[8]

LOCKER-ROOM CULTURE

Quite shocking to many first-time visitors to ancient Greece is the overt male-on-male sexuality associated with all aspects of athletic practice (see also pp. 35ff). Male lovers will arrange to go to the gymnasium together to exercise. Older men hang around the gymnasium to eye up the talent. The poet Theognis of Megara wrote of his happiness at exercising nude and then spending the rest of the day with a boy lover. Anyone going to the gymnasium to train makes himself open to sexual advances.

The homoerotic potential of naked men-only athletics hardly needs stressing. On a busy day, the open-air *palaistra* is a display of bronzed, oiled, fine-muscled young bodies. Intimate physical contact is a feature of many exercise routines. Wrestling practice in particular has an erotic charge.

The locker-room provides the main setting for sexual approaches. The rituals of disrobing, oiling, and washing which take place here have obvious erotic potential, and young athletes will sometimes engage in goosing and other antics. And here, too, older men will sometimes make approaches to youths who have attracted their fancy during exercise, attempting to entice them with gifts and other inducements.

Socrates once took in hand a love-struck youth, Hippothales, who lacked the confidence to approach the object of his affections, one Lysis. Where did he take Hippothales? To the *palaistra*, naturally, where they found Lysis watching a game of knucklebones in a corner of the locker-room. Lysis 'stood among the boys and young men wearing a garland on his head, and had a distinct appearance, worthy to be called not just beautiful [*kalos*], but imbued with beauty and goodness [*kalokagathia*]'.[9]

TRAINERS

As well as athletes, you will see many trainers at Olympia, some of whom are minor celebrities in their own right. The most successful of these run stables of leading athletes and become very rich indeed on the fees they earn. When a certain Thucydides of Athens (not the famous historian) wanted to turn his sons into first-class wrestlers, he knew whom to employ: Eudoxos for one, Xanthias for the other, the two top combat trainers in the city. When Alkimedon of Aigina won the boys' wrestling in 460 BC, his was the thirtieth crown won by athletes trained by the famous Melesias of Athens, a specialist in the training of *paides* ('boys') and *ageneioi* ('beardless youths').

Melesias was typical in two senses. First, he was an ex-athlete himself, with two Nemean crowns to his credit, one for the boys' wrestling and one for the men's *pankration*. Second, he was from Athens, a city of intellectuals which produces a disproportionate number of trainers. This may seem surprising, but the Greek approach to athletic training is scientific, and a trainer is not just an instructor in routines and techniques, but also dietitian, hygienist and physiotherapist. Many keep small libraries of medical treatises and how-to manuals. Among the classics is a seminal manual by Ikkos of Taras, whose advice includes special diets, moderate living, and sexual abstinence during intensive training. Also important are works by such leading doctors as Hippokrates of Kos (discoverer of aspirin), Demokedes of Kroton, and Alkmaion of Kroton.

Many trainers also read philosophical works. How useful these are is debatable. Greek scholars tend to be classroom-bound theorists who prefer to speculate on the basis of general principles than to conduct fieldwork or carry out experiments. Nonetheless, many trainers are clearly impressed, and allow themselves to be guided by one

23. A trainer (right) puts pentathletes through their paces. One is preparing to throw a discus, the other a javelin. Note the pickaxe, for breaking up the ground to create a soft *skamma* for the long jump, and also the pipe-player (left), who helps the trainee athletes achieve rhythm in their exercise.

or other of the various 'schools'. Some favour the inflexible four-day cycle: light exercise on day one, intensive exercise on day two, relaxation on day three, moderate exercise on day four, and repeat. Others favour a less rigid approach. Equally, there are differences of approach to diet, drinking, sexual activity and other lifestyle matters. Choice of trainer is important, and no small matter is the school of thought to which he subscribes.

How important is a good trainer? The poet Pindar, famous for the many victory odes he composed for champions at the crown games (see pp. 187ff), implies that the ingredients of sporting success are divine favour, noble lineage, family tradition, natural ability and good training – in roughly that order. But then he was a hired bard, and he who pays the poet calls the rhyme. Pindar's job was to sing the praises of his clients, not their trainers. Even so, when celebrating young Alkimedon's success, he tells us at length about his trainer, and lays stress on the importance of his work: 'not to be prepared beforehand is stupidity, for the minds of the unpractised are insubstantial things'. In other words, any fool can fail, so if your aim is to succeed in sport, you need proper training. Elsewhere, he defines the trainer as the 'builder' of an athlete, and describes the training programme he imposes as 'toil'.

Accurate information about the pay of trainers is hard to come by, but it ranges from a modest annual salary of about 500 drachmas, which is roughly what a municipal trainer at a local gymnasium earns, to five-figure sums for top private trainers like Melesias, who will be charging rates commensurate with the prize money being won by the athletes under their instruction. When the top Krotoniate doctor Demokedes was head-hunted by city-state rivals, his annual salary went up from 6,000 drachmas at Aigina, to 10,000 at Athens, to 12,000 at Samos. But these are top-of-the-range salaries.

Looked at from the client's point of view, by the way, an athlete just starting out can probably get a full training course from a reputable local trainer for around 100 drachmas a year.[10]

DIET

It has to be said that Greek sports science rests on distinctly shaky foundations. Philosophy, natural science and medicine are overlapping disciplines. The well-being of the human body is thought to rest on the 'balance' between, according to some, various 'elements', or, according to others, 'humours'.

The Sicilian school of medicine, which favours the former, was founded by Empedokles of Akragas, a philosopher rather than a doctor, who argued that all things were formed of four elements – fire, air, earth and water – each with a corresponding characteristic: hot, cold, dry and wet. The fact that Empedokles believed that in a previous life he had been a bush, and that he eventually chose to jump into the crater of Mount Etna, apparently on the assumption that he would be reincarnated, does not inspire confidence.

The Hippokratic school, on the other hand, named after Hippokrates of Kos, stresses the four humours, all of which turn out to be bodily excretions, being, in order of unpleasantness, blood, phlegm, yellow bile and black bile. A further layer of mystification (or refinement, depending on your point of view) comes with a contrast between nasty gases (*physai*) and healthy breath (*pneuma*), the former arising mainly from undigested food residues in the gut and having an unfortunate tendency to drive out the latter.

Environment and lifestyle are thought to affect the balance of both elements and humours. 'The soil,' explains Hippokrates in one of his best-known papers, *Airs, Waters, and Places*, 'may be barren and waterless or wooded and well-watered, hollow and humid or dry and cold. The inhabitants will have different lifestyles: they may drink heavily, take a midday meal, and be rather inactive, or take a lot of hard exercise, have a good appetite, and drink little.'

Since disease and ill-health are explained in terms of 'imbalance', Greek medical practice revolves around attempts to achieve a proper mixing of elements or humours by reducing some and increasing others. Purging, bloodletting and the use of emetics are favoured methods, but they are somewhat indiscriminate. Changes of diet allow for greater subtlety.

Diet faddism has reached epidemic proportions in Greece. It is a cultural phenomenon that links scientists and philosophers, doctors and priests, trainers and athletes, the whole of the body-beautiful set, and sundry mystics and cranks. Food and drink are classified according to their supposed properties and effects. Beef is strong and binding; beans are astringent and laxative; seafood is dry and light; cheese is strong and nourishing; and so on.

Needless to say, as with all fads, such is the mix of pseudo-science and out-and-out charlatanism that dietary advice is a matter of fashion. Charmis, the Spartan winner of the Olympic short sprint in 668 BC, is said to have adhered to a special diet of dried figs. More typically, early Olympians seem to have lived frugally on bread – barley bread or unleavened wholemeal wheat bread – and cheese. Then a trainer called Pythagoras (not to be confused with the famous guru discussed below) started promoting meat.

One early product of the new meat regime was the mountainous Milon, with his unequalled thirty-one circuit victories. Soon after came middle-distance runner Dromeus of Stymphalos, who won twice at Olympia, twice at Delphi, three times at Isthmia and five times at Nemea. His spectacular athleticism was attributed to the new meat-based diet. The new food regime having been endorsed by both runners and wrestlers, everyone promptly switched from cheese tarts to rump steak – encouraged by Hippokrates of Kos, who, keen to be seen as cutting-edge, denounced cheese as 'wicked food'.

At present, debate rages about beans, which are banned by the Pythagorean mystics of Kroton, but have the backing of some doctors – provided they are boiled enough to avoid flatulence.[11]

PYTHAGORAS, FOOD-FADDISM AND THE SPORTOCRACY OF KROTON

You may hear reference to Pythagoras of Kroton. It is as well to know the background, so that you can nod sagely if the subject comes up — it is advisable not to venture an opinion on this controversial subject until you know the company.

Pythagoras was a philosopher, mathematician and mystic of the sixth century BC. He seems to have been a native of Samos, but emigrated at some point, perhaps to escape the dictatorship on the island, and took up residence in the city of Kroton in southern

Italy. The charismatic foreign guru was soon the centre of a mystical cult which attracted both men and women. Mainstream philosophers denounced him as a fraud, but it made no difference: his popularity continued to grow up to the time of his death and beyond.

Central to the cult was a belief in reincarnation. The soul was thought to be rational, responsible and capable of making both good and bad decisions. The virtuousness of the soul determined what sort of body it ended up in. The ultimate aim was such purity of soul that it could achieve release from bodily form. Crucial to this was the avoidance of all kinds of pollution. Sad to say, 'pollution' seemed to be caused by pretty well anything pleasurable, from sex to pastries. Virtue, as so often, depended on abstinence and pain. Abstinence meant that people had time on their hands, so meditation was also encouraged.

Food-faddists and sex-deniers they may have been — with such neurotic characteristics as a particular antipathy to beans — but the Pythagoreans were not some fringe group of drop-outs and cranks. Organised in numerous, tight-knit, semi-secret cells, they were an influential and well-connected political force that came to dominate the government of Kroton. Their impact, moreover, extended well beyond the city. The Pythagoreans won converts among the social and intellectual elite across southern Italy and Sicily. The philosopher Empedokles of Akragas was one (see pp. 173–4), the sports writer Ikkos of Taras another (see p. 171).

Obsessive about purity and pain, the Pythagoreans were also sports-mad. Kroton, under their influence, promoted a strong culture of sports science and athletic training, becoming one of the very few places in Greece to give substantial public support to athletes from humble backgrounds. The city was, in effect, run by a mystical cult group of vegetarian sports nuts officially committed to a programme of spiritual eugenics.

Under the sportocracy, Kroton became an athletic powerhouse in the late sixth century BC. This single city dominated the Olympics for the best part of a century, winning forty-four per cent of the short-sprint races, and twenty-eight per cent of all events. In this period, while Kroton won twelve short sprints, the home city of Elis, traditionally pre-eminent at its own games, could manage only two crowns. This was the era of such Krotoniate sporting giants as Milon, a mountainous champion wrestler, with thirty-one wins on the crown circuit, including five at Olympia (see pp. 230–1). It was as the popular proverb avers: 'He who finishes last of the Krotoniates is first among the rest of the Greeks.'

Such was the superiority of Krotoniate athletes that large bribes were offered to secure transfers. Astulos of Kroton, thrice winner of the Olympic short sprint, declared himself a Syracusan on the latter two occasions; it seems likely he had been bought by the immensely rich tyrant of Syracuse. The Krotoniates retaliated by turning Astulos's house into a prison and destroying his portrait in a local temple.

With plenty of work for them to do, this was also the era of the great Krotoniate doctors. Demokedes was one, an expert on foreign diseases and the effect of environment, who, after working for the Persian emperor, was successively head-hunted by

Aigina, Athens and Samos. The historian Herodotos described him as 'the most skilful doctor of his time', and the man mainly responsible for the fact that 'the Krotoniates came to be reckoned such good doctors'. Alkmaion, who popularised the notion that good health depended on a balance of bodily fluids, was another of the great doctors of Kroton.

Sport became an industrial-scale enterprise at Kroton, with a network of public gymnasia, schools of trainers and private consultancies. Everything was sacrificed to Olympic glory. It was all too much. Provoked beyond endurance by the tyranny of aristocratic gymnasium hearties, the left-wing fatties of Kroton finally rose from their couches to overthrow their tormentors. The Pythagorean elite were killed or exiled, their organisations broken up, and some badly needed 'balance' was restored to the life of Kroton. The world's first — and so far only — experiment in government by sports-stars was ended by democratic revolution in the middle of the last century. Kroton's achievements at the Games, like her politics, have since been more moderate.[12]

EXERCISE

Nowadays, most athletes exercise, practise and train in public gymnasia (see pp. 118-19). The best-appointed facilities, as we have seen, include open and roofed running tracks, a large open-air courtyard with specially prepared sand-pits, and rooms for changing, oiling, storage and specialist practice (such as with a punch-bag).

These grand establishments may be found only in the richer cities, but even very ordinary cities usually now have some sort of public provision; only the most impoverished and remote communities, places with no Panhellenic record or aspiration in athletics, are wholly without.

At the gymnasium, of course, athletes need their own kit: *aryballos* (oil-flask), *stlengis* (oil-scraper or strigil) and *spongos* (sponge). The *aryballos*, usually ceramic, is a small rounded jar, about the size of a large apple, with a narrow mouth. Corked and suspended on a cord, it is ideal for transporting a personal oil-supply. The *stlengis* is a small curved tool, concave in section, usually made of bronze, occasionally iron, and with a handle formed all of a piece. The *spongos*, a natural sponge (though many make do with a rag), is used for the wash-up after the scrape-down.

Arriving for a workout, the athlete first undresses and oils himself. He may do both in the

24 and 25. A bronze figurine of an athlete with his strigil. The oil-flask and oil-scraper (pictured right) and the sponge are the three trademark items carried by all athletes.

apoduterion – the changing-room, or more precisely, the 'undressing-room', where benches are often also supplied for relaxation and conviviality – or he may pass after disrobing into the specialist oiling-room (*aleipterion*). Wrestlers and pankratiasts, you will remember, also coat themselves in dust or powder (*konis*) to ensure that sparring partners can get a grip. Sometimes the dust of the *palaistra* must suffice, but fine sifted powder is often supplied; in the best-appointed establishments, athletes may have a choice of black, red or yellow from the containers in the dust storage-room (*konisterion*).

The training session is likely to be intensive, with drills to develop particular muscles and rhythms, and repeated practice to master specific techniques. These, of course, are described in the many manuals available, and form the basis of the formal instruction given by trainers. But they become second-nature only with the conditioning, strength, agility and skill acquired in the *palaistra*. You will see the trainers – easy to spot as they remain clothed – pacing around their athletes, barking instruction and comment, brandishing rods, and using them freely when occasion demands. You will also see athletes undergoing more relaxed toning and rhythm exercises to the accompaniment of pipes.

Different sports have different requirements. Precautions are necessary in the combat sports, of course. Though wrestlers usually practise by actually wrestling, both boxers and pankratiasts tend to spar lightly in order to avoid injury, and also to pummel various sizes of punch-bags in the *korukeion* (punch-bag room).[13]

SPARTAN SPORT

If you have been to Sparta, you will know that it is like nowhere else in Greece. The city has the appearance and feel of a large village. The monumental temples, porticoes and statuary you see elsewhere are largely absent. Sparta cannot boast famous philosophers, scientists or artists: the city does not concern itself with 'culture'. Nor is it, like Athens, Corinth or Syracuse, filled with foreign merchants and exotic imported wares: Sparta is not a place of commerce either. It is a city of soldiers and serfs; and the business of the state is war and internal security.

The peculiarity of Sparta has deep roots. The ruling class is descended from Dorian invaders, who conquered Lakonia (the southeastern quarter of the Peloponnese) in the distant Dark Age between c. 950 and 750 BC. Some of the indigenous people were allowed to keep their land: these are the *perioikoi*, 'those who live round about'. Others lost it to new Spartan landlords and were forced to work for them as serfs or 'helots'.

In two further wars during the succeeding Archaic Age, the Spartans conquered Messenia (the southwestern quarter of the Peloponnese), turning the previously independent Messenian Greek population into helots, like so many of the Lakonians.

The Spartans are a military elite supported by a mass of agricultural serfs. The adult male citizens who form the Spartan army number only a few thousand, each one supported by a state farm staffed by helots. To maintain their position, they have to hold down tens of thousands of reluctant subjects. It is for this reason that the whole of Sparta is organised as a military camp, and that every adult male Spartan is a full-time professional warrior.

War, sport and education form a tight nexus throughout Greece; but nowhere more so than in Sparta. The Spartan *agoge* (its military training system) is a ruthless process of weeding out and toughening up. Weak or deformed babies are put out to die. Boys attend boarding school from seven to eighteen years of age, where they are subjected to a brutal regime of deliberate neglect and mistreatment. Underfed and ill-clad, they learn survival by fighting or stealing for food, but face floggings if they get caught. Games, of course, form the core of the curriculum: an endless round of exercises, competitions and violent sparring, all performed naked, all under the watchful eye of a state-appointed inspector. The out-of-shape are flogged.

Grouped in age-based *agelai* ('herds') while at boarding school, young men pass directly into age-based *sussitia* ('mess-groups') when they graduate at the age of twenty. For the next ten years, they spend most of their time living in military-style dormitories, feeding on the infamous Spartan 'black broth' (the precise composition of which remains something of a mystery in wider Greece).

Sparta does not require separate sports facilities: the whole state is a factory for mass-producing military athleticism. This applies to girls as well as boys. Sparta is the only state in Greece that puts special emphasis on games for girls. These originated as fertility rituals, but rather than becoming marginalised by male games — as, for example, the Games of Hera have been by the Games of Zeus at Olympia itself — Sparta's female games have grown in importance. Naked teenage girls can often be seen racing, wrestling, and throwing discus and javelin. The reason for this is practical and eugenic: as the Athenian political commentator Xenophon puts it, the Spartans 'believe that stronger children come from parents who are both strong'. Sparta worries about the health of its women because it sees them as incubators for breeding soldiers.

The *agoge* seems to have conferred a substantial advantage on Sparta in the early Olympics, with some thirty-two victories during the seventh century BC. But Sparta's athletic pre-eminence thereafter diminished, achieving only five athletic and five chariot wins between 550 and 450 BC. Sparta rallied thereafter, but these new sporting triumphs were in equestrian events, with an almost unbroken string of chariot victories between 448 and 420 BC.

What seems to have happened is that the widening of the Olympics from a Peloponnesian to a Panhellenic event, coupled with the spread of gymnasia and a mass sporting culture across the rest of the Greek world, offset Sparta's early advantage. Later, though, with the prowess of the Spartan army making some of its leaders rich, chariot-racing became both affordable and desirable as a mark of status.

What are we to make of it all? In a sense, the whole world is divided into 'Athenians' and 'Spartans'. It is easy to understand why Athens should be admired for its art, its theatre and its intellectual brilliance. What is more controversial is that many also admire Athens for her democracy. And this is what explains the contrary admiration of Sparta. For anti-democrats, Sparta – austere, boorish, militaristic – is the necessary counterpoint.[14]

No doubt, at large in the intensely politicised atmosphere of Greece, your natural inclinations and prejudices will soon have you gravitating towards one side or the other.

CELEBRITY CULTURE

AGON AND *ARETE*

Celebrity culture can seem very shallow – much like the minds of many celebrities themselves. Do not be too sniffy. It is the most visible manifestation of a value-system with deep roots in Greek tradition.

Greek celebrities are defined by reference to two key concepts: *agon* and *arete*. *Agon* means competition, contest, struggle, battle. Greeks imagine the whole of life to have an essentially 'agonistic' character. Whether they are considering war, politics or sport, they think in terms of a series of clashes between opposing forces. This perception underlies their exceptionally competitive character.

Also implicit in the word *agon* is the idea that competition is public: men are tested and graded in contests which take place before mass audiences of fellow citizens.

The implication is clear from the original meaning of the word, which is 'assembly'. *Agon* is therefore, by definition, competition under the concentrated glare of a critical crowd – resulting in either honour or shame.

The complimentary concept of *arete* means goodness, excellence, virtue; and this in turn, in a society as individualistic, competitive and patriarchal as that of Greece, comes to mean the manly qualities of courage, strength, endurance and male physical beauty.

Arete is an absolute. There are neither team games nor runners-up at the Olympics. In every event, there is a single champion. In this respect, as in so many others, recent democratic veneers cannot conceal the deeply aristocratic and traditional character of the Games. Modern athletes are like Homeric heroes. They may nowadays be seen to represent their city-states, but it is not the city that competes – as it would be, in a sense, if a team were to be entered for an event – but the individual athlete.

When, in Homer's *Iliad*, Achilles is dishonoured by being stripped of a prize, he withdraws from the fighting and leaves his Greek comrades-in-arms to suffer defeat and heavy loss. But in a 'heroic' society of warrior-aristocrats, this is not mutiny and a matter to be settled by court-martial; it is the understandable – if unfortunate – action of a true blue-blooded noble. As Achilles had been told by his father, the very essence of his moral code was 'always to be best and to be eminent beyond others'.

The personal honour of the Olympic athlete is also at stake when he competes in the Games. He recognises the gods as patrons of success. He looks forward to the plaudits of his home city. He acknowledges the importance of noble lineage, family support and a good trainer. But the *agon* is above all a test of his own *arete*, and his primary motive is that supremely aristocratic motivator, *philotimia*, 'love of honour'. And his deepest anxiety is fear of defeat and the attendant shame – fear that he will be exposed before the gaze of thousands as second-rate.

Pindar captures this in his victory ode for the wrestling champion Aristomenes of Aigina: 'On four bodies you sprang from above with hurt in mind; for them, no homeward way was decreed at the Pythia happy as yours, nor did welcome laughter give rise to encompassing joy when they returned to their mothers, but, shunning their enemies, they slink home down alleyways, gnawed by failure.'

Sport for its own sake is alien to the Greek mindset. Striving, effort, doing your best: these are nothing if you do not win. The aristocratic ideal of the heroic super-warrior lies at the root of this attitude. But the age of aristocratic social supremacy and of internecine baronial warfare has passed. The Games foster the old ideal, allowing it to persist in a world of city-states and democratic assemblies, by channelling, reconfiguring and containing individualistic competitive impulses that might otherwise prove socially destructive. Greek sport is, if you like, an exercise in social dominance by other means.[15]

Think of the celebrities you see at the Games as windows on this old-world value system of which they are the most notable living examplars.

EARNINGS

Athletes win wreaths and glory at the crown games, but no money prizes. Olympia, Delphi, Isthmia and Nemea form a circuit (*periodos*), and the ultimate glory is to win the grand slam by taking a crown at all four festivals. The champion athlete then becomes a circuit winner and joins the gallery of all-time greats (*periodonikai*). But you cannot eat glory, can you?

Yet all top athletes are rich. The rewards that make them so are twofold. First, motivated by a patriotic desire to win the prestige associated with sporting success (or, to view the matter less generously, to get one over on their rivals), many city-states encourage citizens to compete in crown games by providing their own schedule of rewards. Athens, for example, pays 500 drachmas for an Olympic crown, 100 for an Isthmian. In addition to such one-off payments, a growing practice is to make lifetime awards of a state pension, tax exemption, and the right to free meals at the city hall, as well as such honorific privileges as entitlement to front-row seats at public events.

Second, to ensure appearances by top sports stars, those hosting local games usually do offer money prizes (see pp. 124-6). Some of these – like the Panathenaic at Athens – have been so successful that they have achieved quasi-Panhellenic status. But this has not allowed them to dispense with money prizes; on the contrary, lacking the hallowed status of the crown games, their continuing stature depends in no small part on the size of the rewards they offer. As we have seen, at a premier festival like the Panathenaic, all of the first five competitors in a single event might win a prize, ranging in value from one to five years' average pay.[16]

Success, celebrity and wealth, as in most human endeavours throughout history, are intimately associated in Greek athletics.

FAME

Up to a certain point, athletes become famous by winning in front of tens of thousands of spectators. When these disperse to their homes, news of the athletic achievement they have seen spreads far and wide by word of mouth. But this is rarely enough. Athletes, their kinsmen, and their cities seek to magnify the fame that has been won. Celebrity is deliberately inflated using a variety of messages and media. Let me tell you about four of them.

RECORDS OF ACHIEVEMENT

All sport is competitive, but, as we have seen, none more than that of Greece. The Olympics have nothing to do with fostering unity and friendship: they are driven by the rivalry between athletes, their fans and their cities.

To win is everything. However many prizes there may be for runners-up at the money games, there is only one crown for each event at the sacred games. For these crowns, the competition among top athletes, the touring professionals of the circuit, is intense and unrelenting. The primary aim, of course, is to win as many crowns as possible, but records of achievement can be more nuanced than a mere tally.

This is not a matter of distances and times. The Greeks do not measure these, so it is impossible to say who achieved the greatest ever javelin cast or ran the fastest ever sprint. But you will recall that the sacred crowns are ranked in order of prestige: Olympian, Pythian, Isthmian and Nemean. Over and above that, however, is the status of grand-slam winner: an athlete who wins a crown in the same event at all four crown games. Then there are 'dustless' victories to be paraded by combat sportsmen whose reputations are so fearsome that no challenger appears and they take the crown uncontested. Also, wrestlers and pankratiasts will sometimes boast of victories won without a fall. The mighty Milon is remembered at Olympia as the champion who 'was victorious seven times and not once felled to his knees' (see pp. 230-1).

Then there are those extraordinary men who can boast of winning in more than one event at the same festival, perhaps even on the very same day. They are rare, but they exist. Theagenes of Thasos won both the boxing and the *pankration* on the same day at Pythia, but was then disgraced in his efforts to repeat the achievement at Olympia (see pp. 158-60). Xenophon of Corinth won three events at the same Panathenaia, the short- and long-sprint at Delphi, and then, his greatest glory, both the short sprint and the pentathlon at Olympia.

These records of achievement are discussed, and compared by athletes and sports fans across Greece. They are both measure and magnifier of fame.[17]

THE TRIUMPHAL HOMECOMING

Many cities will organise a grand reception for a returning hero. When Exainetos of Akragas in Sicily won his second short-sprint victory at Olympia in 412 BC, he was met on his return by an escort of 300 chariots pulled by white horses, and a section of the city wall was knocked down for his entrance. The privileges already referred to – like free meals and front-row seats – thereafter act as continual reminders of the achievement of the individual athlete and the prestige he has won for the community.[18]

On your way home after the Games, you might want to pause awhile and watch one of these celebrations if you happen to be passing. They are always genuine outbursts of happiness, solidarity and pride on the part of the home crowd towards their returning hero.

THE VICTORY ODE

One thing you are bound to come across – recited aloud or inscribed on stone – is the victory ode. Poet and athlete have had a close relationship since the time of Homer, and probably long before. In Greece, prose is used to frame laws, provide factual information, and write philosophical, historical and scientific works. It is not used, generally speaking, in storytelling. The *Iliad* and the *Odyssey* are epic poems. Every play of Aeschylus, Sophocles and Euripides is written in verse.

One reason for the enduring popularity of the verse form is that few people read. It is not that they are unable to. Most Greeks have at least basic literacy. But this is not a scroll-reading society. Most news is transmitted by word of mouth. Most entertainment involves public performance before an audience. Philosophers give lectures, historians read from their works, and poets give recitals of their compositions. The rhapsode (*rapsodos*: one who makes his living by delivering public recitations, usually of Homer) is a familiar figure in society.

Anyone, therefore, who wishes to elevate themselves and their achievements above the everyday might seek to broadcast them in the form of poems designed for public recitation. The victory ode is now long-established as an appropriate genre for this purpose. It is technically a 'choral lyric', meaning that it is composed to be sung by a chorus of singers on a special public occasion. You will see specialist poets crowding around the stars to tout their various services during the Games. Length and quality are, of course, adjustable to suit clients' purses.

If it is immortality an athlete seeks, the work of the best composers of victory odes is certainly long remembered – men like Simonides of Keos, Bacchylides of Keos (nephew of the former), Ibykos of Rhegion and, above all, the incomparable Pindar of Thebes (518–438 BC). Pindar is considered to have perfected the genre, writing odes for victors at all four of the crown games, the shortest around twenty lines, the longest more than 300, and typically involving direct praise of the victor and his city, an appropriate mythological story, a heavy dose of moralising, and often something about the poet, the ode and its performance.

Odes have recurring themes. Some are of general significance: for instance, admiration for the skill, strength and stamina of the athlete, for his dedication and drive, for his surpassing 'excellence' (*arete*). Others are likely to have appealed to the traditionalist impulses of the poet's wealthy clients, such as by emphasising family, lineage and noble birth. Where there are tensions – between, say, aristocracy and democracy, or between the outstanding individual and the wider community – Pindar is a deft hand at glossing over them. His ideal is aristocratic athleticism – the athleticism of those who can afford his services.

Pindar was the supreme propagandist of athletic achieve-ment. 'I am no sculptor,' he wrote in deference to his role, 'to create

26. Pindar, the greatest composer of victory odes.

images which stand motionless on their base; no, sweet song, you must go forth from Aigina on every ship and merchantman, carrying the news that Lampon's powerful son Pytheas has won the *pankration* crown at Nemea.' Unlike 'motionless' bronze and stone, Pindar's choral lyric has the power to broadcast fame widely. Nor need it be any less enduring as a record: 'When men die, it is songs and stories that recall their fine deeds.'

First and foremost, victory odes are composed for singing to the accompaniment of lyre and pipes at a formal celebration, such as the 'revelling procession' that Pindar refers to in one of his Olympian poems. But, ideally, they are also for eternity. And to ensure the words survive to tell the tale, they are often inscribed and put on public display. You can, for example, see the ode Pindar composed for the great Diagoras of Rhodes in celebration of his boxing victory at Olympia in 464 BC engraved in gold letters and dedicated in the Temple of Athena at Lindos.

Given all of this, it seems surprising that the victory ode has been in decline now for many decades. No great poet has emerged since Pindar, and athletes seem increasingly reluctant to grant commissions. It is not clear why. Perhaps the poets priced themselves out of the market. Pindar paraded the fact the he was 'a profiteer and hired hand', his 'sugar soft-voiced songs silver-plated for sale by Terpsichore [the muse of choral lyric]'. He was not joking, it seems: he is reputed to have charged as much as 3,000 drachmas for a single poem.

Statues, on the other hand, are very much in vogue – though they are not cheap either.[19]

THE HONORIFIC STATUE

Some athletes commission paintings to celebrate their victories. Alkibiades of Athens, after his spectacular chariot victory in 416 BC, had himself depicted being crowned by a female personification of Olympia. But two-dimensional images have their limitations. Better is a lifesize statue in bronze or marble, especially if it is executed by a true master, like Myron of Athens, Polykleitos of Argos, or Kallikles of Megara.

You will see hundreds of them in the Sanctuary, many standing in tight clusters representing family groups, citizens of a single city-state, or champions in the same sport. Each statue is identified by an inscription on the base giving the athlete's name, patronymic, city, and a full list of his victories. The Sanctuary is a true sporting hall of fame.

To erect a statue, permission must first be sought from the EOC. If granted, a choice must then be made between bronze or marble, and an appropriate artist commissioned to do the work. The effect of bronze and marble is very different. Bronze statues, which are hollow cast, are polished to glisten in the sunlight like the tanned and oiled body of the athlete. In the finest work, the mix in the metal alloy is varied to produce subtly different colours (with a redder hue for lips and nipples, for example) and the face is made to look uncannily real with the addition of staring glass-paste eyes, and sometimes even finely-carved ivory teeth. Marble, on the other hand, especially if the stone is of good quality and well polished, has a wonderful sheen, against which the garishly painted detail of lips, eyes, hair and garlands are strangely fascinating.

As well as deciding on material and quality of work, the athlete must also choose a pose. Simplest of all is a figure standing stationary and erect. More refined is one in the increasingly fashionable 'casual' pose where the weight is on one leg and the torso slightly tilted. This imparts greater vitality to the statue, and in some cases the figure is made to appear as if slowly walking forwards. These poses are all appropriate to a depiction of the victor in triumph – carrying discus or javelin from the field, scraping-down with a strigil, or simply garlanded with the olive-wreath crown and receiving the accolades of the crowd.

But for something truly sensational, a modern athlete might opt for an action pose. Inspired by a handful of supreme masters, sculpture has been enjoying an unprecedented period of innovation and experiment for more than two decades. The result has been a continuing stream of revolutionary new forms. A central theme has been the artists' attempts to make their sculptures look as if they are about to move by rejecting static standing poses and portraying athletes in a fleeting moment of action and effort – runners in full flight, wrestlers hurling an opponent, pentathletes swinging to cast discus or javelin. Myron's *Diskobolos* is a stunning example. The athlete's right leg is stepped forward and tensed, his right arm swung back to its fullest extent, ready to throw. Muscles bulge with energy. Veins run in long ridges across the surface of the skin. Everything anticipates the mighty swing forwards that, in a second or two of exploding power, will win a sacred crown.

Yet, even in the most action-packed representations, there is no triumphalism. The athletes never boast or cheer or wave clenched fists above their heads. The mood is one of humility and decorum; for, when all is said and done, the victory belongs to Zeus. The statues are monuments not only to athletic success, but also to piety and pilgrimage. They celebrate *arete*, but carefully avoid any risk of *hubris*.[20]

PIN-UPS FOR THE GIRLS

Quite enough has already been said about the attractiveness of young sportsmen to both their male peers and older men (see p. 170). What has not been discussed so far is their effect on women.

The sexuality of citizen-women is tightly controlled. Neither teenage girls nor married women have any opportunity to express their sexuality outside the context of their arranged marriages. That this creates a bulging dam of frustrated desire is obvious. It is obvious to the Greeks, being the stock-in-trade of a good proportion of their output of myths, plays and poems. Even ultra-conventional Pindar cannot help making occasional reference to it. For example, the maestro of the victory ode describes how when Telesikrates of Kyrene, the Pythian champion of the race in armour in 474 BC, competed in local games back home, every girl harboured a secret wish that he were 'her dearest husband'. He boasts to Hippokleas of Thessaly, winner of the boys' long-distance sprint at Pythia, that his victory ode broadcasting the achievement would make the athlete 'an object of desire for young unmarried girls'.

But, of course, these girls can do little if anything to pursue any lustful fancy they may harbour. The best they can hope for, if seriously besotted, is that a champion athlete might commend himself to a girl's family if she drops appropriate hints, given his likely good birth and wealth.

Other women may be more proactive. *Hetairai*, the most glamorous and expensive of Greek prostitutes (see pp. 30-3), are women renowned for their self-confidence and sophistication, and have been known to actively pursue sporting celebrities who may keep them in the style to which they have become accustomed.[21]

HERO WORSHIP

Sporting celebrities are rich and famous in their lifetimes, and are remembered afterwards as men whose achievements set the benchmarks for their successors. As well as earning prizes, subsidies, privileges and statuary during their careers, they may be honoured with a grand tomb after death. A champion discus-thrower was buried at Taras in southern Italy in a stone sarcophagus wearing a gold wreath and accompanied by four amphoras won at the Panathenaic Games. It is at this point that celebrity seems to blur into something more: hero worship – in a literal, not metaphoric, sense.

Do sporting superstars perhaps have a touch of the divine about them? Are the all-time greats, so much larger than life, something more than mere men? Are they modern-day equivalents of mythic heroes like Herakles and Odysseus? Many Greeks appear to think so.

After his death in battle, the Olympic champion Philippos of Kroton was honoured with a hero-shrine. The statue of Theagenes of Thasos, recovered from the sea and re-erected in a place of honour in the city market-place in conformity with a Delphic oracle, is venerated and worshipped, and the regular recipient of sacrifice (see pp. 158-60). Local people claim it has miraculous powers: by mere proximity one absorbs strength, health and good fortune. Kleomedes of Astypalaia, despite killing his boxing opponent and sixty children, is also hero-worshipped in his home city under injunction from Delphi (see pp. 154-5). The same is true of Diognetos of Crete, who also killed his opponent in the boxing, but then received a hero's honours at home.

If sporting heroes may become divine beings after death, their images charged with magical properties, what of their status in life? Some have been venerated as demigods – like Polydamas of Skotoussa, the Olympic *pankration* victor (see p. 238), whose statue in the Sanctuary will supposedly cure a fever, or Euthymos of Lokri, three-times winner of the Olympic boxing, whose divinity seemed apparent when he drove away a ghost that had been haunting Temesa and rescued the beautiful girl whom the locals had offered up to it and with whom he had fallen in love. Euthymos was later credited with a divine father, the river god Karkinos, and was reported not to have died like ordinary mortals, but to have departed 'in some other way'.

So do not be too surprised when you see men touching and embracing the statues in the Sanctuary, nor when you see the enthusiasm with which they jostle around famous athletes eager to feel the oil and sweat on their skin. It is partly the lure of celebrity, the magnetic attraction of the famous. But it is also religious: sporting champions are favoured by the gods, blessed by the gods, closer to the gods. To touch one is to touch something magical and otherworldly.

It is also to touch something dangerous. Like Homer's heroes, Olympic champions occupy a liminal space between mortals and the gods, a borderland where society's rules apply with reduced force. The boxer, the wrestler and the pankratiast, pumped up with muscle and aggression, sometimes explode through the constraints of law and custom. The power to smash an opponent at the Games becomes the power to collapse the roof of a school. The combat athlete is both good and evil, superstar and murderer, god and monster. Celebrity can sometimes wear a dark and sinister aspect.[22]

This is a grim note on which to end our discussion of the superstars. But perhaps it is a useful reminder of the complex, multilayered, contradictory character of the Olympic Games. You have much food for thought as you immerse yourself in the spectacle and excitement of the festival. It is time for it to begin.

7 THE PROGRAMME

On the eve of the festival's official opening, there will be an air of tense anticipation, even infectious excitement. For although the Games are to begin tomorrow, a marvellous spectacle awaits you tonight: the grand procession from Elis.

It sets out from the city – thirty-six miles northwest of Olympia – two days before the Games begin. It is led by the nine *Hellanodikai*, the fifty-strong Olympic Council, the Heralds, the Trumpeters, the Whip-bearers, and various other EOC officials, along with their staffs of functionaries and slaves. Following them come the athletes and their trainers, perhaps as many as 200 of the former, along with a great throng of horses and chariots, jockeys and charioteers, owners and stablehands. In the crowd, too, are various family members, groupies and hangers-on,

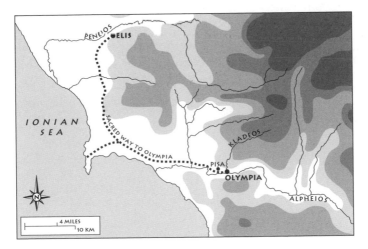

Map 5. The processional route taken from Elis to Olympia by the EOC, the athletes and local spectators.

along with the most enthusiastic of the fans and cultural tourists, those who have deliberately turned up early and headed down to Elis in order to join the procession. Most numerous, however, are the ordinary citizens of Elis, some of them departing with the procession when it leaves the city, others joining as it passes through local villages.

All who join the procession become pilgrims, and the route from Elis to Olympia is a sacred way. The first part of the road runs more or less due south, parallel with the coast. But after an overnight stop, where some thousands camp out under the stars, they leave the coast and head inland, following the road southeast down the valley of the Alpheios. At the Fountain of Piera, on the boundary of the Olympic province, the procession stops to sacrifice a pig. The *Hellanodikai* are ritually purified by being sprinkled with pig's blood and then washed in the sacred spring. Then they all walk the final stretch to Olympia.

Once the approaching procession is sighted from the Hill of Kronos, news spreads fast among the waiting tens of thousands. As it arrives, it is received with rapture. Amid the surging crowd and roars of acclamation, everyone strains to catch sight of the sporting superstars, Sicilian dictators craning to see no less than Peloponnesian herdsmen, aristocratic princes alongside humble peasant farmers. Foreign visitors like yourself – assuming you can see anything at all – will find plenty of amateur sports experts in the crowd willing to point out the famous faces. Do not be afraid to ask. People will be keen to help, eager to show off their knowledge.[1]

DAY 1

THE OPENING CEREMONY

The first day of the Games is devoted to the Opening Ceremony, minor events and fringe performances: there are no major competitions until Day 2.

The Opening Ceremony is fairly low-key. If you want to watch it, you should make your way to the Council House (see pp. 45-6). All participants – athletes, trainers, guardians and Judges – are required to be present in order to swear a sacred oath before the altar and statue of Zeus *Horkios* ('god of oaths'). The Priests sacrifice a wild boar. Athletes, trainers and guardians are required to swear an oath on slices of the boar's flesh that the obligatory ten months' prior training has been performed, that they will obey the rules, and that they will do nothing to bring the Games into disrepute. The *Hellanodikai* swear that they will not accept bribes and will judge fairly.

Be aware that this is a solemn religious ritual; you would invite serious trouble if you were in any way disrespectful. However, expect a great deal of pushing and shoving as people struggle to get a view, and, towards the back of the crowd, where no-one can see, arguments breaking out among the bored and fractious.

There is nothing exceptional in the solemnity of the occasion. The entire festival is one long ceremony in honour of Zeus. The sporting events have been added to an existing schedule of ritual observance, and the exertions of the athletes in competition are no less religious in significance than prayers around an altar. The best advice, therefore, is always to do as others do. Matters can become very rowdy at times, but then a solemn calm can suddenly descend. Do not get caught out.

The drawing of lots to determine starting positions in the races and who fights whom in the combat bouts immediately follows the swearing-in. This, like so much else, may appear to be a purely secular administrative matter. The athletes gather in a circle, an urn is placed before them, and each comes forward to select a token inscribed with a letter. For the combat sports, for example, the urn contains two of each letter, and these give the pairings for the bouts.

But there is more to it than appears on the surface. For one thing, the athletes are required to strip off and display their physique. The sight can be intimidating – as is partly the intention – and athletes selected to fight a particularly formidable opponent have been known to bottle it and withdraw even at this late stage. The drawing of lots also has a religious dimension. It appears to be mere chance which lane a runner is allocated or who is paired with whom in a boxing bout. That is not the local view of matters. The lot allows the gods to decide. The 'sortition' (*kleros*) is itself a sacred act.

It is the *Hellanodikai*, however, who make the final decision on age classifications – no divine assistance here – and there is always the possibility of a last-minute change of mind. In practice, the decision is usually made during the month's training in Elis. But technically, nothing is finally settled until the public declaration at the Opening Ceremony, and young athletes are sometimes traumatised by the anxiety that they might suddenly find themselves pitted against full-grown men.[2]

CONTESTS FOR HERALDS AND TRUMPETERS

These contests were introduced only eight years ago in 396 BC, following representations by the Olympic Heralds and Trumpeters, among whom competition for the honour of serving at the Games is intense.

In the run-up to the Games, large numbers of Heralds

and Trumpeters are employed by the EOC and despatched across Greece to announce the forthcoming Games and declare the Sacred Truce. You might even have seen them on the road during your own travels across Greece. But there is work for only one of each during the actual festival, since just one event runs at any one time. The two winners of these contests will therefore become *the* Herald and *the* Trumpeter for the present Olympiad: in effect, the public-address system for the Games of 388 BC.

The contestants – often distinctively stocky and barrel-chested – take turns on a special raised platform near the entrance to the Stadium, and are judged according to volume and clarity by Judges ranged at various distances. The winning pair, who receive olive crowns and are ranked as Olympic champions, will work closely together throughout the festival, the Trumpeter calling the crowd to order and silence, the Herald functioning as an oral timetable and results service.[3]

THE BOYS' SPRINT, WRESTLING AND BOXING

Other festivals offer a wide range of competitions for boys, but Olympia offers only three – the short sprint, wrestling and boxing. All of these events take place on the first day. They are in the way of a warm-up for the crowd.[4]

Watching the boys' events in the Stadium, you will get your first experience of the Olympic crowd. It is as loud, critical and partisan as any in the sporting world. The fans from different city-states tend to group together on the banks and will roar encouragement to fellow-citizens among the athletes. If no-one from home is competing, they will give support sometimes to famous champions, sometimes to an underdog. Everyone considers himself an expert, many offering running commentary, some arguing furiously about the merits of respective competitors.

Your biggest problem is likely to be getting a decent view in the Stadium. Everyone sits around until an event is announced, then stands to watch, often bobbing around with excitement. During the Games, 'What happened?' is probably the most frequently asked question on the Stadium banks. This is a problem without a solution. Olympia originally developed as a local religious sanctuary with space for a few thousand at the most. The simple fact is that it cannot cope with 100,000 people.[5]

If it all gets too much, take yourself off for some sightseeing or fringe performances (see pp. 38ff). Remember that the Sanctuary offers antiquities, art and architecture, and a sporting hall of fame; when most people are busy watching the sports can often be the best time to view it all. And with orations by philosophers, readings by historians, and recitals by poets, many of them famous names, the Olympic fringe is a veritable cultural festival in its own right; again, you avoid the crush when the athletics are running. There is always something to do, and usually too much. You cannot get bored at Olympia.[6]

DAY 2, MORNING

THE EQUESTRIAN PROCESSION

The second day of the Games begins with the equestrian procession, which is one of the festival's greatest spectacles. The procession assembles in the northwest corner of the Sanctuary by the Committee Room, where the Olympic flame, the sacred fire of Hestia, burns (see p. 70). It is led by the Priests of Zeus together with the *Hellanodikai*, the latter resplendent in their purple robes and displaying their rods as symbols of authority.

But all eyes are on the equestrians who follow them in procession across the Sanctuary – all of the competitors in the Hippodrome events can now be seen on parade. Despite the crowds, you should find an opportunity to get close, for the procession moves slowly, pausing to pay homage at no fewer than sixty-three altars and, as a result, it tends to straggle among the clutter of shrines and statues.

Once these ritual observances are complete and the official procession is approaching the Hippodrome, the Trumpeter blasts the news across Olympia that the time has finally come for the first of the major competitions to begin. Thousands will already have taken their place on the banks; thousands more now rush to join them from the Sanctuary and the Village. You should hurry and follow them to secure your vantage point in the Hippodrome.[7]

THE FOUR-HORSE CHARIOT-RACE (*TETHRIPPON*)

Date of introduction: 680 BC
Distance: twelve laps or seventy-two *stadia* (43,200ft)

As the procession enters the Hippodrome, the competitors shake themselves into an orderly file, and as each passes, the Herald announces his name, his father's name, and his native city. Any final challenges to the good character of those selected to participate must now be made. This is rare: the Judges' investigations during the month-long sojourn at Elis have been thorough. It is time for the first contest.

For many, the *tethrippon* is the supreme event. Though modern Olympiads are named after the winner of the short sprint, it may not always have been so. In Homer's day, the chariot-race had greater prestige, and just as it was scheduled first at the funeral games of Patroklos, so it is at Olympia. Doubtless this reflects its aristocratic character. Poorer athletes can run and jump, but only the rich can afford chariots and teams of horses. The chariot-race is not least an opportunity to display wealth and power.

In 416 BC, the flamboyant Athenian aristocrat Alkibiades entered no fewer than seven four-horse chariots. His motives are undisputed: to an ambitious young politician, Olympia offered the best opportunity in Greece to display both patriotic virtue and personal excellence – while avoiding the risk of caste-contamination inherent in the non-equestrian events. He secured the crown and also the second and fourth positions (and a victory ode composed by the famous playwright Euripides).

Rumour has it that this year, 388 BC, Dionysios, the unpopular dictator of Syracuse, the richest and most powerful man in Sicily, plans to enter several teams. He may even be present in person. Many other wealthy horse-owners certainly will be. Typically, they are men in their forties or fifties wearing smart clothes, attended by slaves, and accompanied by small retinues of staff and hangers-on – all part of the theatre of power.

There is space for up to twenty competitors across the 800ft-wide track. The starting-gates – ranged like the prow of a ship and with an elaborate mechanism for a staggered start, you will recall (see p. 75) – are designed to prevent bunching and accidents at the start of the race, and to ensure that competitors in the middle of the field, who are closer to the turning-post at the far end than those in the outer lanes, do not gain an advantage.

As the chariots are manouevred into their gates, you will have a chance to study them. The horses, of course, are among the finest in Greece, young but full-grown animals in peak condition, well cared-for and highly trained. Good racehorses are prized possessions and much loved. Many are famous, they always have names, and plenty of fans can rattle them off. Horsemania knows few bounds. When you have a spare moment, take a look at the monument of Kleosthenes of Epidamnos in the Sanctuary. A horse-breeder and winner of the *tethrippon* in 516 BC, he paid for a statue of himself, his driver, his chariot and his horses. You can read the horses' names on the dedicatory inscription: the yoke horses were Knakias and Samos, the trace horses, Phoinix and Korax.

The chariots are of the most slender construction – a modified racing design based on the war-carts of the Homeric age. (Only the Persians and other barbarians use the chariot in war today.) They are built mainly of wood, wicker and leather thongs. The basic frame of the vehicle is provided by a central pole. This is attached to a wheel-axle at the back, and rises at the front to support a yoke, to which the collars of the two inner horses are harnessed. Straps are suspended from the yoke to the top of the chariot frame for added stability.

The two wheels are lightly built with four spokes which narrow towards a rim sheathed in metal. Above the axle is a wooden platform with a footboard at the back and a flimsy superstructure of bent wood and wicker towards the front, rising to provide a handrail. Chariots are usually brightly painted, and often decorated with sheet bronze cladding and finials, sometimes inlaid with silver.

The inner horses (*zugioi*) are harnessed directly to the yoke, but the outer ones (*seiraphoroi*) are trace horses. All four have reins attached by bit or noseband. Unlike war chariots, which require both driver and warrior, racing chariots are designed for speed alone and therefore have a single charioteer. He wears an ankle-length *chiton* with a broad band around the waist and ties elsewhere to minimise wind resistance. Though equipped with a crop, he has little opportunity to use it, for he must manage four sets of reins with split-second finesse. To prevent him losing the reins, the charioteer fastens all the ends to his waistband. He then operates them as two sets, one in his right hand, one in his left.

When all have taken their places, the Judge gives a signal, the Trumpeter sounds the start, and an official triggers the complex mechanism that drops the gates in careful sequence. First to move are the horses in the outer lanes, then those next to them, and so on as the staggered start works its way towards the centre of the field. Finally, all the competitors are in motion. Clouds of dust swirl across the track amid the thudding of hooves and rattle of chariots. Roars of encouragement from the banks swell into an ear-splitting cacophony, and trumpet blasts ring out periodically above the racket to signal the laps.

The race, fast and long, a high-speed chase over some eight miles in all, is exceptionally demanding of the stamina of horses, the skill of charioteers, and the fortune bestowed by the gods. Animals froth and steam, and are soon drenched in sweat. Spokes disappear in the whirl of wheels. Charioteers grip their reins in clenched fists, tugging and easing as they struggle to swerve, to overtake, to get ahead.

Each turn of the *kampter* is a crisis. The track has no central spine and no lanes. There is nothing but the turning-posts at either end. Here, the skill is to minimise distance by turning close to the post, pulling in the left trace-horse, giving the right its head. But the tighter the turn, the greater the risk of hitting the post. And as others bunch to attempt the same, the close proximity of fragile vehicles moving at high speed makes collision likely.

Disaster, when it strikes, is rarely deliberate. The likelihood is that any vehicle used as a ram will itself be destroyed in the resulting crash. Cutting in ahead of another vehicle is banned by the rules, and the Judges watch carefully for fouls at the turning-posts. Dangerous driving of any kind is resented. Even so, there is a premium on risk-taking, the line between panache and penalty is hazy at best, and the stakes are very high. So do not expect chivalry at the turning-posts.

As the field spreads out, most eyes stay fixed on the turn, the crowd eager to witness the smashes. We are all the same – all fascinated by disaster and a mangled body. This is one reason that the charioteers are often slaves. If not, they are likely to be highly-paid professionals. For wealthy citizens to compete in person is generally considered too risky, though there are exceptions: owners who crave the excitement and the added lustre of personal participation.

Many in the crowd, by the way, as well as taking a voyeuristic interest in disaster, seem to take a grim pleasure in seeing aristocratic *hauteur* brought low in chariot crashes. After all, few of the spectators will earn the cost of a chariot-racing team in a lifetime of hard work. Equally appealing is to witness the failure of teams entered by dictators and oligarchs. Expect enthusiastic cheering if any of Dionysios of Syracuse's teams comes to grief.

If a wheel snarls at speed, it will splinter into fragments in seconds, collapsing the cart and pitching the charioteer forwards. Some can be thrown under their own horses' hooves, some impaled on the wreckage of the vehicle. Others become entangled in the reins and are dragged down the track, or are thrown clear of their own vehicle only to be trampled by another. As often as not, one collision leads to another, and a multiple pile-up can leave the track strewn with loose horses, capsized chariots, and bruised and bloody bodies. The most famous case occurred at the Pythian Games in 462 BC, when the winning chariot of King Arkesilas of Kyrene was the only one in a field of forty-one entrants to complete the course.

For sheer spectacle, the Olympic chariot-race is unbeatable. A high-speed chase with acute risk of crashes, pile-ups and battered bodies, it always has the crowd hyper-charged with excitement. From start to finish, the banks sway and echo with the curses and groans, the cheers and shouts, the furious bickering, and the wild leaps and gesticulations of tens of thousands of rival fans. Finally, as the victor crosses the line, expect a surge from the banks onto the track as the mob races forwards to pelt the new champion with flowers and leafy twigs.[8]

THE HORSEBACK RACE (*KELES*)

Date of introduction: 648 BC
Distance: one lap or six *stadia* (3,600ft)

Next up at the Hippodrome is the Olympic horseback race, a wild charge once up and once down the track: a distance of about two-thirds of a mile. The jockeys are trained

THE KYNISKA SCANDAL

The equestrian events provide the only opportunities for women to compete in the Games – and only because these events do not require personal participation or even attendance at the festival. The most famous recent example of a female 'sports-star' is Kyniska of Sparta.

After Sparta was readmitted to the Games in 396 BC (see pp. 156–7), their attempt to re-establish their equestrian supremacy was led by Kyniska, the sister of King Agesilaos. Her team was victorious in both 396 and 392 BC. Her motives for entering the Olympic fray are as enigmatic as whether it was really she, or a coterie of her male relatives with their own

agendas, that directed Sparta to equestrian victory.

Opinion is divided. Some say Kyniska was just a sports enthusiast from a posh horsey background ambitious to win Olympic glory. Some also detect a note of Spartan feminism in the proud inscription beneath her victory monument of bronze horses in the Santuary: 'Kings of Sparta were my fathers and brothers. Kyniska, victorious at the chariot-race with her swift-footed horses, erected this statue. I assert that I am the only woman in all Greece who won this crown.'

Another view holds that Kyniska was put up to it by her male relatives in an elaborate

boys, usually slaves, and
they ride naked, bareback
and without stirrups. Reins
attached to a bit are the
only tack. The jockeys also
carry riding crops.

For the young jockeys,
simply staying on the horse
is achievement enough.
They hook their legs and
squeeze them tight against
the flanks of their mounts, trying to hold their buttocks
wedged across the animal's spine, their upper bodies in

scheme to discredit the Olympics, driven by political resentment and sexual scandal. During the recent ban on Spartan participation at Olympia, arch-rival Athens was able to romp to victory in the chariot-race of 416 BC. The champion, Alkiblades, defected from Athens to Sparta soon after, but did nothing to endear himself to his new Spartan allies, seducing the wife of their king and subsequently returning to his motherland to resume service in the war against Sparta. Alkibiades was murdered in Phrygia, Asia Minor, in 404 BC, and the finger of blame points towards the Spartan king. Thoroughly dishonoured by the famous Athenian playboy, he certainly has a motive.

Unsurprisingly, tainted by an Olympic ban, the triumph of a rival, and the cuckolding of a king, chariot-racing appears to have lost something of its lustre at Sparta. Consequently, as some commentators have it, King Agesilaos 'wanted to show the Greeks that an equestrian victory was the result of wealth and expenditure, not in any way the result of excellence'. In this light, Kyniska was merely a female pawn in a devious interstate and interpersonal game, her role — dictated by her male superiors — nothing less than the emasculation of the Olympic chariot-race.

If this were indeed their intention, you may conclude from the undiminished popularity of the race a few years on that they have not been successful.[9]

27. An archaic bronze figurine of a rider, probably a jockey, since he lacks the arms and armour of a warrior.

wild motion, swinging and leaning, pulling at the reins, flailing with the whip.

The race is fast and furious. Fouls are punished by floggings, and the Judges watch especially at the turning-post, where crowding affords opportunities to shove, lash or unseat a rival. The Judges' job is unenviable: the speed of the race, the clouds of dust, and the chaos at the turn make for close calls.

For a jockey to lose his seat is exceptionally hazardous. Boys have been trampled to death or suffered crippling injuries in the Olympic horseback race. Frequent falls during years of hard riding to reach Olympic standard are also responsible for much long-term damage. This is one reason that the jockeys are almost always slaves. Whereas chariot-racing is quintessentially aristocratic, horse-racing lacks good Homeric precedent: in this case, the risks inherent in participation carry little reward for the high-born. The grim truth is that jockeys are expendable. It is the horse that matters, and the owner who will get the crown; the winning jockey must make do with a ribbon. In the Games of 512 BC, a mare named *Aula* ('Breeze') threw her rider at the outset, but, well trained, completed the race and came in first, winning for her owner, Pheidolas of Corinth, the olive crown.

Often enough, getting ahead at the first turn can prove decisive, but with so many competitors and a high chance of mishap, it is rare for any race not to be open down to the final moments. So expect the cheering and shouting to reach a crescendo as they come to the finishing line.

It is all over in a couple of minutes. But what minutes! It is the short distance that energises the race, making it a heart-stopping flash of sweat, dust and fury, an unforgettable test of lightning speed.[10]

THE TWO-HORSE CHARIOT-RACE
(*SUNORIS*)

Date of introduction: 408 BC
Distance: eight laps or forty-eight *stadia* (28,800ft)

The morning of the second day ends with a relatively new addition to the programme: the two-horse chariot-race. It is perhaps curious that this is such a recent addition. Four-horse chariots have only ever been used for racing, whereas the two-horse chariot was widely used in war in Homer's time. Yet it was only twenty years ago, two or three centuries after it became militarily obsolete, that it made its first appearance at the Olympics.

There is little to be added here to what has already been said about the four-horse race. Apart from the size of the teams, and the somewhat shorter distance over which the race is run, the *sunoris* is very similar to the *tethrippon*.[11]

OLD NESTOR'S CHARIOT-RACING TIPS

Old Nestor, an ageing but revered hero in Homer's *Iliad*,
gave this advice to his son Archilochus before the chariot-race
at the funeral games of Patroklos.

✳ 'It is by skill that charioteer beats charioteer. The driver who relies only on his horses and chariot is careless at the turn and wheels wide this way or that, and his horses wander on the straight, without control.'

✳ 'If a man has cunning, even though he is driving inferior horses, he always keeps his eye on the post and turns right, and does not miss the proper use of ox-hide reins to stretch his horses from the start, but drives them on unswervingly, and keeps close watch on the leader.'

✳ 'You must cut in very close as you drive your chariot and pair around the post, and let your body, where you stand on the well-sprung platform, lean a little to the left of the horses.'

✳ 'Goad your right-hand horse and shout him on, and make sure your hands give him rein: and have your left horse cut close into the post, so that the nave of your well-built wheel seems to be just touching it – but be careful not to hit the stone, or you will damage your horses and smash the chariot, and that would delight the others and bring shame on you.'

✳ 'If you can pass them at the turning-post as you come up behind them, then there is no-one who could close the distance to catch you or overtake you.'[12]

DAY 2, AFTERNOON

THE PENTATHLON
Date of introduction: 708 BC
Events (in order of performance): discus,
long jump, javelin, short sprint and wrestling

All equestrian events are completed during the morning
of the second day. After lunch (see pp. 21ff), everyone
reassembles in the Stadium for the five separate events of
the pentathlon.

Like the equestrian events, though to a lesser degree, the
pentathlon has an aristocratic flavour. To be accomplished
in five sports, and outstanding in at least three, requires
an exceptional level of training, and therefore greater
investment of time and money. General athleticism is also
the Homeric ideal: the true noble is an all-rounder, a man

28. Three of the five events comprising the pentathlon, showing, from
left to right, athletes preparing for long jump, javelin, discus, and again
javelin.

excellent in all respects, unlike the low-born specialist (see p. 219). The pentathlete is also more likely than specialist athletes to conform to the Polykleitian ideal of balance, proportion, and male beauty; and this, too, is considered an aristocratic virtue (see pp. 166ff). Perhaps it is their common elitist character that explains the fact that both the equestrian events and the pentathlon are held on the same day and ahead of the foot-races and combat sports.

The five events of the Olympic pentathlon include two (the short sprint and the wrestling) that also feature as separate events in their own right. Your guide to these therefore appears under the appropriate heading below (see pp. 225ff and 228ff respectively). Here, we deal only with the three events peculiar to the pentathlon: discus, long jump and javelin.

Though achievement in these sub-events depends much on muscular power, it is also a matter of rhythm, timing and good measure. Because of this, a pipe-player stands beside the starting line, and as the crowd falls silent in anticipation of each athlete's performance, you will catch the whistling of the pipes on the wind. By a curious arrangement, the origins of which are forgotten, the official Olympic pipe-player is always the most recent victor of the pipe-playing contest at Pythia. You can see the honorary relief-sculpture of the most famous of these champion pipe-players, one Pythokritos of Sikyon, who won six times running at Delphi (574–54 BC), in the Sanctuary.

Mishaps are common in the pentathlon. To ensure that each athlete has the opportunity to display his true prowess, his score for both throws and the jump is given by the best of three attempts.[13]

THE DISCUS

Athletes use stone, iron and bronze discuses (*diskoi*), but for the Olympic competition they are required to use the three bronze discuses kept specially for the occasion and traditionally stored in the Treasury of the Sikyonians. A standard Greek discus is about 20cm in diameter and weighs about 2.5kg, but precise sizes vary. The three Olympic discuses are no exception. In this event, each competitor throws each discus just once.

The athlete stands on the track behind the *balbis*; he must not step over the front groove during his throw. As he waits, he limbers up, and shifts the discus from hand to hand, feeling for the most comfortable fit.

29. A bronze discus as used by a Greek pentathlete. Thrown by Exoidas when he won a contest, it was inscribed and dedicated to Castor and Pollux, the twin sons of Zeus.

When he moves forward to take position, he puts his weight on his right rear leg, and holds the discus vertical at head level, resting it in his left hand, gripping the top edge with his right. Then he folds his body back and down; the right hand takes the discus, the right arm swings backwards, and the body twists around with it, like a corkscrew, the weight still resting on the right leg.

As the throw begins, he whirls back in the opposite direction, shifting the weight to the left leg, which provides extra thrust as body and right arm extend to cast the discus forwards. It is all done in a single flowing movement. Powered by torsion and propulsion, the bronze object spins through the air and lands around a third of the way down the Stadium track, to the gasps and cheers of the crowd. Once all three discuses have landed, an official moves forward to mark the athlete's furthest cast with a distinctive wooden peg. The discuses are then brought back down the track for the use of the next competitor. The athlete who achieves the longest single cast wins the discus.

A word of warning in relation to the discus. There are no nets in the Stadium, and it has been known for the discus to miscarry and kill a bystander. You are advised to stay alert.[14]

THE LONG JUMP

For the second event, the long jump, an area of ground in front of the Judges' box is specially prepared. The arrangements include a *bater*, from which the actual jump is made, and a *skamma*, where the earth has been loosened to soften landings using picks, rakes and water.

At his turn, the athlete advances to the *bater* carrying a jumping weight (*halter*) in each hand. The simplest weights are spherical, made of stone, and carved with a seat for the hand and a finger-hole for enhanced grip. But weights can also be made of lead or bronze, and the form can be more elaborate, with cylindrical, elongated and curving varieties. *Halteres* weigh between 1.5-2.5kg, and their purpose is to increase the momentum of the jump and therefore the distance.

30. Two lead jumping-weights of the kind used by Greek pentathletes in the long jump.

Jumping weights are prized personal possessions – every athlete uses his own special pair – and for this reason they have become the trademark attribute of the pentathlete. Many inscribe their names on their weights, and some can think of nothing more precious to offer up to Zeus in thanks for victory.

31. A long-jumper in motion.

The EOC does not attempt to regulate weights. There is no need: the matter is self-regulating. Too light, and they are ineffective; too heavy, and they weigh the athlete down. Every pentathlete knows that there is an optimum size for his *halteres*.

The pentathlete leans back, bracing himself on his right leg, extending his left forwards, and holding his arms outstretched with a weight in each hand. The muscles tense. He rocks to the music. Then, he bursts into a run, gathering speed and momentum as he goes, until he launches himself into the air, weighted arms thrown out in front, legs folding against buttocks beneath. For a moment, he seems to fly. The legs open and thrust forwards, reaching into the distance, pulled there by the weighted arms. Finally, coming in to land, the arms swing back, the weights are cast away, the feet crash to earth, and arms and torso catapult forwards to complete the jump.

An official comes forward to mark the distance with a peg. After two more jumps, the next competitor, who has been standing by and warming up, steps forwards to the *bater*.[15]

THE JAVELIN

The javelin (*akon*) used in sport is not to be confused with the military thrusting-spear, which has a broad blade of iron with a sharp point and razor-like edges. The *akon* is a throwing-spear – similar to the weapons used by some light infantry – and is aerodynamically designed. It comprises a long thin shaft of elder wood, perhaps 1.9m in length and 3 or 4cm in diameter, and a small bronze pyramidal head.

Preparing for his cast, the athlete winds a thin leather thong (*ankule*) around the middle of the javelin, the centre of gravity, where it is sometimes slightly thickened. The end of the thong is looped, and the athlete holds the javelin by gripping the shaft with two fingers and thumb, and placing his other two fingers in the loop of the thong. During the throw, the loop provides leverage, the thong as a whole acts like a sling, and the twist it imparts to the javelin has a rifling effect, causing it to spin and fly straighter.

32. The iron head of a javelin used by a pentathlete.

The *ankule* can add at least five per cent to the distance of a throw. More importantly perhaps, it helps ensure that the javelin travels true and pitches into the ground when it lands; otherwise, it leaves no mark for measurement, and the throw must be discounted. But the *ankule* is fiddly and demands skilful handling. Consequently, pentathletes take the greatest care when wrapping before a throw. You will see each competitor loop the centre of the thong around a big toe, place the loose ends on the centre of the javelin shaft, and then roll downwards to cover the loose ends and wrap round the two arms of the thong. Once wrapped, to keep the *ankule* taut and prevent it unravelling, the athlete holds the point of the javelin in his left hand, and pulls back on the loop with his right. He is ready.

As the crowd falls silent and holds its breath, you will hear again the whistle of the pipes. The athlete pounds forward towards the *balbis*, gathering speed as he goes, still gripping the javelin tip with his left hand, keeping it level with his ear. As he reaches the casting line, the left arm is flung forwards, the right arm pulls the javelin backwards and downwards, tipping it to thirty degrees, and the right leg flexes, taking the body's weight, poised like a spring. Then, in a single flowing sequence of movement, the body swings from left to right, the javelin flashes forwards, the *ankule* drops away, and the athlete hops to a halt, taking care not to cross the *balbis*. The javelin spins upwards and away, arcing through the air, before dropping into the track halfway down its length.

As with the discus and the long jump, the only criterion of victory is distance, and, as before, each competitor's achievement is marked by an official.[16]

The winner of the pentathlon is the competitor who shows himself to be supreme in at least three of the five sub-events. The contest proceeds by elimination. At the end of the first three sub-events – discus, long jump and javelin – if any athlete is the victor in all three, he is immediately declared the overall winner. Otherwise, athletes without any victories are eliminated, since they could not now win the contest, leaving only two or three competitors. If the short sprint does not then produce an overall winner, one or more wrestling bouts decide the outcome. In this way, the pentathlon can be either something of an anticlimax, or it can build to a brutal finish.

In either case, there will be a crescendo of shouting and cheering as the new champion triumphs. Then, the Trumpeter blasts for silence, the Herald formally announces the victor, and a Judge ties a woollen ribbon around the victor's head. Finally, he runs his victory lap around the Stadium, and the crowd surges around him, cheering again, and throwing up showers of flowers and ribbons.[17]

ODYSSEUS
AND THE PENTATHLETIC IDEAL

If the pentathlon is the contest for the aristocratic all-rounder, Odysseus is one of mythology's leading role-models.

During his long journey home from Troy to Ithaca, he visited the mythological Phaiakians and watched their games. At first he declined an invitation to participate, but one of the young bloods, Euryalos, responded by throwing doubt on his aristocratic status: 'No, stranger, for I do not see you are like one versed in contests . . . but rather like one who plies his ways in a many-locked vessel, master over mariners who are also men of business, a man who, careful of his cargo and grasping for profits, goes carefully on his way. You do not resemble an athlete.'

A profiteering merchant? What insult! His caste in question, his anger stirred, Odysseus rose to the challenge. He took up the discus and cast it beyond the mark of any of the Phaiakians' throws. Then he

rounded on the impudent youth: 'Now reach me that mark, young man, and then I will make another throw, as great as this . . . or one even better. Let any of the rest, whose heart and spirit are urgent for it, come up and try me, since you have irritated me so, either at boxing or wrestling or in a foot-race . . . I am not bad in any of the contests where men strive. I know well how to handle the polished bow . . . I can throw with the spear as far as another casts with an arrow.'

There was an awed silence, followed by fulsome contrition. The point was sufficiently made: Odysseus was an athlete, an all-rounder, and therefore unquestionably an aristocrat. Time-worn and travel-weary, anxious to be off and headed for home, he was disinclined to do more, and nor needed he, having proved his excellence and noble birth. Henceforth his hosts treated him with due honour and respect.[18]

DAY 2, EVENING

The second day's contests may be over, but not its rituals. It is high summer and this day is always the eve of the full moon. You may now wish to join the holy procession through the Sanctuary to the Shrine of Pelops, located between the Temples of Zeus and Hera, where a black ram will be sacrificed to the heroic founder of the Games (see pp. 90-3).

As dusk descends on a long, hot, electrifying day, the Olympic Village fills with flaming lamps and sounds of revelry. Expect it to continue into the early hours and even until dawn, as the victors and their friends and supporters celebrate the day's triumphs. The equestrian parties, in particular, can be lavish. Men still talk of the bash thrown by Alkibiades the Athenian in 416 BC, when his chariot won the *tethrippon*; he borrowed all the state's official golden vessels and pretended they were his in order to impress his guests. And people still relate the story from an earlier age of Empedokles of Akragas, a vegetarian discipline of Pythagoras (see pp. 175-7), who had an ox of dough made, garnished with costly herbs and spices, and distributed it among the spectators.[19]

DAY 3

THE FESTIVAL OF ZEUS

Everyone will be exhausted this morning. Many of those who attended parties will have got drunk and retired late, and probably will not arise before midday. Those who did not will have struggled to sleep with the racket of the revellers breaking the stillness of the night.

Fortunately, there are no contests, and you can afford to take it easy. It is the day after the full moon, and therefore the day reserved for the rites of Zeus.

33. A sacrifice at an altar. The figure on the left is pouring a libation from a wine-cup. A bull's head is roasting in the fire. Two young men wearing wreaths carry joints of meat on spits. A musician plays the pipes on the right.

Around mid-morning the procession assembles at the Committee Room, with the Priests, Judges and other Olympic officials near the front, and the athletes close behind. All athletes are pilgrims, so whatever their condition on the morning after the night before, their attendance now is obligatory. Spectators may either join the rear of the procession or seek a place to watch along its route.

Next come the ambassadors of the city-states, parading the rich vessels and incense-burners reserved for state occasions – like those borrowed by Alkibiades in 416 BC. Behind the VIPs come the sacrificial beasts, 100 oxen, what the Greeks call a *hekatombe*, the number required in holy rites of the highest importance.

A small army of herdsmen and butchers leads the beasts to the altar. They are garlanded with flowers and ribbons. After the procession has meandered its way past all the major shrines in the Sanctuary, it arrives at the Altar of Zeus (see pp. 65-6), where the Priests deploy themselves to receive their victims.

One by one, amid mounting panic and bellowing, the oxen are led forwards to have their throats slit. Jets of blood spray across the worshippers. The dying hulks of the beasts flop to the ground, heaving and quivering, great black pools spreading outwards across the ground. The butchers are already at work, hacking with axes, chopping with knives.

The fat thighs are cut away first, for these are Zeus's portion. The dripping lumps are passed up the sides of the altar, a milky-grey heap of ash debris several centuries old and now several metres high. The Priests at the top, drenched in blood and smeared grey and black by the fire at the top of the altar, give each lump reverentially to the flames. These soar and spit with each addition as the fat boils. Fresh smoke billows upwards. God is getting his share.

The rest of the meat is cut up and carted away, to be roasted by the Olympic cooks for the official evening banquet. This takes places in the Committee Room, and it is an exclusive event dominated by EOC officials. But there is far more meat than they can consume, so much, in fact, that there should be a small portion for all who want it. If supplemented with bread, vegetables, wine and sweets purchased from petty-traders in the Olympic Village, you may have your own feast.

But getting your portion can be a challenge. Expect chaotic scenes around dusk. This may be a day of solemn ritual, but thousands of Greeks pushing and shoving around an open-air kitchen for free meat at dinner-time is not a pretty sight.[20]

DAY 4, MORNING

THE MIDDLE-DISTANCE RUN (*DOLICHOS*)

Date of introduction: 720 BC
Distance: ten laps or twenty *stadia* (12,000ft)

The fourth day of the Games is as busy as the second. The trumpet blast announcing the first of the contests rings out early, and many join the rush to secure decent vantage-points in the Stadium for a good view of the foot-races. Others may be slower. The first race is something of a warm-up for spectators, and many will still be shuffling in after the previous day's partying as it begins. Perhaps you will find yourself among them.

Do not delay too long. The Stadium is much smaller than the Hippodrome, with space for only about 40,000 spectators. Latecomers risk seeing nothing.

Once the purple-robed Judges have taken their seats in the box, the Trumpeter calls for silence, the Herald announces the event and then, as the athletes troop onto the track one by one, he dutifully gives the name, patronymic and city of each. Cheers rise from different sections of the Stadium, where patriotic fans are ranged in their city-groups, as each athlete is identified.

It is a moment of transition. Passing from the sacred space of the Sanctuary, through the shade of the tented changing-area behind the Stadium, the athletes, their naked brown bodies gleaming with oil, emerge into brilliant sunlight and instant fame as they are acclaimed by tens of thousands of their fellow Greeks. Many will be veterans, but for some this will be their first Olympic appearance – the first unequivocal affirmation that they are among the supermen at the summit of athletic achievement. Life has become unreal. Divinity seems within reach.

The *dolichos*, a middle-distance run, lacks the frenzied urgency of the two sprint races to follow. The athletes have to pace themselves, so they jog along with knees low and arms close to their sides, their limbs swinging gently in a relaxed-looking gait. On the other hand, they must not fall behind; those who do will probably never close the gap.

For the *dolichos*, a ten-lap race, two turning-posts are required, one at either end of the track. These are offset slightly to the right – as viewed by the oncoming competitors – to compensate for the tendency of runners to turn tight and swing wide as they bear around the post. The offset turning-posts keep the race in the centre of the track.

Barging and tripping are illegal, but sometimes hard to spot from the Judges' vantage point. Watch especially for fouls as athletes negotiate the hairpin turn at the post.

It is widely recognised that, with a single turning-post at the far end of the track, competitors placed in the middle-right of the field in the line-up at the start of the race have an advantage, being closer to the post, with those placed outer-left at particular disadvantage. No-one has come up with a satisfactory solution to this problem. The Greeks satisfy themselves with the reflection that, since position in the line-up is determined by lot, the gods take responsibility for fairness.[21]

Runners tire in a long race. Others save themselves and try to speed up over the final lap or two. Occasionally, someone will fall, maybe even injure themselves, perhaps hobbling away from the track in silent anguish. The crowd will groan, especially if it is a favourite who fails to finish or is beaten in the final rush to the line.

As the leading pack nears the end, the cheers, groans and shouting swell into a mighty roar as the fans of every runner become frantic with excitement – as if the group with the loudest bellow will secure the crown. When it ends, the noise subsides for a moment, and then swells again as thousands pour onto the track to hail the victor, while others fall to heated debate about the race.

THE SHORT SPRINT (*STADION*)

Date of introduction: 776 BC
Distance: one *stadion* (600ft)

The short sprint is the second event of the day. It is the oldest in the Olympic programme, and the victor in this race gives his name to the entire festival – becoming, in effect, part of the Greek calendar (see p. 11).

The presiding Judge calls the athletes to the starting positions. There is space for up to twenty runners across the 30m width of the track. Once every athlete has taken his place in the line-up, the noise of the crowd dies away. Tens of thousands of souls, standing under the mid-morning sun of a Greek summer, are united in tense anticipation.

The Judge's voice rings out across the Stadium: *Poda para poda!* ('Foot by foot!'). The sprinters move forwards to take their places on the *balbis*, left foot slightly forwards with toes hooked over the front of the stone, right foot set back with toes in the groove. They lean forwards with arms outstretched.  Many athletes might prefer a four-point start with hands resting on the ground, but this is illegal under Olympic rules: all must run from a standing start.

False starts are possible, even likely, in a crowded field of hyped-up superstars. The EOC has explored installing wooden hurdles with waist-high horizontal bars in front of each competitor, but no-one has yet come up with a satisfactory design for a reliable mechanism of ropes and pulleys to drop the gates. Fear of a flogging is, however, a serious deterrent, not least because of its likely effect on athletic performance.

The athletes being correctly positioned and ready, the Judge shouts again: *Apite!* ('Go!').

It is all over so quickly. The race is decided in barely twenty-five seconds of furious pounding, with high-kicking knees and punching arms all working like pistons. Such is the frenzy that the close-packed runners sometimes collide. A stumble is the sprinter's greatest fear. With not a second to spare, it guarantees defeat. Every runner knows the story of Ajax, who was beaten by Odysseus in the foot-race at the funeral games of Patroklos because he tripped and fell, ending up with a mouthful of dung.

At the far end, Judges are ready at the finishing-line, where another grooved stone fixed across the track demarcates the line the winning athlete must cross ahead of his rivals to secure the crown. Their task is unenviable. In any full field, the outcome is likely to be close; there may be no more than a split-second between first and second places, and the Judges must make the call before the critical gaze of tens of thousands.

Before you have had time to catch breath, a new Olympic champion, beribboned and waving a palm branch aloft, will be doing a victory lap through a surging crowd of admirers.[22]

THE LONG SPRINT (*DIAULOS*)
Date of introduction: 724 BC
Distance: one lap or two *stadia* (1,200ft)

The *diaulos* ('double-pipe') is similar to the *stadion* race, except that a doubling of the distance introduces the complication of a turn. To facilitate this, a line of wooden turning-posts corresponding to the number of competitors is erected along the *balbis* at the far end of the track. There is less chance of a pile-up, though athletes have been known to come undone at the post, crashing off the course.[23]

THE HERMES BOOST

Zeus and Hera may be the principal deities worshipped in the Olympic Sanctuary. Zeus may be the divine recipient of the *hekatombe* on the third day. But it is Hermes and Herakles who are most often called upon for assistance in the Olympic Stadium.

Multitasking is characteristic of all Greek gods. Hermes is the rustic god of herdsmen, and his son, Pan, is the god of shepherds. Hermes is also the god of merchants and of thieves (an interesting conflation of roles). But he is best-known as messenger of the gods, appointed such by Zeus himself, a role that requires frequent travel between Olympos, Earth and the Underworld.

Consequently, he is commonly portrayed as the well-equipped traveller, wearing sun-hat, cloak and boots, often with the handy addition of wings on either headgear or footwear. His snake-entwined magic wand gives him access to secret places. A god of travel, then; and also — such are the demands on his time — by necessity, a god of speed.

It is for this reason that he is honoured by runners and pentathletes. Panting competitors pounding the track will call on him for an extra, final, winning burst of speed. During the festival, the Herms of Olympia — square pillars with erect phalluses surmounted by heads of the deity — are especially venerated. You will see them festooned with garlands and ribbons, and athletes standing before them offering prayers of supplication or thanks.[24]

DAY 4, AFTERNOON

THE WRESTLING (*PALE*)

Date of introduction: 708 BC

The three 'heavy events' that take place on the afternoon of the fourth day are the most popular of all. These are the combat sports of wrestling, boxing and the virtually no-holds-barred *pankration*.

There is no ring, but there are officials on hand to ensure that a combat event does not degenerate into the comedy of a chase around the Stadium. The officials are equipped with a long rod, called a *klimax*, which they hold horizontally to act as an improvised bar if necessary. And, of course, to run away is an offence likely to result in a flogging: the spectators have come to see a fight, not a race, and the Judges aim to ensure that is what they get. *Klimax* and

34 and 35. Two wrestlers exercising in the gymnasium under the eye of a trainer, executing different moves: the 'flying mare' (above) and the 'body hold' (right).

whip restrict the competitors to the *skamma* and secure a gruelling close-quarters fight.

There might be several contests, depending on how many men have qualified in the month-long ordeal of training and selection at Elis. The bouts have already been arranged by the drawing of lots on the first day of the Games (see pp. 197-8). There are no weight classifications in any of the combat sports, so wrestlers, boxers and pankratiasts are invariably mountainous. The feet of Lygdamis of Syracuse, the first Olympic *pankration* winner, are said to have been a cubit (around 45cm) long.

The Olympics recognises two forms of wrestling. The *pankration* (see pp. 236ff) is an especially brutal form of mixed upright and ground wrestling, whereas the *pale* is upright wrestling, where the aim is to stay on your feet and bring the other man down. In Olympic terms, Herakles was really a pankratiast rather than a wrestler. The pictures of his fights show him rolling on the ground as often as standing on his feet. It is Theseus, among the mythic heroes, who is the true wrestler Olympic-style.

Because there are no weight limits, big men have the

advantage, but skill – nifty footwork, a distracting move, a sudden lunge, an efficient body-lock – can sometimes make the difference. Before each bout begins, the presiding Judge, brandishing his rod for good effect, reminds the contestants of the rules.

Each pair comes forward to a roar from the crowd. The wrestlers face each other, completely naked, tree-trunk legs planted, shoulders and arms bulging over barrel chests, heads thrust forward on bull-like necks: these are men swollen by high-protein diets and years of pounding physical exertion. Hair is shaven or close-cropped, or perhaps a leather skull-cap is worn, denying opponents an

SPORTING LEGENDS: MILON THE WRESTLER
(Kroton, Calabria, southern Italy)

Following victory in the boys' wrestling at Olympia in 536 BC, Milon of Kroton had one of the most illustrious careers in Greek sporting history. He won thirty victories on the Panhellenic circuit, including five olive crowns at Olympia.

On at least one occasion, such was Milon's reputation that no opponent would face him, and he therefore won the Olympic title 'without touching the dust'. Embarrassingly, Milon, who used to boast that he was never brought to his knees, slipped on this occasion on his way to collect the crown. The crowd joked that he should not win since he had fallen down all by himself. Milon shouted back that it was not the third fall, only the first, and challenged anyone to throw him the other two times.

Milon was finally defeated at his sixth attempt at the Olympic title in 512 BC, when, at the age of forty, he faced a young exponent (from his own city of Kroton) of the new 'high-handed' technique, which minimised the advantage conferred by Milo's legendary size and strength. Even so, the crowd raised the Olympic veteran onto its shoulders and cheered him around the Stadium.

easy hold. Bodies are coated in dust and dirt, glued on by the layer of oil beneath. The rule is that bodies have to be grippable, though some contestants have been known to run an oil-smeared hand over shoulder and thigh at the last minute.

Of chivalry, there is none. Instead, in the initial squaring up, there is psychological warfare. Opponents glare and snarl, trading insults, sneers and boasts, and the crowd joins in, identifying the better-known contestants by their nicknames – 'the Bear', 'the Lion', 'the Eagle' – while loudly comparing rival physiques and shouting out their allegiances.

Milon is said to have carried his own statue into the Sanctuary of Zeus at Olympia, to have borne a four-year-old bull around the Stadium on his shoulders, and to have stood on a greased discus and dared anyone to rush at him and try to knock him off. His appetite was prodigious: he would consume twenty pounds of meat, twenty pounds of bread, and eight quarts of wine at a sitting. It is said that he could snap a cord tied around his head by holding his breath to make his veins swell.

He always boasted proudly of his prowess: he is, for example, said to have entered battle against the neighbouring city of Sybaris in 510 BC wearing not only his Olympic crowns, but also dressed as the mythic wrestling hero Herakles, with a lion-skin cloak and wooden club.

Milon's brawn was formidable, but lack of brain may have been the death of him. They say he was killed by wild beasts. While walking in the countryside of his native Kroton, he happened upon a dried-up tree trunk into which wedges had been driven ready to split it. Milon decided to attempt the feat with his bare hands, but the wedges sprang out, the wood closed on his fingers, and he was held trapped, eventually to be gnawed to death by a pack of wolves.[26]

Then it begins, the wrestlers moving together, heads down, arms locking. 'Their backs creaked under the strain of their strong intertwined arms,' says Homer of such a contest between the heroes Ajax and Odysseus. 'Sweat poured down their bodies, and bloody welts rose up on their shoulders and ribs.'

The rules are simple. The aim is to throw the opponent. Holds have to be above the waist, except that foot-trips are permitted; punching, kicking and gouging are definitely banned, and there is a specific rule forbidding the deliberate breaking of fingers. Well-matched opponents circle, lunge, grapple, and then part again, pouring sweat and gasping for air in the hot dry dust, chests pounding.

Each man probes for an opening for one of the standard grips and a chance to throw, seeking to grasp his opponent's arm, neck or torso. But each knows the moves and how to parry. Among the most spectacular is the 'flying mare', when a wrestler grabs his opponent's arm, turns in an instant, crouches down, and then heaves him over his shoulder so that he crashes down on his back. Or the 'body hold', in which a wrestler grasps his opponent round the waist in a bear-hug, lifts him off the ground, and then either hurls him through the air – if possible, head-first – or smashes him to the ground with maximum force.

The flying mare and the body hold are the bull-like methods of big, heavy men. Lighter men – 'Lions' rather than 'Bears' – hope to win by speed, agility and footwork. Traditionalists hold such 'arms-length' methods – dubbed *akrocheirismos* or 'high-handedness' – in contempt. But if they bring a hulk crashing down in sand and dust, they secure victory just as surely.

A bout ends whenever a fall is declared – defined as a contestant touching the ground with hip, back or shoulders – and three falls secure victory.

The victors – the 'treblers' – progress immediately to the next round. The final therefore tends to be a contest between two exhausted men, and as much a test of stamina as of strength and skill. And luck. A wrestler who has been drawn against weak opponents in the heats will have an advantage in the final against an opponent whose energy has been drained by hard contests. But there can be no argument: instant disqualification is the penalty for questioning the rules – especially as it is Zeus himself who manages the lots.[25]

THE BOXING (*PUGMACHIA*)
Date of introduction: 688 BC

Next up is the boxing, the most lethal of the Olympic combat sports. Padded gloves are used in training, but not in contests. Instead of gloves, boxers wear 4m-long leather thongs softened with oil or animal fat, which are wound tightly around hands and wrists, leaving only the fingers free, and secured using a loop at each end. The fingers are left free so that they can be clenched to punch or opened to parry.

The purpose of the thongs is to protect the hands of the wearer (fancy versions are lined with fleece). They do nothing to soften the blow to the victim; on the contrary, they often result in severe cuts. Though the technical name for them is *himantes,* they are nicknamed *murmikes* ('ants') because of the stinging wounds they inflict.

Wearing nothing but their *himantes* and sometimes fleece armbands to wipe away sweat, the contestants advance at one another with murderous looks and touch fists. There is no bonhomie, no friendly banter, no gentlemanly handshakes.

Once the Judge has ordered the start, the struggle is relentless: with neither ropes to which a contestant can cling for safety, nor intervals between rounds for respite, a Greek boxing contest is a single brutal slugging match that continues until one man is either knocked insensible or offers his submission by raising the middle finger of his right hand. The rules ban blows to the body – the head is the sole legitimate target – and they place no restriction on relentless pummelling, even when a man is knocked to the ground. The only real restriction is that gripping an opponent – to hold him so he can be battered – is illegal.

Boxers dance warily around one another, fists raised close to the head, ready to parry sudden blows. 'They faced each other and put up their massive fists together,' says Homer of the fight between Epeios and Euryalos at the funeral games of Patroklos, 'then fell to, and there was a flurry of heavy hands meeting. There sounded a fearful crunching of jaws, and the sweat poured all over their bodies.'

Some aim to tire a heavier opponent in a long fight, until his reactions slow and his guard slips. There are even boxers who boast that their faces are unscarred, such is their success with these tactics. Others, sure of the weight of their punch, seek opportunities to attack from the outset.

Almost any type of blow except gouging is allowed, and boxers deliver upward hooks, upper cuts, rabbit punches, blows with the side and heel of the hand, even violent jabs with hand outstretched and fingers flat. Both right and left hands are used as opportunity allows.

Fights can be long, the combatants becoming lacerated and bruised, sometimes pouring blood from noses, cheeks or brows. With the summer sun overhead, streams of sweat sting the eyes, and dust parches mouth and throat. The finalists, moreover, may have to fight like this several times before the day is out.

You will have no trouble spotting the seasoned boxers in the crowds: it is not just their massive shoulders, arms and fists that give them away, but also their facial scars, broken noses, lumpy brows and cauliflower ears. Wrestlers

36. A boxer resting after a hard fight. His leather thongs are designed to protect his fists but deliver brutal injuries to his opponent's face.

and pankratiasts can be beautiful; veteran boxers are invariably scarred and battered.

If the fight drags on without result, a tie-breaker may be announced. Each man then stands to receive his opponent's punch in turn, until one is knocked out. But this is rare, and the end can be sudden as men tire. As Homer describes it: 'Then, as Euryalos peered for an opening, god-like Epeios moved in for the punch and struck him on the cheek-bone – he did not stay on his feet long: his bright body collapsed under him where he stood ... His dear companions surrounded him, and carried him through the assembly with legs dragging, spitting out thick blood, and lolling his head to one side.'

Boxing is the bloodiest, cruellest and most violent of the Greek sports. It is not unknown for men to die, sometimes at the moment of defeat, preferring death to disgrace. Prepare yourself for a gruesome, heart-stopping, and sometimes sickening spectacle.[27]

THE *PANKRATION*

Date of introduction: 648 BC

The *pankration* (literally 'all-power event') is the top spectator sport in Greece. An all-in wrestling contest in which virtually anything is permitted, there are no rounds, so once underway, it is a relentless struggle to win by inflicting maximum pain to secure a submission. Biting and eye-gouging are banned, but not much else in this brutally violent sport. The genitals, for example, are legal targets. In prize games, the rewards for pankratiasts top

those for all other sports – not because it is more prestigious, but because of the risks and the suffering.

The groundsmen saturate the *skamma* to create an area of sticky mud known as the *keroma* ('beeswax'). Each pair of contenders at first confront one another upright, punching at the face, kicking at the groin, arms lunging and locking as they seek a grip and a chance to twist and throw. But they will soon be on the ground, their naked bodies, coated in oil and dust before the bout, becoming smeared in dirty brown slime as they heave, strain and grunt in the mire.

To the uninitiated, the *pankration* can appear little more than a primeval clash of boneheaded hulks, devoid of either skill or intelligence. To its fans, it is a highly nuanced dance of method, strength and pain. Techniques are numerous and varied. As well as kicking and punching, there are arm locks, leg twists and foot jerks.

The 'heel trick' involves seizing an opponent's foot in order to throw him and then keeping hold of it as he falls to twist it out of its socket. In the 'ladder hold', the pankratiast jumps on his opponent's back, wraps his legs around his stomach, and then locks his arms around his neck, pulling back the head, choking off the wind-pipe. In the 'stomach throw', he grabs hold of his opponent, rolls onto his back, places his feet on the man's stomach, and then catapults him into the air to land crashing against the ground, winded and quite possibly broken.

Fingers and toes are snapped, ribs cracked, shoulders dislocated, and limbs pulled from sockets. Men are held and twisted and squeezed to the point of searing agony or imminent suffocation. Endurance of pain is part of the pankratiast's craft, endurance for long enough to engineer escape from a crippling hold.

This is what the spectators come to see: the experience of pain. It is this that makes the *pankration* so popular, its champions the most revered of Olympic victors. What is it about these Greeks?

Let us recall some of the previous discussions about Greece. For all its civilisation, it is a very violent place. For sure, there is art, drama, philosophy and science; there is high culture and a world of 'good taste'. But there is also killing, pain and hatred.

The noble city of Athens – the city of Sophocles and Socrates – is at war three years out of every four. Part-time national service is universal, and men are hardened and brutalised by the exigencies of war and preparations for war. The myths demonise real and imagined enemies, and depict a world of slaughter, ethnic cleansing and murderous atrocities. The gods certainly sanction – and practise – retributive violence. Slaves are flogged, women battered, foreigners bullied.

No doubt also the homoeroticism of the *pankration* has an appeal. Many must experience a sexual frisson watching

---

SPORTING LEGENDS:
POLYDAMAS THE PANKRATIAST
(Skotoussa, Thessaly, Northern Greece)

Reputed to be 'the biggest man of his times', Polydamas of Skotoussa won the *pankration* at Olympia in 408 BC. Although he lost the Olympic title in 404 BC, his sporting triumphs were prodigious, and he is widely regarded, with Theagenes of Thasos (see pp. 158–60), as one of the two greatest pankratiasts of all time.

As with Milon of Kroton, another giant fighter (see pp. 230–1), legends have accumulated around Polydamas's name. Brought up in the shadow of Mount Olympos, he is said to have killed a huge wild lion with his bare hands, emulating the achievement of Herakles, his hero and role-model. Another story told of him is that he went into a herd of cattle and deliberately seized the most

powerful bull, grabbing it by the hind legs and holding it fast as it kicked furiously to escape. The bull got away – but such was the power of his grip that Polydamas was left clutching its hoof. He is also reported to have brought a racing-chariot to a dead halt by grabbing the back of the vehicle as it shot past.

Polydamas's strength seems to have been his undoing. He entered a cave with a group of friends to shelter from the sun on a hot summer's day. But the refuge proved unsafe, the roof cracked, and his friends fled outside. The veteran pankratiast rose to a perceived challenge and attempted to hold up the roof with his arms – and was crushed by the rock-fall.[29]

the naked hulks, glistening with oil and sweat, smeared with mud, groping and grunting, twisting their bodies into tight, intimate embraces. Not for nothing do many athletes, wrestlers and pankratiasts especially, tie a string knot around their foreskins to prevent the inconvenience of an involuntary erection during a contest.

And the sado-masochistic angle? Civilisation has its discontents – its libidinal frustrations and psychic tensions. The cost of social order is conformity, obedience, restraint and denial: a repressive psychic complex that may produce libido-charged surges of sublimated anger, hatred and violence. Perhaps the combat sports, above all the *pankration*, are catharsis for the mass neuroses of the Greeks.[28]

SPORTING LEGENDS:
ARRICHION THE PANKRATIAST
(Phigalia, Arkadia, Peloponnese)

Twice Olympic champion in the *pankration*, Arrichion of Arkadia is famous for having fought to the death to defend his crown at the Games of 564 BC. He had reached the final, but faced defeat when his opponent, using his legs to lock him in a scissor grip, began to throttle him with his hands.

Arrichion may have been on the point of surrender, but a shout from his trainer reminded him that death was preferable: 'What a noble epitaph, not to have conceded at Olympia!' The veteran pankratiast managed to grab and break one of his opponent's toes, dying of strangulation at the very moment that his opponent, crippled by pain, announced his submission.

The crowd went wild: here was the ultimate expression of the supreme Greek values of *agon* and *arete*. Arrichion had not submitted and was therefore declared the winner. The dead body was duly crowned with Olympic olive.

You can still see a statue of the champion in the marketplace if you visit his home town of Phigalia in Arkadia.[30]

THE RACE IN ARMOUR (*HOPLITODROMOS*)

Date of introduction: 520 BC

Distance: one lap or two *stadia* (1,200ft)

The race in armour is a relatively late addition to the Olympic programme. It reflects the rise of the hoplite, the citizen of moderate wealth who equips himself to fight as a heavy infantryman with bronze helmet, body armour, large round shield, long thrusting-spear and sword (see pp. 116-17). It was just thirty years after the race in armour's introduction to Olympia that an Athenian hoplite phalanx charged at Marathon and routed a Persian imperial army.

Athletes, however, do not run the race in full armour; they have a helmet, shield and sometimes greaves – and these are heavy enough. Greek helmets weigh about 1.5kg and greaves around 0.65kg a piece. They are also inconvenient, the helmet obstructing view and liable to slip, the greaves cumbersomely banging against the foot.

But the main burden is the shield, typically a metre wide and weighing 7kg. A set of twenty-five standard-weight shields is stored in the Temple of Hera for use in the

Games. Each man is therefore encumbered with about 10kg of awkwardly arranged weight, and the race, it must be said, has a somewhat comic appearance. Sometimes shields are dropped, participants stop to retrieve them (or they will be disqualified), and collisions may result.

What is one to make of this curious event? Most spectators do not seem to take the race in armour very seriously. Comic playwrights make jokes about

37. The comic chaos of the race in armour. One athlete's helmet has fallen off, while another has dropped his shield.

it, and armed runners never achieve true superstar status. It could hardly be otherwise coming, as it does, after the combat sports. It is the light relief at the end of the long fourth day of the festival. Speculative comment to the effect that it symbolises the end of the Sacred Truce seems a little tendentious.[31]

DAY 5

THE CLOSING CEREMONY

Every event in the Olympic programme is suffused with sacred significance, but some are more religious than others. The contests themselves are rowdy affairs, and the award of ribbons to the winners, and the victory laps around the track that they traditionally run, take place amid a swirling mass of cheering fans. The Closing Ceremony on the final day, on the other hand, is a carefully choreographed holy rite – though again, like every one of the Olympics' major open-air spectacles, accessible to all.

A gold and ivory couch stored in the Temple of Hera is

38. A life-size statue of a victorious athlete. An Olympic hero is created when the winner is first beribboned (as here) in the Stadium immediately after his contest, and then crowned with a wreath of wild olive in the Sanctuary during the Closing Ceremony.

carried forth and set down in front of the Temple of Zeus. On it are placed crowns of wild olive, the branches cut from the Sacred Tree that grows behind the Temple. The tree – the *Kotinos Kallistephanos* ('the olive beautiful for its crowns') – is remarkable for the symmetrical pattern and pale green hue of its leaves. One branch is cut for each contest by a young boy both of whose parents are alive – a boy, that is, unpolluted by death – and he does this using a golden sickle.

A procession of the champions winds its way through the Sanctuary to the place where the couch has been placed. They parade naked, except for their victory ribbons, for the holy rite of transition from simple sportsman to one of the blessed of the gods is yet incomplete. The victors are called forth, one by one, to be crowned by the Judges, the Herald announcing the name, patronymic, city and contest of each. Despite their achievements, despite the prowess of these supermen, their demeanour now is modest and humble, for here, in front of the Temple of Zeus, they stand before God.

When each has been crowned, the tension breaks,

the mood lifts, and the crowds surge around their heroes, showering them with fruit and foliage, symbols of the fertility which the festival is designed to ensure.

As sultry summer afternoon passes into balmy evening, the final bout of celebration, feasting and revelry begins. The champions and their retinues – trainers, kinsmen, friends – process around the Sanctuary, garlanded and singing victory hymns. Magnificent banquets are prepared. Many of the richer victors extend open invitations to eat with them. As on the third day, the parties often last until dawn.

The journey home still awaits you – and unfortunately it promises to be as long and arduous as the outbound trek. Hiring a horse or a mule, or securing space on an ox-cart or the deck of a merchantman (assuming you can afford it) will be nigh-on impossible for several days, with tens of thousands setting out from this remote corner of Greece.[32]

But hey, that is tomorrow's problem. Now is a time to party. You have survived five days at Olympia. You have endured the sun and the stink, the crowds and the noise, the flies and the mosquitoes. You have been part of the greatest athletic spectacle in the ancient world. You have watched the most famous sporting celebrities perform. You have seen new champions crowned with sacred olive.

So, forget tomorrow, pour another cup of wine, and drink a toast to the gods and heroes of ancient Olympia.

REFERENCES

I **THE BASICS**
1. Harl 1998; Jones 1984, 71; Swaddling 2008, 7 and 52.
2. Hanson 1999, 72-3.
3. Kyle 2007, 115-16, 129.
4. Callwell 1906, 59.
5. Hodges 1974, *passim*, esp. figs 129-32 and 201; Jones 1984, 71-2.
6. Golden 1998, 35-6.
7. Finley and Pleket 1976, 14; Miller 2004a, 87.
8. Hughes 1997, 68-71.
9. Finley and Pleket 1976, xiii.
10. Harl 1998.
11. Finley and Pleket 1976, xiii; Harl 1998; Jones 1984, 184-5.
12. Pindar, 'Olympian 13', 36-9, 153-4.
13. Jones 1984, 104, 117-18; Miller 2004a, 226-7.
14. Batchelor 2008, 193.
15. Jones 1984, 118.
16. Batchelor 2008, 194-5.
17. Bury and Meiggs 1975, 55-7.
18. Swaddling 2008, 48.
19. Thucydides, 2.49, 152-3; Kagan 2003, 78.
20. Jones 1984, 190-2, 296-7.
21. Miller 2004a, 16.
22. Garland 1995, 92-6.
23. Graves 1960a, 31, 79, 173-5.
24. Kyle 2007, 133-4; Spivey 2005, 82-5.
25. Finley and Pleket 1976, 54.
26. Loi 2004, 17.
27. Davidson 1997, 3-35 *passim*; Loi 2004, 33-4.
28. Davidson 1997, 3-35 *passim*; Loi 2004, 17-38 *passim*.
29. Davidson 1997, 5.
30. Loi 2004, 32-3, 38-40.
31. Ibid., 19, 192-219 *passim*.
32. Davidson 1997, 40-3.
33. Ibid., 61-9.
34. Ibid., 54.
35. Ibid., 186-90.

36. Spivey 2005, 129–30; Kyle 2007, 172; Swaddling 2008, 53.
37. Davidson 1997, 22–3, 144–59; Loi 2004, 22.
38. Kyle 2007, 225–8.
39. Swaddling 2008, 41.
40. Graves 1960a, 264–6, Graves 1960b, 187; Miller 2004a, 151–2.
41. Davidson 1997, 73–136 *passim*, 196–7.
42. Golden 1998, 65–9; Spivey 2005, 121–2; Swaddling 2008, 62.
43. Miller 2004a, 11–17.
44. Kyle 2007, 85–90.
45. Pedley 1990, 89–94 and Plate VIII.
46. Davidson 1997, 166–7.
47. Ibid., 96–7.
48. Spivey 2005, 30–69 *passim*.
49. Kyle 2007, 89–90.
50. Garland 1995, 4.
51. Graves 1960a, 115–18.
52. Kyle 2007, 137–9, 159–60.
53. Spivey 2005, 190–1.
54. Ibid., 44–5.
55. Herodotus, Bk 8, Ch. 144, 273; Spivey 2005, 190–1.
56. Kyle 2007, 134.
57. Miller 2004a, 86.
58. Finley and Pleket 1976, 100.
59. Ibid., 26–7; Miller 2004a, 119.
60. Miller 2004a, 119.
61. Ibid., 167–75.

2 FINDING YOUR WAY AROUND

1. Spivey 2005, 82–5.
2. Swaddling 2008, 25, 39.
3. Ibid., 20, 27.
4. Woodford 1981, 28–40; Woodford 1986, 128–30.
5. Yalouris and Yalouris 1998, 98–101; Miller 2004a, 92.
6. Swaddling 2008, 34.
7. Finley and Pleket 1976, 40; Kyle 2007, 111–12, 129–30.
8. Tomlinson 1989, 33–5; Swaddling 2008, 17–19.
9. Yalouris and Yalouris 1998, 104–16.
10. Ibid., 104, 117–29.
11. Ibid., 130–9.
12. Swaddling 2008, 19.
13. Graves 1960b, 100–206 *passim*; Bellingham 1989, 49–67 *passim*.
14. Pindar 2007, 'Olympian 3', 11; Spivey 2005, 126–7; Kyle 2007, 117.
15. Swaddling 2008, 16–17.
16. Pausanias, 5.17, 247; Yalouris and Yalouris 1998, 10–11, 79; Miller 2004a, 89; Spivey 2005, 215; Swaddling 2008, 22–3, 31.

17. Yalouris and Yalouris 1998, 22; Swaddling 2008, 23–4.
18. Pausanias, 5.14, 240; Bellingham 1991, n.p.; Swaddling 2008, 8.
19. Pausanias, 5.13, 235–6; Yalouris and Yalouris 1998, 11–14; Miller 2004a, 90; Spivey 2005, 215; Swaddling 2008, 24.
20. Spivey 2005, 180–1; Swaddling 2008, 27–9.
21. Yalouris and Yalouris 1998, 14; Miller 2004a, 87; Swaddling 2008, 25.
22. Miller 2004a, 235–8.
23. Bury and Meiggs 1975, 268–75.
24. Spivey 2005, 186–8; Swaddling 2008, 21.
25. Miller 2004a, 33–45, 94, 109–10, 121; Miller 2004b, 105; Kyle 2007, 112–13, 217; Swaddling 2008, 29–31.
26. Miller 2004a, 81–2; Kyle 2007, 113; Swaddling 2008, 34–7.
27. Graves 1960b, 33–4; Miller 2004a, 81–2; Spivey 2005, 220.

3 MYTHS

1. Thomson 1961, *passim*, esp. 204–48; Miller 2004a, 113; Spivey 2005, 235–6.
2. Hesiod, *Theogony*, 6; Pausanias, 5.14, 240; Graves 1960a, 178; Bellingham 1991, 10; Swaddling 2008, 8.
3. Graves 1960a, 37–44; Bellingham 1991, 10–25 *passim*.
4. Pausanias, 6.21, 348; Graves 1960a, 89–96; Spivey 2005, 119–20.
5. Pausanias, 5.16, 245–6; Golden 1998, 125–32; Miller 2004a, 155–6; Spivey 2005, 120–1; Swaddling 2008, 31, 43.
6. Garland 1995, 41–5; Spivey 2005, 174–8.
7. Pindar, 'Olympian 6', 17–18; Sophocles, *Antigone*, 167; Spivey 2005, 174–5.
8. Graves 1960b, 25–39; Spivey 2005, 209–13.
9. Golden 1998, 12–14.
10. Pausanias, 5 and 6 *passim*; Spivey 2005, 215–17.
11. Graves 1960b, 43–64.
12. Pindar, 'Olympian 10', 32; Spivey 2005, 227.
13. Golden 1998, 146–50.
14. Bellingham 1989, 49–50; Spivey 225–30.
15. Waterfield 2009, *passim*.
16. Kyle 2007, 23–37, 92–3 *passim*.
17. Ibid., 23–53 *passim*.
18. Homer, *Iliad*, 23, 372–92.
19. Golden 1998, 91–3.
20. Homer, *Iliad*, 23, 372–4; Poliakoff 1987, 149–57.
21. Pausanias, 5.4, 204–5, 5.5, 256; Graves 1960b, 158–62; Kyle 2007, 102–4.

4 HISTORY

1. Golden 1998, 63–5; Kyle 2007, 15–16, 105–9.

2. Homer, *Iliad*, 23, 374–92.
3. Cotterill 1922, 54–9; Coldstream 1979, 332–8; Yalouris and Yalouris 1998, 53–89.
4. Hesiod, *Works and Days*, 56.
5. Finley and Pleket 1976, 42–3.
6. Ibid., 42.
7. Kyle 2007, 26–53.
8. Miller 2004a, 20–30; Kyle 2007, 54–71.
9. Graves 1960a, 292–303, 336–48; Bellingham 1989, 74–8.
10. Hanson 1999, 33–41; Spivey 2005, 1–29 *passim*.
11. Finley and Pleket 1976, 83–4; Golden 1998, 25–7.
12. Spivey 2005, 33–44.
13. Ibid., 56–8.
14. Jones 1984, 87, 174.
15. Homer, *Iliad*, 2, 69–71; Spivey 2005, 57–8.
16. Spivey 2005, 190–2.
17. Poliakoff 1987, 19; Kyle 2007, 80–3.
18. Finley and Pleket 1976, 24, 68; Miller 2004a, 129–45; Kyle 2007, 136–49; Swaddling 2008, 11–12.
19. Miller 2004a, 145–9; Kyle 2007, 148–79.
20. Jones 1984, 300; Miller 2004a, 132–5; Swaddling 2008, 59–60.
21. Pindar, 'Olympian 2', 7; Bury and Meiggs 1975, 110–11, 223; Finley and Pleket 1976, 22–3; Golden 1998, 16, 34–6; Miller 2004a, 84, 96, 102, 107, 218–20.

5 MANAGEMENT

1. Finley and Pleket 1976, 59–60; Poliakoff 1987, 19–20; Golden 1998, 15, 42, 106; Miller 2004a, 114–15; Miller 2004b, 66–7; Kyle 2007, 114–16; Swaddling 2008, 50–1.
2. Golden 1998, 82; Miller 2004a, 115; Kyle 2007, 115–16.
3. Finley and Pleket 1976, 54–5; Kyle 2007, 116; Swaddling 2008, 61.
4. Miller 2004a, 116; Miller 2004b, 93–4.
5. Miller 2004a, 117–18; Swaddling 2008, 49–50.
6. Finley and Pleket 1976, 60; Jones 1984, 47–8, 227–37; Miller 2004a, 116–17.
7. Herodotus, 5.22, 9; Lane Fox 1986, 30; Worthington 2004, 7–8; Spivey 2005, 193.
8. De Ste Croix 1983, 133–74 and *passim*; Pomeroy 1994, 68–70; Golden 1998, 3–4.
9. Homer, *Odyssey*, 1.36; Euripides, *Trojan Women*, 111–12; Aristophanes, *The Poet and the Women*, 105; Golden 1998, 123–4; Spivey 2005, 117–19.
10. Poliakoff 1987, 80–1; Golden 1998, 9, 104–13.
11. Finley and Pleket 1976, 63–4; Swaddling 2008, 50–1.
12. Thucydides, 6, 426, 442–3, 447; Pausanias, 6.6, 302; Garland 1995, 37–40; Finley and Pleket 1976, 63.

13. Golden 1998, 139.
14. Homer, *Iliad*, 14, 15, 250–1, 256; Garland 1995, 4–5.
15. Thucydides, 5.49–50, 380–1; Xenophon, 3.2.21–31, 110–13; Finley and Pleket 1976, 98–100; Golden 1998, 16–17.
16. Finley and Pleket 1976, 15–16; Golden 1998, 15.
17. Kyle 2007, 116.
18. Herodotus, 8.59, 235; Thucydides, 5.50, 381; Miller 2004a, 17–18; Finley and Pleket 1976, 66–67.
19. Thucydides, 5.49–50, 380–381; Swaddling 2008, 39–40.
20. Pausanias, 6.9, 311–312; Poliakoff 1987, 123.
21. Thucydides 5.49–50, 380–381; Xenophon 3.2.21–31, 110–13; Kyle 2007, 192–4; Miller 2004a, 220–1.

6 THE ATHLETES

1. Pausanias, 6.11, 315–17; Kyle 2007, 200–1.
2. Plutarch, Themistocles, 1.164; Poliakoff 1987, 107, 129–30; Spivey 2005, 55; Kyle 2007, 175, 208–16.
3. Golden 1998, 143; Kyle 2007, 210.
4. Finley and Pleket 1976, 68–77; Golden 1998, 155, 160–1; Miller 2004a, 212–14; Perrottet 2004, 13–14; Kyle 2007, 208.
5. Homer, *Iliad*, 23, 379–80, 386; Golden 1998, 108–9, 118–19.
6. Golden 1998, 107–8.
7. Pausanias, 6.10, 312–13; Poliakoff 1987, 124; Howatson 1989, 251–2.
8. Finley and Pleket 1976, 89; Spivey 2005, 40–1, 56–63, 94, 150.
9. Miller 2004a, 189–93; Kyle 2007, 89.
10. Herodotus, 3.131, 273; Pindar, 'Olympian 8', 25–6 and *passim*; Finley and Pleket 1976, 89–97; Golden 1998, 83; Miller 2004a, 187, 214; Spivey 2005, 145–6; Swaddling 2008, 46.
11. Finley and Pleket 1976, 93–5; Jackson 1998, 16–22; Miller 2004a, 213; Spivey 2005, 63; Swaddling 2008, 47.
12. Herodotus, 3.129–38, 271–6; Pausanias, 6.13, 320; Finley and Pleket 1976, 94–5; Howatson 1989, 476–7; Jackson 1998, 16–17; Miller 2004a, 217; Swaddling 2008, 47.
13. Poliakoff 1987, 11–18, 51–52; Miller 2004a, 14–17, 54; Swaddling 2008, 51.
14. De Ste Croix 1972, 89–94 and *passim*; Forrest 1980, *passim*; Miller 2004b, 106; Kyle 2007, 181–7.
15. Pindar, 'Pythian 8', 75; Finley and Pleket 1976, 20–2; Poliakoff 1987, 104–7, 112–15; Miller 2004a, 13–14, 19, 231–2, 237–40; Kyle 2007, 55–6, 198–9.
16. Finley and Pleket 1976, 77–8; Golden 1998, 10–11, 33, 76–7, 155, 165; Miller 2004a, 111–12, 205, 218.
17. Finley and Pleket 1976, 75; Golden 1998, 4–5; Spivey 2005, 160.
18. Spivey 2005, 132.
19. Pindar, 'Olympian 7', 'Nemean 5, 6', 20–3, 99–104, 147 and

passim; Golden 1998, 76–88; Miller 2004a, 237–8; Miller 2004b, 195; Spivey 2005, 135–47; Instone 2007, vii–xxi *passim*; Kyle 2007, 203–5.

20. Osborne 1998, 159–63, 226–30; Spivey 2005, 147–65.
21. Pindar, 'Pythian 9, 10', 79, 82; Golden 1998, 74–5.
22. Poliakoff 1987, 121–4, 128–9; Miller 2004a, 160–5; Spivey 2005, 163–5; Swaddling 2008, 93.

7 THE PROGRAMME

1. Miller 2004a, 118; Swaddling 2008, 52.
2. Finley and Pleket 1976, Plate 24c; Miller 2004a, 120; Spivey 2005, 78–83; Kyle 2007, 119.
3. Finley and Pleket 1976, 43–4; Miller 2004a, 84–5, 121.
4. Miller 2004a, 46; Swaddling 2008, 53.
5. Finley and Pleket 1976, 57–8; Swaddling 2008, 53.
6. Miller 2004a, 119.
7. Ibid., 121.
8. Homer, *Iliad*, 23, 378–84; Sophocles, *Electra*, 89–91; Pausanias, 6.10, 314; Finley and Pleket 1976, 27–31, 57; Golden 1998, 82–3, 99–100, 121–2; Miller 2004a, 75–82, 122; Spivey 2005, 86–91; Kyle 2007, 58–61; Swaddling 2008, 83–7.
9. Finley and Pleket 1976, 30–1; Kyle 2007, 188–96.
10. Golden 1998, 82–3; Miller 2004a, 75, 78–9; Swaddling 2008, 87–9.
11. Miller 2004a, 79–80.
12. Homer, *Iliad*, 23, 379–80.
13. Finley and Pleket 1976, 32–4, 56; Miller 2004a, 73, 83–4; Spivey 2005, 91–7.
14. Miller 2004a, 60–3, 228–9; Spivey 2005, 92–5; Swaddling 2008, 63–6.
15. Miller 2004a, 63–8; Swaddling 2008, 68–71.
16. Miller 2004a, 68–73; Swaddling 2008, 66–8.
17. Golden 1998, 69–71; Miller 2004a, 122–3; Spivey 2005, 91–2; Kyle 2007, 121–3.
18. Homer, *Odyssey*, 8.124–7; Kyle 2007, 65–8.
19. Miller 2004a, 123–4; Swaddling 2008, 53, 93.
20. Finley and Pleket 1976, 34–5; Miller 2004a, 124–5; Swaddling 2008, 55.
21. Miller 2004a, 44–5; 126; Spivey 2005, 111–15; Kyle 2007, 113.
22. Miller 2004a, 31–8, 44, 126; Kyle 2007, 62, 113.
23. Miller 2004a, 44–5, 126.
24. Bellingham 1991, 38–9; Miller 2004a, 184.
25. Finley and Pleket 1976, 40, 56–7; Poliakoff 1987, 8–15, 23–53 *passim*, 116; Golden 1998, 52–3; Miller 2004a, 46–50; Swaddling 2008, 72–5.
26. Finley and Pleket 1976, 38–9; Poliakoff 1987, 117–19; Miller 2004a, 50, 160–1; Kyle 2007, 200.

27. Homer, *Iliad*, 23, 387; Poliakoff 1987, 68–88 *passim*, 90–1; Miller 2004a, 51–7; Spivey 2005, 103–5; Swaddling 2008, 77–81.
28. Poliakoff 1987, 54–67 *passim*; Spivey 2005, 47, 105–11, 122–3; Kyle 2007, 124–6; Swaddling 2008, 75–7.
29. Pausanias, 6.5, 299–300; Miller 2004a, 161; Kyle 2007, 202.
30. Pausanias, 8.40, 471–2; Poliakoff 1987, 91; Miller 2004a, 59–60.
31. Miller 2004a, 32–3; Spivey 2005, 115–17; Kyle 2007, 121.
32. Kyle 2007, 117–18, 203–4; Swaddling 2008, 90–3.

SOURCES

Aristophanes, 1964, The Wasps, The Poet and the Women, *and* The Frogs, trans. D. Barrett, London and New York, Penguin.

Batchelor, S., 2008, *The Ancient Greeks for Dummies*, Chichester, John Wiley & Sons.

Bellingham, D., 1989, *An Introduction to Greek Mythology*, London, Apple Press.

Bury, J.B. and R. Meiggs, 1975, *A History of Greece to the Death of Alexander the Great*, 4th edn, London, Macmillan.

Callwell, C.E., 1906, *Small Wars: Their Principles and Practice*, London, HMSO.

Coldstream, J.N., 1979, *Geometric Greece*, London, Methuen.

Cotterill, H.B., 1922, *A History of Art*, vol. 1, *Down to the Age of Raphael*, London, George Harrap & Co.

Davidson, J., 1997, *Courtesans and Fishcakes: the Consuming Passions of Classical Athens*, London, Fontana.

De Ste Croix, G.E.M., 1972, *The Origins of the Peloponnesian War*, London, Duckworth.

—— 1984, *The Class Struggle in the Ancient Greek World*, London, Duckworth.

Euripides, 1973, The Bacchae *and Other Plays*, trans. P. Vellacott, Harmondsworth, Penguin.

Finley, M.I. and H.W. Pleket, 1976, *The Olympic Games: the First Thousand Years*, London, Book Club Associates.

Forrest, W.G., 1980, *A History of Sparta*, London, Duckworth.

Garland, R., 1995, *Religion and the Greeks*, London, Bristol Classical Press.

Golden, M., 1998, *Sport and Society in Ancient Greece*, Cambridge, Cambridge University Press.

Graves, R., 1960a, *The Greek Myths: 1*, Harmondsworth, Penguin.

—— 1960b, *The Greek Myths: 2*, Harmondsworth, Penguin.

Hanson, V.D., 1999, *The Wars of the Ancient Greeks*, London, Cassell.

Harl, K., 1998, 'Greek coinage and measures', accessed at www.tulane.edu, September 2011.

Herodotus, 1910, *The History of Herodotus*, trans. G. Rawlinson, London, Dent.

Hesiod, 1988, Theogony *and* Works and Days, trans. M.L. West, Oxford, Oxford University Press.

Hodges, H., 1974, *Technology in the Ancient World*, London, Book Club Associates.

Homer, 1968, *The Odyssey*, trans. R. Lattimore, New York, Harper & Row.

—— 1987, *The Iliad*, trans. M. Hammond, London, Penguin.

Howatson, M.C., 1989, ed. *The Oxford Companion to Classical Literature*, Oxford, Oxford University Press.

Hughes, E., 1997, *Tales from Ovid*, London, Faber & Faber.

Instone, S., 2007, 'Introduction', in *Pindar: The Complete Odes*, Oxford, Oxford University Press.

Jackson, R., 1988, *Doctors and Diseases in the Roman Empire*, London, British Museum Press.

Jones, P., 1984, *The World of Athens: An Introduction to Classical Athenian Culture*, Cambridge, Cambridge University Press.

Kagan, D., 2003, *The Peloponnesian War*, London, HarperCollins.

Kyle, D.G., 2007, *Sport and Spectacle in the Ancient World*, Oxford, Blackwell.

Lane Fox, R., 1986, *Alexander the Great*, Harmondsworth, Penguin.

Loi, M., 2004, *Ancient Dining*, Athens, ISP International Athletic Editions.

Miller, S., 2004a, *Ancient Greek Athletics*, London and New Haven, Yale University Press.

—— 2004b, *Arete: Greek Sports from Ancient Sources*, Berkeley, University of California Press.

Osborne, R., 1998, *Archaic and Classical Greek Art*, Oxford, Oxford University Press.

Pausanias, 1979, *Guide to Greece*, vol. 2, *Southern Greece*, trans. P. Levi, London, Penguin.

Pedley, J.G., 1990, *Paestum: Greeks and Romans in Southern Italy*, London, Thames & Hudson.

Perrottet, A., 2004, *The Naked Olympics: the True Story of the Ancient Games*, New York, Random House.

Pindar, 2007, *The Complete Odes*, trans. A. Verity, intro. S. Instone, Oxford, Oxford University Press.

Plutarch, 1864, *Plutarch's Lives*, 3 vols, trans. (revd) A.H. Clough, London, J.M. Dent & Sons.

Poliakoff, M.B., 1987, *Combat Sports in the Ancient World: Competition, Violence, and Culture*, London and New Haven, Yale University Press.

Pomeroy, S.B., 1994, *Goddesses, Whores, Wives, and Slaves: Women in Classical Antiquity*, London, Pimlico.

Sophocles, 1953, *Electra and Other Plays*, trans. E.F. Watling, Harmondsworth, Penguin.

Spivey, N., 2005, *The Ancient Olympics*, Oxford, Oxford University Press.

Swaddling, J., 2008, *The Ancient Olympic Games*, London, British Museum Press.

Thomson, G., 1961, *Studies in Ancient Greek Society: the Prehistoric Aegean*, New York, Citadel.

Thucydides, 1972, *The Peloponnesian War*, trans. R. Warner, London, Penguin.

Tomlinson, R.A., 1989, *Greek Architecture*, London, Bristol Classical Press.

Waterfield, R., 2009, *Why Socrates Died: Dispelling the Myths*, London, Faber & Faber.

Woodford, S., 1981, *The Parthenon*, Cambridge, Cambridge University Press.

—— 1986, *An Introduction to Greek Art*, London, Duckworth.

Worthington, I., 2004, *Alexander the Great: Man and God*, Harlow, Pearson Education.

Xenophon, 1979, *A History of My Times*, trans. R. Warner, Harmondsworth, Penguin.

Yalouris, A. and N. Yalouris, 1998, *Olympia*, Athens, Ekdotike Athenon.

INDEX

An index should be useful. Accordingly, this one omits minor passing references, makes entries under English or Greek names as seems best (translations in parentheses), and offers brief descriptions where appropriate as an alternative to having a separate glossary.